ACCULTURATION AND PERSONALITY AMONG THE WISCONSIN CHIPPEWA

AMS PRESS
NEW YORK

Vol. 52   OCTOBER, 1950   No. 4, Part 2

AMERICAN ANTHROPOLOGIST

Organ of the American Anthropological Association, the Central and
Western States Branches of the American Anthropological Association,
the American Ethnological Society, the Anthropological Society of
Hawaii, the Anthropological Society of Washington, and the
Philadelphia Anthropological Society

ACCULTURATION AND PERSONALITY AMONG THE WISCONSIN CHIPPEWA

VICTOR BARNOUW

No. 72 of the Titles in the Memoir Series of the American Anthropological Association

Published by the

AMERICAN ANTHROPOLOGICAL ASSOCIATION

Library of Congress Cataloging in Publication Data

Barnouw, Victor.
  Acculturation and personality among the
Wisconsin Chippewa.

  Reprint of the author's thesis, Columbia
University, published in 1950 by the American
Anthropological Association, Menasha, Wis.,
which was issued as no. 72 of its Memoirs and as
v. 52, no. 4, pt. 2, of American anthropologist.
  Bibliography: p.
  Includes index.
  1. Chippewa Indians.   2. Acculturation—
Wisconsin.   3. Chippewa Indians—Psychology.
4. Indians of North America—Wisconsin—
Psychology.   I. Title.   II. Series: American
Anthropological Association. Memoirs; no. 72.
III. Series: American anthropologist; v. 52,
no. 4, pt. 2.
E99.C6B3   1980   970.004'97   76-43646
ISBN 0-404-15481-6

Reprinted from the edition of 1950, Wisconsin. [Trim size
and text area have been slightly altered. Original trim size:
15.4 × 23.5 cm; text area: 12 × 18.4 cm].

TABLE OF CONTENTS

3

4

INTRODUCTION

THE EXPRESSION OF PERSONALITY IN BEHAVIOR

IN culture and personality studies and in recent delineations of "basic" personality and character structure, various techniques have been used as cross-checking devices to supplement the ethnologist's fallible portrait of his people, to help him delve below the surface of his subjects, and to reveal central personality characteristics which may or may not have escaped observation. Projective tests such as the Rorschach and Thematic Apperception Tests have been employed,[1] drawing analysis has been attempted,[2] and the psychological analysis of dreams and visions, of art, folklore, and of religious rituals have provided converging avenues of approach to personality.[3] But the oldest way of gauging personality, uncertain though it may be, still remains indispensable; this is the analysis of actual behavior. When the psychologist or the ethnologist watches people in living situations—either in situations deliberately structured by the observer[4] or occurring spontaneously in the course of day-to-day social relationships[5]—he can see personality expressing itself in action, sometimes in response to common frustrations, and occasionally in tense moments of crisis or tragedy.

The ethnological field worker often witnesses the unfolding of human relations within a family circle, the varieties of love and punishment meted out to children, and the emotional responses of children to grown-ups and to one another. Such behavioral material alone, if sufficiently representative, may sometimes tell us a great deal about the adult personality which is characteristic of the group. Certainly the personality picture of any human microcosm would be barren without some information about the typical family institutions, child training patterns, and adult social relations and some picture of the actual day-by-day behavior of individuals. So while projective tests and the other supplementary aids in personality diagnosis are of the greatest value in culture and personality studies, it does not seem exaggerated to claim that the analysis of actual behavior must be primary.

From this point of view, *biography* takes on particular importance. A detailed life-history, at its best, provides the chronicle of how a specific individual has reacted to a long sequence of events—to the delights, frustrations, and opportunities which have been experienced in the course of growing up in

---

[1] Hallowell, 1945; Henry, 1947.
[2] See Schmiedl-Waehner's analysis of Alorese children's drawings in Dubois, 1944.
[3] Roheim, 1945; Hallowell, 1947; Mead and Bateson, 1942.
[4] As in: Erikson, 1940; Henry and Henry, 1944; del Torto and Cornyetz, 1945.
[5] As in: Hallowell, 1938a, 1938b.

a particular culture.[6] The *way* in which these events were responded to illuminate the personality of the subject with a clarity hardly attainable through any other means.

THE EXPRESSION OF GROUP PERSONALITY IN HISTORY

From the same point of view, *history* now assumes a fresh significance. If there really is such a thing as "group personality," "national character," or "basic personality type,"[7] we should expect it to find expression in the history of a society, at least within a limited time range, just as the personality of an individual finds expression in his biography. We are then led to ask questions such as these: How have crises been faced by the members of the society in question? By a creative, co-operative effort? By panic? By conflicts within the group? How has prosperity affected the members of the society? Did they form economic classes and castes, establish privileges, share the wealth? And again, how did the members of the group respond to external attack? How did they accept new inventions? new religions? new social institutions?

To be sure, some would argue that variations in group personality have no vital bearing on these questions at all, and that the pattern of historical events is essentially determined by economic factors. In this kind of interpretation human nature is conceived to be a constant in all societies; while the significant variables in operation are assumed to be the economic conditions and other environmental factors which affect the society.

This kind of determinism is expressed, for example, by George T. Hunt in *The Wars of the Iroquois*, where the author comments:

If Indians of other nations or institutions had lived in the country in which the Iroquois lived, they would have been subject to the same pressure of circumstance; the trade of other nations would have been desirable and even necessary to them; and they would, presumably, have taken about the same steps to obtain it as did the Iroquois. Had the position of the Hurons and the Ottawa been exchanged for that of the Iroquois, it is scarcely a mere conjecture that the Iroquois would then have used the Ottawa River highway and that the tribes living in New York would have blockaded it and attempted to destroy them.[8]

My own assumptions are very different in such an issue. To my mind, the wars of the Iroquois or of any nation are not solely explicable in terms of economic conditions and "pressures of circumstance." It seems to me that the

---

[6] For a general survey of life-histories, see Gottschalk, Kluckhohn, and Angell, 1945. For an outstanding life-history document, see Simmons, 1942.

[7] Dr. Ralph Linton's definition reads: "The basic personality type for any society is that personality configuration which is shared by the bulk of the society's members as a result of the early experiences which they have in common." (Kardiner, 1945, p. viii.)

[8] Hunt, 1940, p. 159. Hunt's economic determinism is not followed consistently. Elsewhere the author remarks that the Fox-Sioux war had "no real motive" (p. 126). Hunt has a weakness for characterizing tribes with group personality descriptions. (See pp. 4, 48, 124, 125.)

history of a society cannot adequately be understood without some knowledge of the characteristic culture and personality patterns prevalent within the group, and consequently I am in agreement with the following statement by Kardiner which contrasts with that of Hunt:

> We can assume with complete confidence that the history of the Alorese would be different from the Comanche even if both were subjected to the same external vicissitudes, because each culture is characterized by different life goals and values.[9]

If we accept the latter point of view and reject the fatalism of the extreme economic determinists, the history of a given society may be regarded as a chronicle which embodies the significant decisions made by the members of the group which in one way or another express their central values. The collective history of a society then possesses the same sort of diagnostic value, with respect to "basic personality type," that a life-history possesses with respect to an individual subject.[10]

It is evident that the imaginary experiment of substitution suggested by Hunt, of placing one society in the shoes of another, is an impossible one. No two societies having different historical traditions and patterns of culture can ever be said to be in the "same" situation, or be exposed, as Kardiner suggests, to the "same" external vicissitudes. But since the problems of group personality and history call for some sort of comparative approach, a reasonable approximation to a controlled experiment may be found in cases where two or more adjoining cultures have been affected by the same general sweep of historical events, by equivalent pressures and social dislocations. An example may be found in North America, where the American Indian tribes were faced with the general problem of adjustment to white contact. In the following chapter I will sketch some of the uniform aspects of what we refer to as "acculturation," pointing out how diverse American Indian groups have made accommodations along similar lines, in the long run, to the pressures of western civilization. But I will go on to point out certain differential features in this process of adjustment. In particular, I will contrast the acculturation of the Wisconsin Chippewa with that of neighboring tribes, such as the Dakota and Cheyenne, and show how some of the Chippewa reactions to white domination reveal culture and personality patterns which were characteristic of the Chippewa but not of the Dakota and Cheyenne. It will also be noted that the general patterns expressed in the course of Chippewa history find parallel reflections in the aboriginal folklore and in individual life-histories.

Since personality is always developed within a social, cultural matrix, I will give some picture of the relevant Chippewa institutions concerning the

---

[9] Kardiner, 1945, p. 414.
[10] In making this analogy I do not mean to suggest that society is an organism with a personality of its own.

family organization, child-training techniques, and attitudes towards religion and the supernatural. Where significant contrasts obtain with the institutions of neighboring groups, such differences will be indicated. Rorschach evidence and other auxiliary aids in personality diagnosis will be referred to in the following pages. But the main stress will be on the analysis of behavior and on the characteristic group responses of the Wisconsin Chippewa to a series of historical events stemming from the impact of western culture.

This paper may then be characterized as an application of the culture and personality approach to the domain of history. Studies of this nature have hitherto been relatively rare,[11] for work in this field has generally been restricted to one time level. In the following pages, however, we will deal with a period which exceeds two centuries in duration.

The first material for this study was obtained in two summers' field work among the Wisconsin Chippewa. In the summer of 1944 I was sent to collect life-history material at the Indian reservations of Court Oreilles and Lac du Flambeau in northern Wisconsin for the purposes of the Linton-Kardiner seminar on Psychological Analysis of Primitive Cultures, which had already devoted a semester to a study of Chippewa culture, presented by Ernestine Friedl. My work was done under the joint auspices of the Columbia University Department of Anthropology and the Milwaukee Public Museum. I spent one month at Court Oreilles and two at Lac du Flambeau collecting biographical data and Rorschach records. Most of my work was done with four individuals, Tom Badger, Julia Badger, John Thunderbird, and Jim Mink.[12] Tom Badger is a conservative Indian of the old school, a *Mide* priest about seventy years of age. Julia, his wife, is half his age. John Thunderbird and Jim Mink are men in their middle fifties who have had some school education. Both of them made an attempt to "become like a white man," to use Jim Mink's phrase. Both gave it up and are now trying to be like Indians, with as little success. Julia Badger has passed through somewhat similar experiences. All three are caught between two cultures, as they themselves realize. The Appendix is devoted to life-history material given by these three informants.

In the summer of 1946 I made another trip to Lac du Flambeau for more material. This time I collected drawings and gave the Thematic Apperception Test in addition to the Rorschach. In the summer of 1947 I spent a few days at Flambeau, working in collaboration with Dr. Bernard Rosenthal, who is making an attitude study of racial self-identification among the half-breed children on the reservation. This trip was financed by The Viking Fund.

---

[11] Some pioneer examples include Fromm, 1941; Benedict, 1946; Kardiner, 1939 (Tanala); and Kardiner, 1945 (Comanche).

[12] These are not their real names. I have altered the names of most Indians mentioned in the following pages. For the benefit of field-workers, a key list giving the correct names will be kept on file at the Department of Anthropology, Columbia University, New York City.

My list of acknowledgments is a long one, for many people have helped me in the course of my work. I am much indebted to Dr. Ralph Linton, the Columbia University Department of Anthropology, and to Dr. W. C. McKern of the Milwaukee Public Museum for making possible my first field trip to Wisconsin. I am also grateful to Dr. Linton and to Dr. Abram Kardiner for many constructive suggestions with regard to field work. On the Court Oreilles Reservation I was very fortunate in having the opportunity to work with Robert Ritzenthaler of the Milwaukee Public Museum and to learn from him about the complexities of ethnological field work. Much of my knowledge about the Wisconsin Chippewa stems from the able field notes compiled by him and by Ernestine Friedl and Joseph Casagrande.

In the fall of 1944 some of my life history material was analyzed in the Linton-Kardiner seminar at Columbia by Dr. Milton Sapirstein. Dr. Sapirstein's very perceptive analysis deepened my respect for the theoretical treatment of culture along the psychoanalytic lines established by Dr. Kardiner in these seminars. Dr. Bruno Klopfer's analyses of Chippewa Rorschachs were also a source of insight into Chippewa personality characteristics.

The first draft of this dissertation was read and criticized by Dr. Ruth Benedict, Dr. Marian W. Smith, Dr. George Herzog, Dr. A. I. Hallowell, and Esther S. Goldfrank. Each made valuable suggestions which have been incorporated in the present paper. Dr. Ruth Benedict in particular indicated lines of research to be explored. I am also much indebted to Dr. Hallowell, whose intimate knowledge of the Canadian Chippewa (Saulteaux) is enriched by his interest in psychological problems, and to Maud Hallowell, who clarified for me some of the Rorschach characteristics of the Chippewa.

Those who read the later draft of this paper include Dr. William Duncan Strong, Dr. Julian Steward, Dr. Conrad Arensberg, and Dr. John Krout. Their criticisms have been much appreciated. Dr. Arensberg's constructive recommendations in particular resulted in certain theoretical revisions of the original argument.

In conclusion, I would like to thank my father and mother for their unfailing encouragement and for their financial assistance.

I. FEATURES OF CHIPPEWA ACCULTURATION

UNIFORM ASPECTS OF INDIAN ACCULTURATION

IT is well known that at the time of the first colonization of North America a great diversity of Indian cultures existed on this continent, with many distinct social groups ranging from the settled pueblos in the Southwest to wandering bands of hunters in Labrador. The process of acculturation which accompanied the white man's advance served in many ways as a leveling agency which eventually reduced the numerous independent and frequently contrasting Indian societies to a comparatively indistinguishable minority group, generally settled on reservations.

While there were many local variations on the general theme, most of these Indian societies underwent a similar sequence of historical events. Their first contact with the white man was usually through the medium of trading goods, the immediate practical utility of which guaranteed their acceptance. Often the trader's pots and pans, knives and traps supplanted native manufactures and disrupted the aboriginal economy, so that a relationship of dependency upon the white man originated. New diseases appeared along with new manufactures, waves of measles and smallpox frequently accompanying the trader and missionary on their journeys.

For various reasons, the coming of the white man aroused mixed feelings—admiration mingled with hostility. In many cases there was a tribal split into "friendly" and "hostile" factions over the issue of acceptance or rejection of western patterns of culture. The problem of intermarriage with whites sharpened such disagreements. Often there were nativistic movements, threats of war, and actual clashes between the white man and the Indian.

After the establishment of the United States government, Indian tribes everywhere were influenced by legal decisions made in Washington. The government tried to follow a uniform policy with regard to its Indian "wards." The reservation system was a part of this policy, which affected Indians in all parts of the United States. So did many acts of Congress, such as the Allotment Act of 1887. Indian groups all over the country were subjected to the same government educational policy—for instance the institution of boarding schools away from the reservation during the 1880's and 1890's, a mechanism which aimed to wean young Indians from tribal life. Everywhere the Indians were encouraged to become farmers or to take up useful trades along western patterns. In all parts of the country the half-acculturated individual faced the great difficulty of reconciling two cultures—the Indian and the white.

At the present time, the leveling effects of acculturation can be noted on most Indian reservations in the United States. No matter what the prevalent form of dwelling may have been under aboriginal conditions, Indians may now be found living in frame houses and shacks which are equipped with tables, chairs, and stoves, and often decorated with pictures of Catholic saints and movie actresses. Houses are often clustered about a strip of Main Street, near a filling station and a grocery store. A Roll of Honor can often be found in the center of town listing the names of those who served in the Armed Services. Men in overalls lounge in front of the store or post-office, discussing politics and greeting the newcomer who drives up in a jalopy. Meanwhile young girls walk by dressed in the prevalent American style of "bobby-soxers" and humming the latest juke-box tunes. Such are the leveling effects of acculturation, which may be observed among Indian groups as diverse as Iroquois, Dakota, and Chippewa.

DIFFERENTIAL REACTIONS TO ACCULTURATION

This general picture must be modified by a strong qualification, lest we lose sight of the fact that each Indian group has experienced its own individual history. Patterns in acculturation have varied greatly from one tribe to another, even when similar problems and conditions were met. At the first advent of the white man, for example, the most diverse reactions took place in different areas—a warm welcome on the part of some groups, abrupt flight on the part of others. Some Indians joyously hailed the white man as a supernatural patron, while others grimly took up arms to drive him away.

Once the domination of the white man was accepted, there were other differential reactions. Some groups, for instance, readily accepted Christianity, while others resisted the indoctrination of new religious ideas. Such variations in response to white contact are hardly surprising in view of the great diversity of geographical, sociological, and economic conditions in the different culture areas of aboriginal North America. Differential reactions to acculturation may also be ascribed to cultural and psychological factors; for in their encounter with new patterns of western culture, each Indian society responded in terms of already existent values and traditions. That is why, as Ruth Benedict has shown, there has been no pattern of excessive drinking in the Pueblo region, although on other reservations the Indian liquor problem has been a difficult one; and that is also why peyotism and the Ghost Dance made no headway among the Pueblos, although elsewhere these nativistic cults won almost universal acceptance.[13] Differential reactions which are probably due to a complex of cultural, sociological, and psychological factors may be noted within the Pueblo area itself. Catholicism, for example, won much readier acceptance among the eastern than among the western Pueblos.[14] Further examples of such contrasting patterns in acculturation could be multiplied.[15]

It is evident that differential reactions of this order often tell us something

---

[13] Benedict, 1934, Ch. IV.   [14] Hawley, 1946.

[15] See, for example, the contrast drawn between the Utes of Colorado and the White Knife Shoshoni in Linton, 1940, p. 204.

about the constitution of these Indian societies, the personality characteristics of their members, and the central values and preconceptions imbedded in the native cultures. We may learn a great deal about the social working of a given society when we ask: Why did the members of X tribe take over this aspect of western culture and not that one? Why did they not respond in the same manner as the members of neighboring Y society?

CHIPPEWA ACCULTURATION

When we use the comparative approach to the study of acculturation and examine Chippewa reactions to white contact as contrasted with those of the neighboring Fox, Dakota, and Cheyenne, one striking feature emerges: *the Chippewa seem to have accepted white domination very readily*. They quickly arrived at a *modus vivendi* with the fur trader and became very dependent upon him. The Wisconsin Chippewa did not fight the white man, as did many equally outnumbered and defenseless Indian tribes. Instead, the white man's political authority was accepted and his supremacy unchallenged.

Among the Plains tribes further south, however, there was violent resistance to white encroachment. The Dakota and Cheyenne fought the white man sporadically for about twenty-five years, until their final crushing defeat and capitulation. No such resistance characterized Chippewa history.

We may note another difference: When the Plains tribes were crushed, a nativistic religious movement, the Ghost Dance, sprang up among them and inspired the Dakota, Cheyenne, and others with a feverish messianic enthusiasm. The Wisconsin Chippewa remained aloof from this excitement. The Ghost Dance was never accepted by them, in spite of the fact that it flourished among the neighboring Dakota, from whom the Chippewa had previously borrowed other religious dances and doctrines.

It is evident that Dakota history possessed elements of turbuience and violence which were lacking among the Chippewa, and that acculturation involved a much more traumatic experience for the Dakota. Moreover, the latter appear to have undergone a change in personality structure since the beginning of the reservation period. Judging from all the evidence, the acculturation process does not seem to have brought about any marked change in personality structure among the Wisconsin Chippewa.

As will be seen in the following pages, there has been a discernible continuity of social patterns among the Chippewa. The social structure was atomistic in the past, and so it remains today, and the personality structure associated with the former way of life persists to a considerable extent. One expression of this continuity, in the sphere of work and co-operation, forms another contrast with the situation on the Plains. During the reservation period, the Dakota and Arapaho managed to retain something of the former group spirit to the extent of developing co-operative ventures such as mutual help groups and cattle associations. Such group ventures have not characterized reservation life among the Wisconsin Chippewa.

The foregoing rough outline of Chippewa acculturation will be filled in and elaborated upon at greater length in the following pages, and an attempt will be made to account for the idiosyncratic features of Chippewa adjustment to white contact. The various aspects of acculturation which have been mentioned —acceptance of white domination, rejection of the Ghost Dance, failure to develop co-operative ventures, etc.—will prove upon examination to be closely interrelated and to have relevance to certain aboriginal patterns of culture and personality as well as to the type of relationship established in the early fur trade period between the Chippewa Indians and the trader.

Let us begin with a discussion of work habits and social organization. A brief picture of Plains social life will be presented first, in order to place Chippewa patterns in some perspective.

CO-OPERATIVE TECHNIQUES ON THE PLAINS

Among the Plains Indians, in former days, co-operative activity in the hunt and in other fields was a matter of daily experience, particularly during the summer months when the buffalo were hunted in common by a large number of men. The camp circle consisted of hundreds of individuals in summer time, sometimes as many as two or three thousand, as among the Cheyenne. These people broke camp together, moved together, and worked together. Political authority was centered in a group of chiefs; executive authority was provided by soldier societies which policed camp, regulated the buffalo hunt, and prevented individual raids on the buffalo.

In winter time this closely integrated society was broken up into its component bands; but a sentiment of tribal unity persisted through the winter months and was rekindled in the spring, when the camp circle was formed once again, and each band resumed its traditional place on the rim of the circle. Llewellyn and Hoebel have graphically described this reunion:

> As the snows melted and game was again plentiful, all the Cheyennes from the far-flung territories began their annual drifting together. Within a few weeks, band after band converged; there was the great ingathering. Each group came marching or riding into the camp, whooping, shouting, and singing as they circled the lodges, while those already there cheered and applauded. The groups arranged their lodges in a large circle by bands, each in a traditional position. . . . The closed space in the center was a good mile across, and when all the Cheyennes were present, there were five or six hundred lodges, each facing east. The circle itself was a symbolic tepee with the open door to the rising sun. When all was ready, a huge chief's lodge of double size was raised in the very center of the circle. . . . [16]

Here we see depicted not only the emotional expression of a strong feeling

---

[16] Llewellyn and Hoebel, 1941, p. 74.

of group solidarity, but also the symbolic manifestation of this unity. Symbols of communal integration were manifold among the Cheyenne. Of these, the Sacred Hat and the Medicine Arrows were perhaps the most important. These religious emblems were taken along whenever the whole tribe went on a war party. Their caretaker, the Sweet Medicine chief, "was symbolically associated with the center of all directions—the heart of the world,"[17] and it was he who presided at meetings of the Cheyenne Council of Forty-Four Chiefs.

In this closely-knit social world, a murder was felt to endanger the whole tribe and to "bloody" the Medicine Arrows. Blood feuds and individual retaliation for murder, the usual mechanisms of justice in simple hunting cultures, were discouraged among the Cheyenne. Instead, the murderer was exiled from the group, whose well-being was threatened by the "murderer's stench"; and a special ceremony was held to purify the Medicine Arrows.

Apart from warfare and the buffalo hunt there were many activities which linked people from different families together. This was true of the women as well as of the men. There were institutionalized "sewing bees" and quilling societies for the women, which paralleled in various ways the male military societies.[18] Children modeled their elaborate group play after the doings of adults, pitching camp, making war, and surrounding the buffalo.[19] In this way they trained themselves for the adult roles in which interaction with others played so large a part.

Settlement on the reservation did much to break up this tradition of mutual interdependence. Margaret Mead, in her description of the "Antlers," speaks of the "artificial dispersal of a sociable and gregarious people through the allotment and isolated house system."[20] This is also what took place among the Dakota. MacGregor writes:

> By establishing ration-issue stations and building homes for the band chiefs in different parts of the reservation, the Agency maneuvered most of the bands into settling in separate localities. After a short time the bands broke up, and the individual families spread along the creeks. Thus a great change was made from the old camp life, with families living at close quarters and under the direction of their chiefs, to a more isolated and independent type of family life. From 1900 to 1917 this pattern of Indian homes separate from each other became crystallized by allotting individual tracts to all Indians. . . . [21]

In spite of this dispersal and separation of formerly interacting social units, the tradition of co-operative activity seems to have persisted among the Dakota.

One of these groups, whose members are nearly all full-bloods, has formed a cattle-association and has pooled land for a joint range. All the men of this association are

---

[17] *Idem*, p. 75.   [18] Grinnell, 1923, Vol. I, pp. 159–169.   [19] *Idem*, pp. 110–117.
[20] Mead, 1932, p. 33.   [21] MacGregor, 1946, p. 37.

relatives either by blood or marriage. This particular development, which has been duplicated several times on the reservation, reveals the continuing strength and importance of the extended family.

There is much social as well as economic participation within the modern extended family neighborhood. The women are frequently seen at work together or chatting in one home or under a bough-covered shade. The small children who form a group of brothers, sisters, and cousins play together around a single house. The men not only share their labor and form economic groups but also meet in one another's homes to discuss local events, programs proposed by the government, or problems of the community.[22]

A similar tendency is also noted among the Arapaho, who, according to Elkin, . . . prefer group work to the relative isolation of most agricultural activity.[23]

In their farming practice, the Arapaho have instituted a system of "return help." In reaping and threshing, a group of neighbors join together for the work, start on one farm and go on to others until it is all completed. The same order of mutual help, though not so well organized, prevails in other types of activity. Those who assist others are not paid but are sure of help in return.[24]

Some of the co-operative patterns related to farming may have been learned from neighboring white farmers or acquired at government school; while others, such as the "sewing bee," may represent a continuity of aboriginal customs. But the historical "origin" of any particular custom need not concern us here. The main point is this: despite the dispersal attendant upon settlement on the reservation and despite the "individualistic" tendencies which were reasserted in consequence of that historic change,[25] the co-operative tradition of Plains groups did not collapse, but managed to survive into the new era.

THE ATOMISTIC CONSTITUTION OF CHIPPEWA SOCIETY

We turn now to the contrasting social picture presented by the Chippewa Indians. The Chippewa were originally a hunting-gathering people. Small crops of corn and squash were grown in summer, wild rice was harvested in shallow lakes in the fall, and maple sugar was tapped in spring. But hunting and fishing provided the main basis of subsistence. Game was relatively scarce in the Chippewa region, particularly after the intensive exploitation of the fur trade. While there seems to have been a greater supply of game in Wisconsin than in the Canadian regions inhabited by the Chippewa, the subsistence level never encouraged large aggregates of population. Before 1870 the situation was probably similar to that in Canada, where summer villages, consisting of about a dozen families, tended to split up in the fall, with family

[22] *Idem*, p. 67.   [23] Elkin in Linton, 1940, p. 237.
[24] *Ibid.*, p. 234.   [25] Goldfrank, 1943.

groups often remaining isolated during the winter months. In Wisconsin, as in Canada, there was no economic co-operation outside of the family unit. There was no communal hunting, like that on the Plains, no camp circle, no organized council of chiefs, no policing system, no regularly constituted military societies, and no symbols of group integration. Every man was for himself or for his own family; and there were few activities which linked the isolated families together.

Even the major religious ceremonies were not conducted for the benefit of the group as a whole, as they generally were among the Dakota and Cheyenne. The *Midewiwin*, the Chippewa Medicine Dance, was limited to members and required a high initiation fee.

Margaret Mead noted the contrast between the Chippewa and the Indians of the Plains, and apropos of the Chippewa remarked:

> Their highly individualistic way of life is completely congruent with the sparse distribution of game animals which makes it necessary for men to scatter widely for several months of the year. But it still remains a problem why the habits of the winter months should so completely dominate their whole outlook rather than the habits of the summer months when they collect in villages. On the other hand, among the Dakota it is the brief buffalo-hunting period in which everyone joins which is most congruent with the co-operative, socialized emphases of the culture.[26]

Elsewhere Ruth Landes has described the individualistic nature of Chippewa economy.[27] In a broad sense, her picture of the Canadian Indians holds true for Wisconsin, except for the fact that there seems to have been very much less emphasis on private property among the Wisconsin Chippewa. Thus there appears to have been no permanent individual family hunting grounds south of Lake Superior, no hunting shacks as testimonials of private possession,[28] no warning signs, no murder or sorcery for trespass. Hospitality was extended with a great deal more generosity than Landes describes. Nevertheless, the general picture of social atomism, though less extreme, was characteristic of the Wisconsin Chippewa and seems to have persisted into the reservation period.

THE CHIPPEWA DURING THE RESERVATION PERIOD

In the case of the Chippewa, settlement on the reservation did not break up an integrated social world, as it did among the Plains tribes. Among the Chippewa there was a greater concentration of population than formerly, rather than dispersal, as among the Dakota. At Lac du Flambeau the erection of a large saw-mill in 1893 brought many scattered groups of Indians to join their relatives camped by the lakeside, and many who had previously left Flambeau returned at about this time to take advantage of the allotment

---

[26] Mead, 1937, p. 464.   [27] Landes, 1937b.

[28] Storage sheds in maple sugar groves provide the nearest equivalent.

system and the timber sales. However, this increase in population density does not seem to have resulted in more co-operative activity. Even today, the average Chippewa household is a world to itself. There is little visiting back and forth, no groups of women working together, no spontaneously formed work gangs or cattle associations like those of the Dakota, no system of "return help" like that of the Arapaho. Occasionally a group of men will band together to harvest wild rice in the autumn, but otherwise the only co-operative social unit is the working team of husband and wife.

To be sure, some efforts in planned co-operative activity have been made by the Tribal Council from time to time. These have usually met with little success; but one successful attempt in this line deserves some mention, to show that such an enterprise is not altogether impossible. In 1943 the Indians at Court Oreilles planted beans on tribal land. Seed was purchased with tribal funds. School buses were used to carry bean-pickers to the field. On some days in 1943 there were 200 pickers at work. The government truck hauled the beans to Hayward, where they were sold to the contracting company. After payment for expenses and wages for pickers were deducted, the tribe came out with a profit of about $500.00.

In this case, a united undertaking which involved many individuals was successfully carried through. But a skeletonized account like this gives no indication of the personal conflicts, stresses and strains which may be experienced in such group ventures. Every year, to cite an example, the Indians at Lac du Flambeau organize a group project: the tourist "pow-wow," for which they choose a treasurer, a ticket-collector, and other officials. Financially, the "pow-wow" is usually successful enough. But this does not tell the whole story. There are always quarrels and dissensions about almost every feature of the project. Men who play a prominent part in its organization are criticised for being "bossy" or for pocketing too much money for themselves, and the honesty of the treasurer is usually called into question. As a result, these officials are generally replaced every summer. A handbill is printed to advertise the "pow-wow." Some of the principal Indian performers are listed. Those not listed may feel angered at the slight and fail to appear at the dance. At least, this was the case with John Thunderbird, whose ego was enormously wounded by this rebuff.[29] There is also rivalry about the job of master of ceremonies and much criticism of speeches that are too long or too short. Little of this criticism is of the face-to-face variety; it circulates in the form of gossip and bickering. In this way, gossip begins to pile up, directed against an unpopular leader, and next year he will be replaced by someone else, who will in turn become a target for criticism. In the summer of 1946, tensions were so strained at a "pow-wow" that a scuffle between two of the dancers broke out in front of

---

[29] See Appendix, p. 91.

the spectators and one of the men (who was intoxicated) was ejected from the arena. The man who ejected him was the leading dancer of the group. He was already unpopular enough among the other Indians for being high-handed and "bossy"; but this last action was seized upon as an outrageous demonstration of authority, and he was universally condemned.

The difficulties experienced when engaging in co-operative activities seem to stem, in large measure, from the personality organization of the Chippewa Indians. But Chippewa personality, in turn, is rooted in the nonco-operative atomistic culture. Partly because the individual is not incorporated, early in life, into a rewarding, interdependent social world, the average Chippewa presents a picture of considerable isolation. As we shall see later, this characteristic is strikingly expressed in the Rorschach protocols.

The isolated character of Chippewa personality must be traced back to the formative influence of aboriginal social patterns, to the geographic isolation of Chippewa households (particularly in winter time), to the prevailing social atomism, and to culturally fostered fears of the surrounding world. Some discussion of these contributory factors may help us to understand more clearly the distinctive aspects of Chippewa acculturation, which will be examined ater.

II. THE INDIVIDUAL IN CHIPPEWA SOCIETY

SOURCES OF FEAR AND ISOLATION

SUSPICION of others, a repressed fearfulness, and a kind of spiritual isolation are characteristics which have often been noted among the Chippewa.[30] In this chapter we shall try to account for the prevalence of these traits.

Many Chippewa fears (as of bears, owls, snakes, underwater spirits, medicine men, enemies, etc.) were deliberately inculcated by parents in their growing children;[31] for the Chippewa seldom resorted to punishment, preferring to institute discipline through "scaring" techniques—by warning children about the giant owl that would carry them off if they did not go to bed, or about the spirits of the dead lurking outside. To make these bogies the more vivid, parents sometimes drew a frightening face on a frying pan, or thrust a mask of bark into the wigwam to cow the youngsters.[32]

It is my impression, partly derived from stories of maternal neglect, that children's ties with their parents were not very close. However, testimony on this point is conflicting. In any case, as many commentators have testified, and as the Rorschach record implies, the Chippewa are not usually demonstrative in their affections. In cases where there was a lack of protective maternal affection, the fears built up in childhood would be apt to assume a more threatening complexion.[33]

As the Chippewa child grew up, he soon acquired more fears. For instance, he learned that all menstruating women were to be avoided. Their touch was believed to cause paralysis or death in a child—a notion widely held even today in northern Wisconsin, where cases of infant mortality are still attributed to this cause.[34] The touch of a man or woman in mourning for a close relative or spouse was believed to have the same effect.[35] Such individuals automatically radiated lethal "vibrations" over which they had no control. It was through no will of theirs that babies died in their presence. They simply couldn't help it. So the wisest thing was to avoid them.

There were also human beings who could cause death deliberately by black magic. Any one might be suspected of sorcery, but medicine men were the most

[30] Hallowell, 1947, pp. 217–225; Jenness, 1935, p. 88; Landes, 1937, p. 102.
[31] For a discussion of "culturally constituted" Chippewa fears, see Hallowell, 1938a.
[32] See Appendix, p. 114.
[33] Long, Kohl, and Peter Jones all assert that the Chippewa were very fond of their children. (Long in Thwaites, 1904, pp. 96–7; Kohl, 1860, p. 309; Jones, P., 1861, p. 61.) However, the same authorities give some conflicting testimony. Jones tells us that Chippewa women while drunk sometimes sold their children for rum or "suffered them to perish for want of proper attention and care." (Jones, P., 1861, p. 61). Kohl remarks that grown-up sons were not "equally grateful and patient with the parents." (Kohl, 1860, p. 309).
[34] See Appendix, pp. 114, 119.   [35] See Appendix, pp. 120, 130.

frequent objects of suspicion, because they had too much supernatural power, and because they were often cranky, ill-tempered men.[36] Therefore children were warned never to laugh or smile in their presence, lest the shaman interpret a giggle as an insult to himself and be driven to retaliate with bad medicine.[37]

There were therefore many categories of human beings within the small in-group whom the child was encouraged to avoid. He was also told scarey stories about the white man, about the Dakota, and other out-groups.

The average Chippewa child had few playmates.[38] With them there was none of the complex organized group play that we find among the Cheyenne. Lacrosse was played by some of the older children; but among the younger ones play was generally aimless—spontaneous, but undirected. Tom Badger, my oldest informant, said that he and his friends seldom played games in childhood—just fooled around. He was even unfamiliar with the Chippewa sport of "snow-snake" about which some other informants had recollections. As a boy, Tom Badger seldom played with large groups of children. Usually he roved through the woods with one other friend; they went swimming in summer, and tobogganing in winter.

The fasting experience may have fostered a sense of isolation in childhood. In order to survive in a dangerous world, a growing child in the old culture had to search for supernatural allies. Soon after he was able to walk and play by himself, a little boy was sent out into the woods to secure a guardian spirit.[39] Until he finally did obtain a fasting dream or vision, he was periodically sent off to fast and wait for a tutelary spirit. Thus, a child eventually learned that his base of security lay in the supernatural realm rather than among human beings.[40]

It may be noted that successful fasting was more vital for a boy than for a girl, because woman's work was mundane and predictable. All that a woman needed was some practical ability and good health. But a man's activities— hunting and warfare, etc.—involved unpredictable elements in which magical support was essential for success.[41]

SORCERY

Some quotations from informants may help to make clear how the fear of sorcery, always in the background of human relationships as a potential dan-

---

[36] See Appendix, p. 131.
[37] Landes, 1939, p. 29. Informants in Wisconsin gave similar testimony.
[38] See, for example, Appendix, p. 95.   [39] See Appendix, p. 93.
[40] See Appendix, pp. 109, 135.
[41] In this connection it is interesting to note that the Rorschachs of our Wisconsin Chippewa males, in all generations, show a greater degree of insecurity than do the Rorschachs of the females. The following data may be of interest to Rorschach workers:

The males have a much longer average time per response than do the females. But a more striking characteristic is the greater frequency of card rejections among the men. Among a group

ger, served to perpetuate the isolation of the individual in Chippewa society.

A woman at Court Oreilles once remarked: "You should never have a person standing in back of you. You should always be facing a person." (In other words, one must never be taken off guard or leave a loophole for the working of bad medicine.)

Another woman described the effects of sorcery upon her father. She said that he had periodic convulsions during which, in an unconscious state, he used to talk to the man who had reputedly bewitched him. Her father visualized this man as standing next to him. The children always knew when their father was going to have a fit when his mouth began to turn to one side.

One day, when he was about to go into convulsions, the father is said to have met his putative sorcerer. To quote the informant:

He spoke to this old man. He told him, "I look as if I'm on a drunk. Well, I always said that if you were ever in my reach, you'd be a goner." He asked the old man why he had "doped" him. Then he grabbed him and hit him on his head a few times, and slapped him right on the face. The old man begged him to let him go, but my Dad said, "I've heard that you've been saying you could give me medicine to cure me right away; but you won't, because you want me to suffer."

Such explosions of hidden rage against one's supposed sorcerers occasionally took place, confirming the native beliefs in bad medicine. The twisted mouth, from which the above-mentioned victim suffered, was commonly interpreted to mean that the sufferer was the target of sorcery.

---

of 20 women over 58 (the most conservative, least acculturated age group), five rejected cards. (One rejected X; two rejected VI; one rejected VI and IX; another III, VI, and IX). Among a group of 15 men over 58, 6 rejected cards. (Two rejected III; one rejected V and X; one rejected I, II, III, and V; one rejected III, VI, VII, IX, and X).

In the more acculturated age group between 30 and 58 the difference was more striking. Eight out of 30 female subjects rejected cards; but rejections were much more common among the males. Of 13 males in this age group, 10 rejected cards; and some of the men rejected several. None of the women were as blocked in this respect as the more extreme male cases. (One male rejected VI; one rejected VII; one III; one rejected I and VI; one rejected IV and VII; one rejected VI, VII, and X; one rejected VII, IX, and X; one rejected III, IV, VII, VIII, IX, and X).

Our informants John Thunderbird and Jim Mink belong in this age group. The former rejected cards II and IX; the latter rejected II, IV, V, VI, IX, and X.

Among 5 younger males below 30, the same tendency toward card-rejection was found. (One 12-year-old rejected IX and X, another 12-year-old rejected VII, IX, and X; a fifteen-year-old rejected I and IV.)

Another indication of the relatively greater resources possessed by the women may be found in their responsiveness to human movement in the Rorschach blots. The average Chippewa woman had one more M response than the average man. Both sexes agreed, however, in avoiding color. (See p. 27.)

The typical Rorschach profile of a Chippewa woman between 20 and 80 would include: 3 M, 3 FM, 9 F, 1 Fc. There was remarkably little change from one generation to the next.

For interpretations of two Rorschach records (John Thunderbird's and Julia Badger's), see the Appendix, pp. 109–110, 142.

The informant who told about her father's convulsions suffered from sorcery herself. Here is her own account:

About six years ago I had high blood pressure and a stroke. I used to see a pine tree coming walking toward me with a shawl. I cried, and my mouth was all twisted. I didn't believe I was doped [bewitched], but I told Tom that maybe I was, because I kept seeing a little Christmas tree coming toward me with a shawl. It seemed to come close and almost smother me.

Tom went to his step-mother and got me some medicines. She told him how to use them. I think I know who might have done it. There was a fellow who used to hang around here. I don't like strangers around. I'm afraid of them. This man kept coming around, and one day he asked to borrow Tom's razor. I said Tom didn't have one. Then he wanted some water. I handed him a cup. He took a drink, and I watched him, close. When he was finished, I threw the water into the fire. Then I washed the cup with hot water and threw all the water outside. I didn't drink out of it either, but I guess I must have done so before supper time. Right after supper, my lip started rolling. Boy, I was scared! My mouth got twisted, and I was sick too.

After I got back from the hospital, that man came around again. I told him I didn't want him to hang around here. I told my husband to tell him to keep away. He offered me some oranges, but I wouldn't eat them. I was afraid of them.[42]

These patterns of suspicion are evidently very old ones in the Chippewa region. After telling about a sorcerer who transformed himself into a bear and killed human beings, one of William Jones' informants concluded, "That was the reason why people long ago used to fear one another. Never in any way, therefore, did the people speak ill of one another. Still yet do some possess evil medicine, especially people that are not Christians."[43] Jenness remarks of the Parry Island Ojibwa:

Probably there is not a single adult on the island who has not been accused of sorcery at some time or other, and who has not himself suffered some misfortune which he attributes to the same cause. . . . So potent is this fear of witchcraft that every Parry Islander takes counter-measures for his own protection, and for the protection of his family. He strives to avoid malice and ill-will by hiding his emotions, and by carefully weighing his words lest he give vent to some angry or ill-timed remark."[44]

UNDEMONSTRATIVENESS

The fear of overt emotionality and its possible consequences seems to have led to a toning-down of human interplay and to have established a pattern of undemonstrativeness among the Chippewa. Kohl, for instance, was surprised by the lack of affective expression when he witnessed a Chippewa family reunion. "There was no waving of handkerchiefs, no shouts of greeting, no laughing and gesticulation. They quietly stepped out of the boat one after the other. . . ."[45] Peter Grant wrote,

---

[42] Friedl, Ernestine. Field notes.   [43] Jones, William, 1919, Part II, p. 251.
[44] Jenness, 1935, pp. 87–8.   [45] Kohl, 1860, p. 35.

Their mode of salutation is most ridiculous: when strangers or long absent friends meet, they remain like statues for a considerable time, with their faces hid or inclined to one side without exchanging one word. After a long pause, they smile or grin at each other, this is understood to be the prelude to asking news, and the conversation becomes general after they have smoken a pipe."[46]

Undemonstrativeness still seems to be a trait of Chippewa personality, especially among the men, giving an impression of studied reserve and a lack of spontaneity. Nevertheless, there are social occasions on which they seem to be relaxed and good humored. It must not be thought that Chippewa are invariably tense and sour-faced. Quite the contrary. They are capable of much laughter and merriment. Hallowell remarks that "Laughter seems to be the catharsis they need for the resolution of tensions."[47] Humorists are always popular among the Chippewa. In former days cross-cousin joking was one standard form of this sort of relaxation. It is still found among the Saulteaux and occasionally among the Wisconsin Chippewa in the form of brother-in-law-sister-in-law joking.

SUSPICION OF OUTSIDERS

As might be expected, the typical Chippewa attitude toward out-groups was one of hostile suspicion. We learn from Tanner's narrative that in the eighteenth century, when a Chippewa hunter encountered an unfamiliar Indian, he would first leap upon him and disarm him before ascertaining the stranger's tribe.[48] Of course, such episodes must be visualized as occurring during the period of long-standing Dakota-Chippewa warfare, when strangers were apparently suspected of being enemies until proven otherwise. Fear and dislike of enemies such as the Fox and Dakota is not surprising. But even allies seem to have been regarded by the Chippewa with some aversion. Elsewhere, Tanner describes the Assineboines as "filthy and brutal."[49] The distant Eskimo and Montagnais are also said to have been considered barbarous and filthy by the Chippewa.[50] And it seems that neighboring allied tribes, like the Menomini and Potawatomi were regarded with hostility and suspicion.

Tom Badger spoke with dislike of the Menomini. He used to go to a Menomini community at Neopit for Drum Dances. The whole Chippewa Drum group from Flambeau would travel there together; but although the Drum Dance was supposed to be a means of spreading good will and brotherhood among the Indian tribes, their stay at Neopit was always an uneasy one. The

[46] Grant, in Masson, 1890, p. 328.

[47] Hallowell, 1947, p. 220. Kohl considered the Chippewa to be very sociable and fond of company. (Kohl, 1860, p. 84.) Peter Jones remarked, "To strangers they are reserved, but among themselves they are notorious talkers and newsmongers." In the next sentence Jones adds, "In the presence of others they are seldom known to hold any conversations with their wives." (Jones, P., 1861, p. 58).

[48] Tanner, 1830, pp. 88, 145.   [49] *Idem*, p. 57.   [50] Kohl, 1860, pp. 324–5, 420.

Chippewa invariably stuck close together on these visits, and never mingled with their hosts. "The Menomini Indians are mean," said Tom. "If we ever went out in the bush there, we never went alone. There were always two of us. I bet you that every one of them has a knife; so that when they get mad, they can stab somebody." Tom also expressed suspicion of the Potawatomi and Winnebago as sorcerers—an opinion voiced by other informants as well.

"SUPERNATURAL POWER" AS A PRIVATE RESOURCE

Now as we have seen, a general air of suspicion marred and inhibited social relationships within the Chippewa in-group. The only defense upon which an individual could rely in this state of affairs was his own supply of supernatural power, aided by his personal guardian spirit.

Among the Chippewa, where every child had to acquire his own guardian spirit and his own stock of supernatural power through the process of fasting for a dream or vision, there was no "pooling" of any such powers, as there was among the Comanche, where a group of warriors could all share in the supernatural resources of one of their members. Among the Comanche, power could be lent or transferred without diminution,[51] but the only sharing of power among the Chippewa was between a god-parent and a newly-born god-child.

Babies were considered to be particularly in need of supernatural support, being weak, exposed, and frail; but they were naturally too young to acquire guardian spirits of their own. Parents would therefore solicit the aid of some elderly person, believed to be strong in supernatural power, who would condescend to share some of his guardian spirit's protection with the child until the youngster was able to fast for his own guardian-spirit vision. Between an old man and his god-child there was expected to be a bond of affection, and the two would call each other by the reciprocal term *weʔe* (god-parent or god-child).[52] Except for this relationship there was no sharing of power among the Chippewa. Nor was any association ever formed among the beneficiaries of a particular guardian spirit, such as the Bear. Every man had his own private pipe-line, so to speak, to his own guardian spirit, and he retained his personal monopoly of those resources.

Such resources were conceived to vary greatly in strength. The Chippewa seem to have invested the living world with a hierarchy of power, in which weak spirits were at the mercy of the strong. As we have noted, infants were particularly vulnerable, exposed to the lethal radiations of mourners and menstruating women; and little children were cautioned not to laugh in the presence of medicine men. Old men were conceived to be more powerful than the young, and potentially dangerous to them.

---

[51] Kardiner, 1945, pp. 64, 92.   [52] See Appendix, pp. 92, 98, 115–116, 137.

UNCERTAINTY ABOUT SUPERNATURAL RESOURCES

However, there was an incalculable element in this system, for one could never be sure just how much supernatural strength a person possessed. The lazy son-in-law motif in Chippewa folklore illustrates this point. In-laws jeer at the apathetic stay-at-home, who never goes hunting. But all the time this man is really saving up strength, as his guardian spirit has advised him. When his wife scolds him for loafing around, the man gets up calmly and kills enough game for the whole village. "He could do all this through his early fasting and dreaming," said the informant. "That's how he got to be good. He just made believe he was lazy. When he fasted, the spirit told him to be lazy for a long time, and then to be good."

Miscalculation of a person's strength is a common theme in the folklore.[53] One simply never knows who is powerful and who is not, so it is best to be on the safe side and act politely to everyone. External qualities are not always adequate indications of a man's supernatural resources, and a man may not even know how much power he has himself.

Given this situation, it is possible to play upon people's fears by a show of aggressive confidence. But the quiet and humble person also has a chance. Who knows? A timid child or a sick, crippled person may be backed up by strong supernatural forces. There are many stories of this kind in the mythology. For instance, one tale tells of a nine year old girl who is the only inhabitant of her village with enough supernatural power to stop a *windigo*, a cannibal giant.

Thus, it was difficult to assess the supernatural powers of others. By and large, however, one could operate on the pragmatic assumption that "By their fruits ye shall know them." It was evident that a successful shaman was rich in magical power. A great hunter or warrior, a successful gambler, a notorious Don Juan—such men were all presumed to be strong in supernatural resources of one kind or another.

BOASTING

It was just these areas that provided a field for boasting. One would suspect that Chippewa males frequently labored under hidden doubts about their own supernatural powers. They must have often wondered just how much influence they actually exerted over their guardian thunder birds and buffaloes. But men kept up a show of bravado in spite of such doubts—or perhaps because of them—and boasted of the aid which spirit helpers gave them in times of crisis. Kohl, who attended a Chippewa war dance with an interpreter, commented on "the unconcealed and vain self-laudation each employed about himself."[54] Men boasted, even lied, about their hunting ability[55] and luck in

---

[53] Compare Jim Mink's stories, pp. 83–86.   [54] Kohl, 1860, p. 21.   [55] Tanner, 1830, p. 83.

gambling.[56] Even in the realm of sorcery men sometimes bragged openly of their triumphs, as old Mashos[57] is said to have done at Flambeau, telling people how many men he had killed with his magic art.

This pattern of boasting can still be observed, under altered conditions, on the reservation. John Thunderbird, Jim Mink, and Julia Badger all boasted a good deal in the course of their work with me.[58] John bragged about his good marks and his "good record" as a student. ("I got a hundred on my examinations—all of them.") and about his athletic prowess ("I played against men twenty-five to thirty years old when I was fifteen. . . . I outplayed them on all positions. I was a good batter, good pitcher, good infield, good everything.") John Thunderbird also boasted about the excellence of the band in which he played; how the members of his Indian band outmarched a white military band on a hot day, and how superior they were to the present-day school band at Flambeau. ("The school kids can't play that well now. It's too hard for them.")

Jim Mink bragged in a similar way about his athletic ability at school, and said that he was the fastest runner at school and about the best football player. Julia Badger boasted about her popularity and how much everybody loved her.

In these cases the boasting seems more indicative of insecurity than of self-confidence; and this was very likely the case in past times—in the "self-laudation" which Kohl observed. But if the boasting betrayed self-doubt, it also stimulated self-doubt in others, making people worried about the relative strength of their own supernatural powers.

If a man excelled in any way, he would be apt to expect the resentment and jealousy of others. Such a man was considered to be a likely target for sorcery merely because he was outstanding. His success was conceived to mock the failures of those less fortunate than himself. Consequently, such a man might fear retaliation.[59]

Expectations such as these made group co-operation a difficult matter. No man wanted to accept the responsibilities of leadership unless he felt very secure in his own supernatural resources. It was probably because of this situation that the white trader (who willingly accepted political authority for reasons of his own) found it so easy to fill the vacuum created in the social structure.

Much of this original mental set seems to have persisted into the present period. It is true that there is less belief in sorcery than formerly, and that

---

[56] *Idem*, pp. 114–15.

[57] Not his real name. This man appears in Julia Badger's life-history (see pp. 131–133) and in John Thunderbird's life-history (see p. 92).

[58] See the Appendix, pp. 97, 100, 101, 104, 111, 125.

[59] See Landes, 1937b, pp. 114–6. Also Tanner, 1830, pp. 136, 230.

the whole fasting complex has been abandoned. But some of the psychological patterns and attitudes associated with these aspects of the old culture are still in evidence today.

THE RORSCHACH EVIDENCE

In the Rorschach test, the emotional isolation of the Chippewa individual finds expression in a characteristic avoidance of color. Out of a total number of 107 Rorschach records taken at Court Oreilles and Lac du Flambeau by Ernestine Friedl, Robert Ritzenthaler, and myself, 53 records were without any color responses at all. Of the remainder only nine individuals gave more than two color responses. According to Dr. Bruno Klopfer, so marked a degree of color-avoidance in our own culture would only be found among extreme compulsion neurotics, patients with psychogenic depression states, and cata- tonics. This does not mean, of course, that the Chippewa can be lumped under one of these clinical classifications; the Rorschachs of the clinical groups have other distinguishing characteristics which are absent among the Chippewa.

Among the Chippewa, color-avoidance is not typically associated with indications of "color shock," except in the case of men between the ages of thirty and fifty-eight. Some of these middle-aged male subjects showed "color shock" through exclamations, laughter, delay in reaction-time, card-rejection, etc. The men in this age-group seemed to show more anxiety than any other group. The older Chippewa were usually not flustered by the color stimulus. If they ignored it, they did so without any manifestations of alarm.

Dr. Klopfer believes that the rarity of color responses among the Chip- pewa implies that the individual is under pressure to become as emotionally independent of his environment as possible, and to expect very little from others.[60] This assessment, of course, is essentially in agreement with the per- sonality picture which has been described in the preceding pages.

CONTRAST WITH PLAINS TRIBES

To recapitulate: we have seen that the social atomism of the Chippewa was reinforced by cultural-psychological factors which served to imbue the individual with a sense of isolation. Culturally induced fears, and particularly the fear of sorcery, led to mutual suspicions which inhibited the development of co-operative activities. How did the situation differ among the Dakota and Cheyenne?

---

[60] Analysis made at the Linton-Kardiner seminar on culture and personality, 1944. However, in an unpublished manuscript dealing with the Rorschachs of Saulteaux children, Hallowell re- ports that the number of color responses fall within the range reported for white children and even exceed some groups of European children.

In the brief space which I have devoted to the Rorschach here, there is no attempt at a full treatment of the Rorschach findings. For further details consult Hallowell, 1942. See also fn. 41, above. For individual Rorschach analyses, see the Appendix, pp. 109–110, 142.

In all tribes of the Plains there was considerable emphasis on individual achievement, leading to rivalry and boasting, as among the Chippewa.[61] Moreover, during the contact period before 1850, there seems to have been a considerable amount of in-group aggression, culminating in many murders and "sorcery-killings."[62] However, Dakota society was also characterized by an over-all cohesive unity, an *esprit de corps*, which became strengthened during the period of armed conflict with the white man. Between 1850 and 1877 there were hardly any recorded traces of in-group hostility in the tribes studied by Goldfrank.[63]

The ideal of co-operation, illustrated in the communal buffalo hunt, pervaded all aspects of Plains culture. Even rivalry, such as the rivalry between warrior societies, functioned for the most part in the interests of the larger group, just as the rivalry of various units of an army may increase the efficiency of the whole.

One culture pattern which contributed to the interrelationship and solidarity of the society was the institutionalization of generosity. Generosity was one of the cardinal virtues of the Dakota, and great care was taken to foster this valued trait in children.[64] One expression of this virtue was the Dakota "give-away" in which property was bestowed on others. The Chippewa do not seem to have had any such standardized expressions of generosity before the introduction of the Drum Dance from the Dakota in the 1870's. So the "give-away" was never an integral part of their culture, nor did it attain any comparable importance. Chippewa children were never so deliberately trained to develop generous qualities, or to learn any comparable sense of *esprit de corps*.[65]

Even more striking, however, is the difference in the development of sorcery in the two cultures. Surely it is significant that so little has been written about Plains sorcery. The pattern of sorcery was known, but deaths do not seem to have often been attributed to this cause. Almost every ethnologist who has studied Chippewa culture has remarked on the prevalence of fear of sorcery. Jenness, Hallowell, and Landes have all discussed Chippewa sorcery at length; but in descriptions of Dakota and Cheyenne culture we seldom find references to sorcery.[66]

One key to this contrast may be found in the sphere of child-training.

---

[61] See Wissler, 1916, p. 74.   [62] Goldfrank, 1943, pp. 70–1.   [63] *Idem.*

[64] See MacGregor, 1946, pp. 107, 126–7, 194. See also Mirsky, 1937, p. 385.

[65] While Gilfillan remarks that Minnesota Chippewa women like to work together, he also comments on their lack of generosity and describes the Chippewa as being calculating and mercenary. "The Indians, strange to say, are not prone to assist each other in misfortune or necessity, as other people are . . . they are apt to exact a very high and extortionate price for anything they do for each other." Gilfillan, 1898–1900, p. 109.

[66] In his careful two-volume work on the Cheyenne, Grinnell devotes only one page to sorcery (Grinnell, 1923, Vol. II, p. 144).

Child training techniques among the Plains tribes seem to have been ably designed to instil a sense of courage and self-reliance in the growing child, particularly in the young boy. In his analysis of the Dakota, Erikson remarks: "It seems as if every educational device were used to develop a maximum of self-confidence, first by parental generosity and assurance, then by gradual training for the overcoming of all weakness in the *boy* who was to be a hunter after game, woman, and spirit."[67]

It may be noted that Dakota and Cheyenne children spent much more time in organized group play and in intimate social interaction with one another so that within the rim of the busy camp circle a sense of social isolation was less likely to develop.

In a later section we shall discuss some additional contrasting patterns of childhood experience. But at this point, since we are equipped with a rough general picture of Chippewa culture and personality, let us turn to an examination of Chippewa history. Our problem is to find out whether "group personality" traits had any bearing on the historical events in which the Wisconsin Chippewa Indians participated, and how these traits may have been displayed in the characteristic ways in which the Chippewa adjusted to acculturation.

---

[67] Erikson, 1939, p. 144. Kardiner strikes a similar note in his discussion of the Comanche whom he characterizes as possessing "a very strong, adequate personality structure" (Kardiner, 1945, p. 81). According to Kardiner, Comanche society embodies a seeming paradox: ". . . a society in which death of the young is constant, but in which anxiety about death is minimal; a high degree of security, notwithstanding the constant threat of annihilation. The emphasis on direct action also renders the individual less interested in receiving bounties and protection from the deity and renders unattractive the concept of achieving illicit ends by the employment of magic. . . . We see therefore little opportunity for the development of neurotic anxiety . . ." (*Idem*, p. 87). According to Linton, there was little fear of sorcery among the Comanche (*Idem*, p. 44).

III. CHIPPEWA ACCOMMODATION TO THE WHITE MAN'S AUTHORITY

A CONTRAST WITH NEIGHBORING GROUPS

LET us first consider the most striking feature of Chippewa acculturation: the ready acceptance of white domination. Tangible evidence of this acceptance is the absence of violence directed against the white man. But we must examine this phenomenon in some detail.

To the south of the Chippewa there were many groups which waged relentless warfare against the whites. The Chippewa stand in marked contrast to them, for their relationship with the white man was generally a peaceful one. To be sure, in the wars between the European powers in America, Chippewa warriors were recruited by the French to fight the British and later a few were recruited by the British to fight the Americans. But here they were in the position of allies or mercenary soldiers. Even Chippewa participation in Pontiac's rebellion may be largely ascribed to the intrigue of French traders.[68] Unlike the Fox, the Chippewa never fought the French. And unlike the Dakota and Cheyenne, they did not attempt to stave off the advance of the Americans.

It is well known that Plains groups, like the Dakota and Cheyenne, faced with dwindling buffalo herds and persistent white encroachment, struggled violently against the white man. Even after the treaty of Fort Laramie, which was designed to protect Indian territory, Dakota war parties continued to attack white immigrants for about thirty years. In striking contrast, the acculturation of the Chippewa was a peaceful process. The Wisconsin Chippewa did not fight the white man, even when urged to do so in alliance with neighboring Indian tribes.[69] On more than one occasion the Dakota tried without success to persuade the Chippewa to join them in attacks upon the white man. The Chippewa were urged to take part in an assault on Fort Snelling, but they refused.[70] Later, a Dakota chief named Little Crow sought the Chippewa as allies in an outbreak against the whites, but did not succeed.[71]

To be sure, the situation in which the Wisconsin Chippewa found themselves was a very different one from that on the Plains. Nevertheless, some of the same factors were present. In Chippewa territory, the rivalry of fur companies and later the advent of lumber camps destroyed resources of game. When the forests were cut down in northern Wisconsin, still more game was

---

[68] Parkman, 1907, Vol. II, pp. 277–8. See below, p. 45.

[69] The Chippewa who took part in Pontiac's rebellion were from Michigan. As will be noted, the Wisconsin Chippewa refused to join in this uprising, although they were solicited by Pontiac's agents.

[70] Kohl, 1860, p. 353.   [71] Adams, 1898–1900, p. 434.

driven away. But the Indians did not rebel. They accepted jobs as lumberjacks and pocketed the money from timber sales. The Chippewa had some monetary compensation and consequently were able to turn to a different source of food— the white man's stores and rations.

Admittedly, the situation faced by the Dakota was a more drastic one, the loss of game more sudden, the press of frontiersmen more severe. But they need not have fought the whites for all that; people do not always fight when driven to such extremities. They might simply have collapsed and become dependent upon the white man. Not only did some other Plains tribes (such as the more remote Crow Indians) refrain from fighting the whites, but large sections of the Dakotas remained at peace and co-operated with the white man even while their brothers were on the war path. So the alternative of co-operation was not only possible, but was followed by a majority of the Dakotas. Nevertheless, a substantial minority of Dakota warriors continued resistance and thereby played a significant role in their tribal history. Among the Chippewa, on the other hand, very few outbreaks against the white man ever took place, and the few that did were quickly terminated.

In trying to account for this contrast between the Chippewa and their neighbors, various possible explanations present themselves at first glance which do not prove upon examination to be wholly successful solutions to the problem. For instance, one might ascribe these differences to the different types of white men with whom the various tribes had dealings. Perhaps the Chippewa were more fortunate in this respect than their neighbors. Or else, perhaps the Chippewa were more "realistic" about white military superiority than were the Fox, Dakota, and Cheyenne. One might also find a clue to the belligerence of the latter groups in their greater institutionalization of warfare and the possession of military societies. Still another possible explanation lies in the atomistic nature of Chippewa society, which lacked the better military organization of the other groups. Before proceeding further, let us consider these alternative solutions a little more closely.

THE WHITE FRONTIERSMEN

The first hypothesis to consider is that the Chippewa were more fortunate in their contacts with the white man than their neighbors were, and that this explains their peacefulness and lack of open hostility against the whites. There is much to be said for this suggestion, although it cannot be the final answer. Parkman long ago contrasted the French and British colonists and their relationships with the Indian. He pointed out that the British were more sedentary and agricultural while the French were more mobile and primarily concerned with the fur trade. The French generally got along well with the Indians, whom they solicited as military allies as well as hunters and trappers. While British operations were similar, they were less skillfully managed. British colonists were much more distant, conscious of their separateness from the Indians, and, according to Parkman, they were hated for their pride.[72]

The French, on the other hand, were said to have been more tolerant of Indian customs and more willing to intermarry with the natives.[73] The fur trade seems also to have been much better controlled in the French area. Macleod describes the superiority of French trade regulations over those prevalent in the colonies to the south:

> . . . in the French dominions the trade with the Indians was centrally controlled, and the traders who worked for the great monopolies were a picked body of men closely checked by their responsible superiors. In the other colonies of North America, however, there was no central organization; each colony controlled the Indian trade within its own borders and competed with its neighbor colonies; and often there was no organization of the trade even within the several colonies.[74]

Cut-throat competition led to all kinds of trouble on the Indian frontier. Unruly British frontiersmen were subject to no supervision and clashes with the Indians were frequent. Macleod says that among the various groups of English colonists the Quakers alone were innocent of bloodshed. The French, however, were never guilty of a massacre.[75]

A contributory factor to Indian warfare in the British sphere was the dreadful custom of scalp bounties offered in some of the colonies. Since money rewards were given for a scalp, many innocent Indians, at peace with the colonists, were murdered by mercenary frontiersmen.[76]

But a more permanent and underlying source of friction was the land-hunger of the British colonists. The French had no hordes of squatters in their territory, moving out into Indian land. To the south, pioneers were always pushing westward and running into trouble with the Indians. In consequence, a hard Indian-hating spirit developed among many of these frontiersmen. This tradition was still alive on the prairies when white settlers came into contact with the Dakota and Cheyenne. General Curtis remarked on the underlying hatred for the Indians when he drew up a report on the Sand Creek massacre, and he explained that the popular cry throughout the west was to exterminate the Indians. "I abhor this style, but so it goes, from Minnesota to Texas."[77]

No such malevolence characterized the French in Canada. It seems very likely, therefore, that the absence of Chippewa hostilities is at least partly due to the fact that they were dealing with tolerant Frenchmen, whose interests lay in a mutually profitable trade, and not with land-hungry Anglo-Saxon

---

[72] Parkman, 1907, Vol. I, pp. 69–84, 179.

[73] Indeed, Champlain offered one hundred and fifty francs as a dowry to each French-Canadian farmer who married an Indian girl. See Macleod, 1928, p. 360.

[74] Macleod, 1928, p. 363.   [75] *Idem*, p. 375.

[76] *Idem*, pp. 399–402.   [77] *Idem*, p. 496.

pioneers. But while this is certainly part of the answer to our problem, it can be only a part of it. For in spite of the contrast ably drawn by Macleod, it must be remembered that the French also had plenty of trouble with some of the Indians. The Fox, in particular, kept up a bloody and unrelenting struggle against the French for two generations. Moreover, the Chippewa had dealings with the British, as well as with the French, who were supplanted after the French and Indian War; and later still they had dealings with the Americans. But the attitude of the Chippewa toward these successive white conquerors did not vary very much.

FAMILIARITY WITH THE WHITE MAN'S STRENGTH

It is evident, therefore, that other factors enter into the picture. Can we attribute the peacefulness of the Wisconsin Chippewa to the fact that they were familiar with the military strength of the whites? As we have noted, Chippewa warriors were recruited by the French to fight the British and by the British to fight the Americans. It was the misfortune of the Chippewa to find themselves on the losing side in both these conflicts, and it was a revealing experience for them. They learned how many hundreds of soldiers the whites were able to mobilize and how well equipped they were with weapons. Later still, a few Chippewa young men took part in the American Civil War, and brought back more tales about the endless military camps and countless battalions of soldiers.

There is no doubt that familiarity with the white man's strength did much to dissuade Indian groups from rebellion.[78] But such knowledge was not always enough to serve as a deterrent to warfare, any more than the knowledge of United States power by the military leaders of Japan served to prevent the attack on Pearl Harbor.

When Edwin James visited the Cheyenne in 1820, they were fully aware of white military strength. "These Indians," he wrote, "seem to hold in exalted estimation the martial prowess of the Americans."[79] But this did not prevent the Cheyenne from fighting the Americans in succeeding generations.

The Dakota had seen endless streams of covered wagons and military detachments crossing the prairies. And yet they also struck back. Something of their indomitable reaction to white encroachment can be grasped in the words of Black Elk: " . . . everyone was saying that the *Wasichus* [white men] were coming and that they were going to take our country and rub us all out and that we should all have to die fighting."[80]

---

[78] The Arapaho provide an illustration. One influential individual, who had had intimate experience with the whites, urged the Arapaho not to fight, since the resources of the enemy were unlimited. Many Arapaho were won over by this appeal, although others preferred to fight along with their Cheyenne and Dakota allies. See Elkin in Linton, 1940, pp. 228–9.

[79] James, 1823, Vol. II, p. 50.   [80] Black Elk, 1932, p. 8.

Black Elk himself saw much of the vast resources of the whites. As a young man he traveled in Buffalo Bill's wild west show to New York, London, Paris, and Germany. But this did not prevent him from fighting at Wounded Knee a few years later. Thus, familiarity with white resources cannot, in itself, be considered an adequate solution to our problem.

ORGANIZATION FOR WARFARE

To consider another alternative hypothesis, the difference between the Chippewa and Dakota cannot be attributed merely to the Plains institutionalization of warfare; the Chippewa were also great warriors. It is true that the Dakota possessed military societies, while the Chippewa did not; but the Chippewa were not the less warlike for all that. They successfully fought the Dakota for a hundred years across Wisconsin and Minnesota, staving off the Fox as well; and before that time they had battled the Iroquois in the east. But one aspect of their warfare may be mentioned in this connection: the individualism of the Chippewa to which we have already referred and their inability to co-operate successfully in large group ventures.

John Tanner, who was adopted as a child by the Chippewa and who spent nearly his whole life among them, explained, "An Indian chief, when he leads out his war party, has no other means of control over the individuals composing it, than his personal influence gives him. . . . "[81] This personal influence (usually correlated with the leader's supposed amount of supernatural power) was often inadequate to hold the men together, and members frequently broke away from the expedition to return home in dissatisfaction. On more than one large war party in which Tanner participated, the component members took to fighting among themselves.[82]

There were no real chiefs among the Chippewa, and political authority, as we have seen, was almost nonexistent, although an occasional individual with authority sometimes attained a position of great prestige and respect. The Dakota and Cheyenne, in contrast, had a well-developed political system with recognized chiefs, military societies, public criers, etc. It was much more difficult for the scattered Chippewa to mobilize for warfare. Nevertheless, in spite of all this, the Chippewa were successful enough in their struggles with the more highly organized Dakota, Fox, and Cheyenne. The successful capture of British Fort Mackinaw by the Chippewa of Michigan during Pontiac's rebellion also shows that the Chippewa were even capable of concerted organized warfare against the whites. But if they were able to achieve this triumph once with so much success, why did the Chippewa never repeat the attempt? And why did the Wisconsin Chippewa refuse to take part in Pontiac's uprising?

---

[81] Tanner, 1830, p. 124.
[82] *Idem*, pp. 124–27, 138–42, 204–7. See also Jenness, 1935, p. 102.

The answer to these questions cannot be found only in the tolerant nature of the French traders, nor can it be found only in Chippewa "realism" and awareness of white resources, nor in the atomistic nature of Chippewa society, although all of these factors provide a partial solution to our problem. Our problem is highlighted by the striking fact that Chippewa acculturation in Wisconsin is characterized not merely by the absence of concerted group warfare but also by the rarity of *isolated* outbursts against the white man, in which respect the Chippewa again stand out in dramatic contrast to their neighbors further south. The significance of this contrast will be made more apparent when we examine in closer detail the actual situation in northern Wisconsin before the 1870's and the kind of relationship which existed between the Indians and the whites.

WHITES A SMALL MINORITY

Until the 1870's northern Wisconsin was almost untouched by the outer world. The few white men who held key positions in the area before this time— traders, priests, government officials, etc.—were greatly outnumbered by the Indians. The proportion of Indians to whites at communities like Court Oreilles and Flambeau seems to have been about sixty to one. Court Oreilles and Flambeau were about eighty miles apart and quite isolated from other communities. According to Schoolcraft's figures, published in 1851, there was a combined total of nineteen white men at these posts.[83] The Indian population was 841 at Court Oreilles and 480 at Lac du Flambeau, according to Neill.[84] Moreover, the white outposts fluctuated in numbers, and some of the early traders, like Malhiot, Cadotte, and Corbine, were often alone among the Indians. This seems to have been typical of the Wisconsin Chippewa area, except further north, along the southern shore of Lake Superior, where the concentration of white men was much higher.[85]

It is noteworthy that, despite this unequal population ratio in an area

---

[83] Schoolcraft, 1851, Vol. III, p. 605.

[84] Neill, 1885, p. 508.

[85] During the early years of the Wisconsin fur trade, the trading center of La Pointe on Lake Superior was the focus of white activity in the area. After the completion of the Sault Canal in 1885, which allowed the passage of ships from the other Great Lakes, the aspect of the southern shore changed very quickly. A mining boom began, to exploit the copper mines and the iron ores of the Marquette, Gogebic, and Vermilion ranges; and ports like Ashland, Superior, and Duluth sprang up as shipping centers, with population multiplying quickly. Between 1871 and 1877 the Wisconsin Central constructed a main line up to the growing port of Ashland on Lake Superior. This was the first railroad to cross northern Wisconsin and to reach the Wisconsin shore of Lake Superior. Railroad lines generally preceded settlement in the area. Communities like Court Oreilles and Flambeau were not much affected by these developments until the coming of the lumber companies to the reservations in the 1870's and 1880's. For a picture of Wisconsin's historical development, see Raney, 1940.

where the Indians were well armed with guns,[86] the outnumbered whites were almost never attacked. And yet there was a considerable amount of Indian resentment against the whites.

REASONS FOR ANTI-WHITE HOSTILITY

There were many reasons for this resentment. One was a temperamental difference between Indians and whites. It would be hard to imagine a greater contrast to the reserved and cautious Chippewa than the first white men who lived among them, the *voyageurs*. By all accounts, the *voyageurs* were energetic extraverts.[87] Their jokes may sometimes have been welcomed by the Indians, but their social dynamism must also have been rather frightening. Indeed, the Indians still consider white men to be very noisy, an attribute they dislike.

Tom Badger said to me, "I used to be scared when the white man at the store talked with my father. The white man was a big fat man, who talked so loudly that I thought he was quarreling with my father." Tom added that white men generally talk louder than Indians. This attribute, allied with the white man's obvious power, gave an impression of overbearing dominance, which was resented by the Chippewa; while on their side the whites regarded the Indians as sullen and lazy and felt superior to them.

Tension in relation to the white man also stemmed from the intermarriage of Indian women with French traders and *voyageurs*. These matches were usually welcomed by the girl's parents because of economic advantages. Harmon wrote that his interpreter married an Indian girl and presented her parents with rum and dry goods to the value of two hundred dollars.[88] Thereafter, the girl would be well clothed and fed at the trader's expense, and her influence at the trading post could be brought to bear in favor of her relatives. This situation was very advantageous to many of the Indians, but not to the young men, who resented the wealthy intruders. Their jealousy was one of the many sources of discontent.

Another, according to Benjamin G. Armstrong, was the defection of white husbands, who frequently regarded their alliances as only temporary liaisons.

. . . the climax came when the traders quit the country and left their families to the Indians' care. This led to family troubles. The abandoned woman would go back to her family, where there were probably several children and dependent persons to support and only one or two men to hunt for their living. The addition to the perhaps already heavy burden was hard to bear. The white race were cursed, family talks resulted in aggravating troubles that were already heavy enough.[89]

---

[86] See below, pp. 39–41. Kohl says that few of the whites in the region were armed (see below, p. 41).

[87] See Nute, 1931.   [88] Harmon, 1903, pp. 23, 57, 58.

[89] Armstrong, 1892, pp. 128, 132.

Still another source of discontent was resentment of authority and of the specific abuses which the Chippewa suffered at the hands of the white man.

To take one example: before the establishment of the present reservations in Wisconsin, the United States government put a great deal of pressure on the Chippewa to move west of the Mississippi. The majority had no desire to comply, because to do so would have meant to be at the mercy of their old enemies, the Dakota. Moreover, the Chippewa did not want to abandon their hunting grounds.

In 1850 the government employed a new maneuver to encourage westward migration. They paid the annuity at Sandy Lake, near the Mississippi River. Many of the Wisconsin Indians preferred not to travel there for their annuities. The Reverend Wheeler at Odanah, who sympathized with their situation, wrote: "They appear to be fully determined to remain on the shores of Lake Superior, and even forego their annuities, if the government choose to withhold them."[90]

The stand of these resisters was strengthened by the shocking conditions attending the annuity payment at Sandy Lake. The Indians who gathered there were kept waiting for seven or eight weeks before any provisions arrived. Since sanitary conditions were poor, epidemics of measles and dysentery broke out. Many returned home without being paid, and many died.[91] This incident greatly angered the Chippewa. Such episodes were not soon forgotten. Nor were the broken treaty promises, a long account of which can still be given by the average Chippewa adult.

After the coming of the lumber camps, the Wisconsin Chippewa also resented the destruction of their tall pine forests, even though the Indians were hired to take part in this destruction, and even though "timber money" was a source of wealth. Trees formed the raw material of most Chippewa manufactures in aboriginal times—birchbark canoes, birchbark containers, winnowing trays, etc. Cedar boughs constituted the most potent purificatory antidote to the dangerous properties of female menstrual blood. Moreover, trees seem to have been symbolic of health, life, purity, and manhood among the Chippewa, just as water apparently symbolized danger, evil, and death.[92]

Therefore, the leveling of the forests was regarded ominously by some of the old-timers at Court Orielles and Lac du Flambeau, and there were strong complaints as well when the Wisconsin and Minnesota Light and Power Company inundated a large stretch of land at Court Oreilles in order to construct a dam. For actions such as this, the white man was regarded as ruthless, rapacious, and insatiable. John Thunderbird expressed these feelings one day in a sudden explosion of emotion:

[90] Davidson, 1895, p. 168.   [91] Neill, 1885, p. 500. See also Pitezel, 1860, p. 298.
[92] On the symbolism of trees, see Kohl, pp. 109–10, 152–3.

Indians call you white people *mačimánidòg* (evil spirits) [John told me]. They call you that because you invent machinery—everything. You're regular devils in making all kinds of equipment—airplanes, automobiles, boats, things the Indian could never do. But they dreamt about them before. *Manido* told them "You'll see white men flying in the air. You'll see iron horses on tracks, automobiles with rubber tires carrying people. They're going to bring fire water too—poison. They're going to use that on you to fool you people." That's the preaching the old-timers used to bring out. They said we'd lose our land on account of those things that would happen when the white man would come. We'd lose our rights, our land, our timber. "White man's going to take it. They're regular devils. They cheat everybody. But there's one thing they can't cheat: that's *Manido*. Watch all the accidents the white man will have on account of the way they treat the Indians. *Manido* will punish them for it. A lot of things will happen after we die. There won't be any Indians left on earth. Only mixed blood. Pretty soon there'll only be white people." . . . Today the Indian sits quiet. He don't say anything any more. There's too much white people around. . . . They keep taking his property away. . . . We just have to let the white man do as he wants in this country. . . . *Manido* can't do nothing to help the Indians now, because the white people are here, and they're too wise.

While John Thunderbird spoke these words, his eyes flashed with angry excitement. But it is interesting to note that when he was through, he was particularly cordial to me, and he and his wife posed for a series of photographs in one of which John wore an Indian bonnet.

SENSE OF IMPOTENCE

The feelings expressed by John Thunderbird are widespread in northern Wisconsin today, and there is evidence that they are not recent. The short-lived Shawano prophet cult, a nativistic movement which reached Court Oreilles in 1808, was an early expression of this resentment and hostility against the whites. And yet, even in those days, there seems to have been an impotent quality to this resentment, an apathetic resignation such as can be noted in John's tirade against the white man. That this feeling of impotence is not a new phenomenon is indicated by a passage written by J. G. Kohl before 1860.

The Ojibbeways have all lost their memory. The Americans have made them weak [said one of Kohl's informants] . . . Our nation has fallen, and this came quite suddenly, since the *Kitchimokans*, or "Long Knives" [Americans] entered our country.[93]

The same feeling of helplessness is also reflected in the record of a Chippewa chieftain's speech taken down by Richard E. Morse in 1856.

My father, look around you upon the faces of my poor people; sickness and hunger, whiskey and war are killing us fast. We are dying and fading away; we drop to the ground like the trees before the axe of the white man; we are weak—you are strong. We are but foolish Indians—you have knowledge and wisdom in your head; we want

[93] Kohl, 1860, p. 367.

your help and protection. We have no homes—no cattle—no lands, and we will not long need them. A few short winters, my people will be no more. . . . [94]

These expressions of impotence seem curious in view of the marked numerical inferiority of white men in the region prior to 1870. And considering the extent of anti-white sentiment, the rarity of open acts of hostility against the white man is also puzzling.

RARE INSTANCES OF ANTI-WHITE AGGRESSION

Warren refers to two outbursts against white men at Court Oreilles. The first involved the murder of a Canadian *coureur de bois* by an Indian during the first half of the nineteenth century. This incident will be described further on.[95] The second occurrence concerned Jean Baptiste Corbine, the principal trader at Court Oreilles. It seems that after a quarrel with his native wife, Corbine gave her a beating and sent her home to her parents' wigwam almost naked. This act touched off a smoldering hostility which had been stirred up by the Shawano prophet cult. In consequence, some Indians broke into the trader's storehouse and plundered his goods. Corbine managed to escape in the excitement and made his way up to Chequamegon Bay.[96] But later on he returned and spent the rest of his life at Court Oreilles.

A much more serious affair was the murder of four white men by a raiding party of Chippewa Indians from Lac du Flambeau in 1824. Truman Warren, then principal trader at Lac du Flambeau, demanded the murderers from the hands of the local chiefs. Despite a show of opposition from some of the old men, this demand was met with, and the four captives sent to jail at Mackinack.[97]

It is hard to find more episodes of this kind in the historical records.[98] To be sure, the Indians sometimes threatened traders when they were drunk, usually demanding more rum. But although the trader was greatly outnumbered, he was usually able to control the situation on these occasions, even though his heart was pounding all the while. Long gives a very interesting description of such an experience, during which he behaved with calm and sagacity, while surrounded by a band of armed Indians who were drunk and menacing.[99] Schoolcraft tells of a trader threatened by forty armed men who

---

[94] Morse, 1856, p. 343.   [95] See below, p. 61.

[96] Warren, 1885, pp. 301–2, 326.   [97] *Idem*, p. 389.

[98] For a few cases of Chippewa murders of white traders, most of which did not take place in Wisconsin, see: Neill, 1885, pp. 411–2, 456, 467; Long, p. 53; Cameron in Masson, 1890, p. 287; Schoolcraft, 1851, pp. 198–200. Gilfillan writes of the Minnesota Chippewa: "One or two white persons have been killed in collisions with the Indians within the past twenty-five years; but not so many as there have been Indians killed by whites." Gilfillan, 1898–1900, p. 92. Julia Badger's grandfather, "Big Bill," killed a white man during a brawl. See the Appendix, p. 112.

[99] Long, 1768–82, in Thwaites, 1904, pp. 100–8.

meant to kill him, but were easily dissuaded from this purpose by a friendly Indian.[100]

Malhiot, the trader at Lac du Flambeau, describes a similar nervous moment.

Several of Chorette's Savages came here last night to get rum and to use violence. For a long while I may say, making use of an expression among the lower orders in Canada, that " *I did not know whether I was eating pork or pig.*" . . . I was alone with Gauthier and they were at least 15 rascals all armed; those who had no knives or spears, had sticks or stones. Fortunately we all got off with calling one another names and threatening one another.[101]

On a later occasion, these Indians attempted to raid the fort, but Malhiot informs us that "After a two hours quarrel we succeeded in getting those wild beasts out of the Fort."[102]

SAFETY OF THE CHIPPEWA REGION

Such raids were rare occurrences. Kohl wrote in 1860:

The *voyageurs* and traders assure me that they generally consider their wares perfectly safe among the Indians, although they travel among them frequently with valuable stores and full purses. Though there are no police or soldiers, it has very rarely happened, since Europeans have traveled the country, that any trader has been attacked for the mere sake of plunder. The robberies which have been committed now and then have been effected by Europeans, or at their instigation, especially at that period when the two great rival fur companies—the Hudson's Bay and North-West—existed here side by side. The agents of these companies often plundered each other's posts and employed the Indians for this purpose.[103]

Kohl goes on to observe that it is only in exception to this rule that there is a Chippewa band known as "Pillagers,"[104] a name derived from a single episode of looting on the part of its members. The episode must have been considered rather unusual—else the name "Pillagers" would never have been applied to them. Yet, the affair was not a very lawless one, to judge by Warren's descrip-

[100] Schoolcraft, 1851, pp. 192–5.   [101] Malhiot, 1804–5, p. 194.   [102] *Ibid.*, pp. 196–7.

[103] Kohl, 1860, p. 68. This seems to have been the case in Malhiot's experience. Note that he refers to his attackers as "Chorette's savages." Chorette was a North West Company employee, who was a rival of Malhiot throughout the latter's stay at Lac du Flambeau.

[104] "In the year 1781 a large band of the Ojibways, who had taken possession of Leech Lake . . . became for the first time known by the distinctive appellation of 'Pillagers,' *Muk-im-dua-win-in-e-wug* (men who take by force)."

After describing the occurrence, Warren continues: "The conduct of the Pillagers in this affair was generally censured by their more peaceful fellows as foolish and impolitic, as it would tend to prevent traders from coming amongst them for fear of meeting with the same treatment. To make up, therefore, for their misconduct, as well as to avert the evil consequences that might arise from it, the Pillagers, on the ensuing spring, gathered a number of packs of beaver skins and sent a delegation headed by one of their principal men to the British fort at Mackinaw, to appease the ill-will of the whites, by returning an ample consideration for the goods which they had pillaged." Warren, pp. 256, 259–260.

tion of it. Moreover, the "Pillagers" sent a delegation to Fort Mackinaw with goods in compensation for their crime.

Kohl's description of the situation at La Pointe, the annuity and trading center of the Wisconsin Chippewa in the 1850's is a very telling one.

We are here a handful of Europeans, surrounded by more than a thousand Indians armed with tomahawks, knives, and guns, and yet not one of us feels the slightest alarm. Hardly one of us Europeans possesses a weapon; only the Indians are armed. There is not a trace of any precautionary measure, as in the towns of Austrian Illyria, where the Montenegrins and other mountaineers are compelled to deposit their arms at the gate before being allowed to enter the town, nor is there a single soldier or armed policeman on the whole island. And yet, for miles around, every bush conceals an Indian, and the wooden booths of the Europeans are filled with the most handsome and desired articles. A whole ship-load of wares has just arrived, and the blockhouse in which they are packed could be broken open with a hatchet. The sum of ready money on the island, in handsome new coinage, amounts to several thousand dollars, and yet we sleep with open windows and doors, and not one of us thinks of locking a door or bolting a window.

To this it may be replied, I grant, that the Indians, for their own sake, would soon detect and give up a single thief, and that they are well aware a robbery *en masse* would be eventually avenged on the whole nation. But to which I answer, first, that these reasons are equally valid in Syria and Spain, but in neither of these countries could money or men be so exposed without a company of gendarmes. . . .[105]

Kohl need not have turned to Europe for his contrast with the Chippewa. Another traveler of this period contrasted the safety of the Chippewa-Cree-Assineboine region with the dangerous territory of the neighboring Dakota, where the white man's life and possessions were much more insecure.

This tribe [the Assineboines] like the Sauteurs [Chippewa] and the Crees, their allies, are not hostile to the whites. A traveler can pass through this nation with more security for his life than in a civilized country; which cannot be said of the Sioux. One cannot travel upon the highlands of the Missouri and Red rivers, without being often seized with horror by the narrations occasioned by the view of places and scenes of a crowd of acts of barbarity and treason, that have been perpetrated by this people, of which, one sees in history but an example from time to time.[106]

Chittenden, in speaking of the Plains country, commented:

Above the friendly tribe of the Omahas . . . the navigator had to pass the country of six or seven tribes who might prove hostile or friendly according as circumstances over which he had no control might turn. It was a very rare thing for a keelboat to run the entire gauntlet unmolested, while in many instances disastrous conflicts were precipitated.[107]

---

[105] Kohl, 1860, p. 68 ff.

[106] Belcourt, 1872, p. 237. On the peacefulness of the Assineboine and neighboring tribes, see also Willson, Beckles, p. 217.

[107] Chittenden, 1902, Vol. I, p. 116. See also p. 160. For some descriptions of encounters with unruly Plains tribes, see James, 1823, Vol. I, pp. 124–127, 149, 229. Vol. III, pp. 72–5.

This brings us back once more to our old question: How can we explain the absence of open hostility among the Wisconsin Chippewa, which is so different from the situation among the Fox, Dakota, and Cheyenne? In order to answer this question we will have to consider the early relationship between the Chippewa and the fur traders, the first white men with whom these Indians came into any close contact.

TIES BETWEEN THE CHIPPEWA AND THE TRADER

We have seen that out-groups were generally regarded with mistrust and dislike by the Chippewa. This is true of attitudes toward the white man as well; but here we have a different complex of associations and ideas. The whites differed in important respects from other out-groups—in their skin-color, way of life, etc. They were immensely more powerful and wealthy than any other human beings with whom the Chippewa had ever had dealings, so that the Indians could not help but regard them as being especially rich in supernatural power. What is more, the whites made a deliberate attempt to woo the Indians, pressing gifts upon them, and making protestations of friendship. The Chippewa recognized the value of the white man's kettles, guns, traps, needles, knives, hatchets, blankets, clothing, etc., which seemed so superior to their own manufactures of stone, bone, shell, and wood. What is more, the whites enriched their lives with tobacco and liquor, blessings which produced exciting experiences unknown before. The Indians were very willing to abandon the native arts and crafts supplanted by new manufactures and to settle down in a relationship of dependency upon the white man. They camped about the trading center, which became the focal point of community activity. The Chippewa, who had never had strong "chiefs" before, now had one; and he was indispensable. If the trader moved, they followed him; for all of the adult male population had become specialized as trappers and hunters, in order to exchange pelts for trading goods.

The Chippewa were bound to the trader by bonds of credit. Before a man set out to his hunting and trapping grounds, the trader customarily equipped him in advance with traps, ammunition, food, clothing, etc. When the Indian hunter brought back his furs later on in the season, this debt was canceled; and the hunter then assumed new debts for as much as the trader would allow.[108] Thus, the relationship between the trader and the Indians was a symbiotic one. He needed their furs; and they had become dependent upon his trading goods.

It was probably in consequence of this situation that the Chippewa migrated into Wisconsin from Canada early in the eighteenth century. In 1830 Edwin James wrote of the Chippewa Indians:

[108] See Gilfillan, 1901, p. 73. See also Tanner, 1830, pp. 70–71, 181–82, Kohl, 1860, pp. 78–80, 130, and Turner, 1891, pp. 62–4.

Such is their urgent necessity for ammunition and guns, for traps, axes, woolen blankets, and other articles of foreign manufacture, that at the approach of winter, their situation is almost hopeless, if they are deprived of the supplies they have so long been accustomed to receive. . . . The practice of the traders now is, whenever they find the animals in any district becoming scarce, to withdraw their trading establishment, and by removing to some other part, make it necessary for the Indians to follow.[109]

In his *History of the Ojibway Nation*, Warren gives us a description of one of the pioneer traders, Michel Cadotte, who led his following westward through Wisconsin.

As game became scarce in the vicinity of their villages [wrote Warren of the Indians at Court Oreilles and Lac du Flambeau], they moved in large hunting camps towards the Mississippi, and on the richer hunting grounds of the Dakotas they reaped rich harvests of meat and furs.

The older and more intelligent men of these bands attribute to this day their steady westward advance, and final possession of the country nearly to the Mississippi, through following the example and footsteps of their first and old pioneer trader, Michel Cadotte. . . . He is mentioned to this day as having not only placed the weapons into the hands of the Ojibways which enabled them to conquer their enemies, but led them each winter westward into the rich hunting grounds of the Dakotas, until they learned to consider the country as their own, and caused their enemies to fall back after many a bloody fight west of the "Great River."[110]

The Chippewa entered Wisconsin at the time of the French warfare with the Fox Indians. So perhaps there were other motives to this migration beside the search for furs. It may be that the French encouraged the Chippewa migration south of Lake Superior as a buffer against the Fox, providing Chippewa warriors with guns to repel the enemy. Whether or not the French pursued this as a conscious policy, the Chippewa were soon at war with the Fox as well as with the Dakota. Another possible explanation of the Chippewa migration to the south is that of Neill, who suggests that it was in the interest of the French to draw the Chippewa as far away as possible from the influence of English traders who had appeared in the vicinity of Mackinaw.[111]

In any case, it is clear that the Chippewa who trailed after their traders into Wisconsin had become extremely dependent upon them. Kohl explains how the traders influenced the destinies of their followers.

At times the traders will make a commercial treaty with the chiefs, and thus enter into a debtor and creditor account with an entire village or tribe. Hence they frequently acquire great political influence, and, as they risk very considerable sums, it may be conjectured that a trader can only be successful through caution and the exercise of tact. I have been told, and have indeed remarked it, that association and difficult nego-

[109] Tanner, 1830, p. 10.   [110] Warren, 1880, pp. 299–300.   [111] Neill, 1880, p. 420.

tiations with the Indians have produced famous diplomatists among these traders, who carry on the *"ars rerum gerendarum"* with great cleverness and tact, and can form an excellent judgment of the character of these savages.[112]

POLITICAL POWER OF THE TRADER

For reasons such as these, it was usually the trader who mapped the crucial plans of action for the band in peace and in war. On one occasion, for instance, Michel Cadotte, referred to above, got together with a French trader attached to a band of Dakota Indians and these two men were able to conclude an armistice between the rival tribes.[113] On other occasions, when it seemed to their advantage to do so, the traders managed to foment or encourage inter-tribal warfare,[114] or even to launch attacks upon rival trading posts.[115]

Warren tells a story about how Jean Baptiste Cadotte attempted to dissuade the Chippewa warriors of his band from launching an attack upon the Dakota. He called a council, presented liquor and tobacco, "and promised them, that if they would give up their present warlike intentions, and hunt well during the winter, in the spring he would give them all the ammunition he might have on hand, to use against their enemies."[116]

In spite of the trader's enormous influence, these appeals were not always heeded; and on this particular occasion an old warrior insisted on going on the warpath after all. Forty-five men accompanied him, "many of whom, it is said, went with great reluctance."[117]

At Lac du Flambeau, the trader Malhiot also begged a group of Chippewa warriors not to go on the war path, for if they went, he would get no furs.[118] Often, as in this case, the lure of military excitement and prestige outweighed such appeals. But the point is that the trader made such requests, and that the young men listened. The trader was really the crucial authority in the band, of greater functional importance than the "chiefs," whom often enough he himself had elevated to chieftainship.[119]

The trader even took a hand in ethical questions. Duncan Cameron, for example, exhorted the Indians to "good conduct," although he probably had reference to repaying credits on time. Cameron also discouraged the Indians

---

[112] Kohl, 1860, pp. 130–1.   [113] Warren, 1880, p. 303.

[114] *Idem*, pp. 316, 318. Tanner writes of a trader giving the Chippewa ammunition to fight the Dakota. Tanner, 1830, p. 138.

[115] Tanner writes: "About planting time, the traders of the North West Company sent messengers and presents to all the Indians, to call them to join in an attack on the Hudson's Bay establishment at Red River. . . . Many of the Indians obeyed the call, and many cruelties and murders were committed. . . . Some of the Hudson's Bay people were killed in open fight, others were murdered after being taken prisoners." Tanner, p. 216.

The influence of the traders had international repercussions. Turner writes that "The leaders in the opening of the war [French-British] that ensued were Northwestern traders." Turner, 1891, p. 41.

[116] Warren, 1880, p. 337.   [117] *Ibid.*   [118] Malhiot, pp. 194–9.

[119] *Idem*, p. 204. See also Cameron, pp. 270, 278, Kohl, 1860, p. 270.

from fishing, since this activity interfered with the prevailing emphasis upon hunting and trapping.[120]

The trader's power lay in his possession of vital supplies, the access to which depended upon his willingness to extend credit. An Indian who was denied credit really faced disaster. To be sure, he might set off in search of another trader; but in such a case the latter might look with suspicion upon the "straggler" who had left his own trading area. Long describes such an individual.

. . . I immediately considered him as a straggler or he certainly would not have traveled so far, unless he had done something to displease the servants at the company's forts, and could not obtain credit. . . . I told him I never gave credit to any but good hunters.[121]

Thus, each trader could count on a band of followers, restless and dissatisfied, but loyal to him in the long run.[122]

The power of the traders is demonstrated by the events which took place during the conspiracy of Pontiac. A group of Chippewa from Michigan and the Lake Huron region took part in this insurrection but none of the Wisconsin Chippewa participated. In both cases, the influence of French fur traders is discernible. The traders in Michigan seem to have done their best to encourage Pontiac's rebellion against the British. In his classic account of the conspiracy, Parkman describes the intrigues of these traders.

The fur-trading French . . . dreaded the English as dangerous competitors in their vocation, and were eager to bar them from the country. They lavished abuse and calumny on the objects of their jealousy, and spared no falsehood which ingenious malice and self-interest could suggest. They gave out that the English were bent on the ruin of the tribes, and to that end were stirring them up to mutual hostility. They insisted that, though the armies of France had been delayed so long, they were nevertheless on their way, and that the bayonets of the white-coated warriors would soon glitter among the forests of the Mississippi. Forged letters were sent to Pontiac, signed by the King of France, exhorting him to stand his ground but a few weeks longer, and all would then be well. To give the better coloring to their falsehoods, some of these incendiaries assumed the uniform of French officers, and palmed themselves off upon their credulous auditors as ambassadors from the King. Many of the principal traders distributed among the warriors supplies of arms and ammunition, in some instances

---

[120] Cameron, p. 281–3.   [121] Long, pp. 152–3.

[122] Turner speaks of Indian groups in Wisconsin being apportioned to different traders. See Turner, 1891, p. 24, Fn. 3. According to a widespread Indian belief, each species of animal within a given locality has its own "chief" or "boss," who leads his followers from place to place. According to Jenness, the "boss" was always colored white. Jenness, 1935, p. 23. One informant at Court Oreilles also volunteered the information that the deer chief was white in color. This piece of folklore may not be a "projection" of the trader-Indian relationship into the world of nature, but it provides a nice parallel in native symbolism. If awe of white animals was an aboriginal pattern, as seems to have been the case, this belief would probably have facilitated the acceptance of whites as superior beings with authority to command.

given gratuitously, and in others sold on credit, with the understanding that payment should be made from the plunder of the English.[123]

Although some of the more eastern Chippewa took part in Pontiac's conspiracy, particularly in the dramatic capture of Fort Mackinaw, the Wisconsin Chippewa remained aloof from this struggle in spite of the solicitations of Pontiac's agents. Here again, the influence of a fur trader seems to have been decisive but this time on the side of peace. As Warren informs us:

It is true that the war-club, tobacco, and wampum belt of war had been carried by the messengers of Pontiac and his lieutenant, the Mackinaw chieftain, to La Pointe, and the principal villages of the tribe on Lake Superior, but the Ojibways listened only to the advice and the words of peace of a French trader[124] who resided at Sault Ste. Marie, and from this point (with an influence not even surpassed by that which his contemporary, Sir Wm. Johnson, wielded over the eastern tribes), he held sway, and guided the councils of the Lake Superior Ojibways, even to their remotest village.[125]

As Alexander Henry observed, "They considered M. Cadotte as their chief. . . . It was by him that the Chippeways of Lake Superior were prevented from joining Pontiac."[126]

It is clear that the relationship between the Indians and the trader is an important one for us to understand because it apparently formed the prototype for later attitudes toward the American government and its representative, the Indian agent, who stepped into the trader's shoes.[127]

THE PATTERN OF GENEROSITY

It was the custom, not only of the trader, but also of the political representatives of the French, British, and American governments, to give presents to the Indians in order to secure their allegiance. Envoys who wished to capture their friendship were forced to be generous. According to Louise Phelps Kellogg, the temporary suspension of this policy was one of the causes of Pontiac's rebellion. At any rate, the lavish giving of presents was renewed by Robert Rogers and continued throughout the American Revolution and thereafter.[128] Later government officials also created "chiefs" as traders and political representatives had done before them. In 1897 Gilfillan referred to "the great number of chiefs which have recently been created by the United States government agents."[129]

One might consider the United States treaties with the Indians to be in line with the old paternalistic tradition of gift-giving, for these contracts generally stipulated that annuities were to be paid to the Indians, some of them "forever." To be sure, the annuities were largely in payment for the cessions of Indian lands and thus perhaps represent exchanges rather than gifts. Prolonged

[123] Parkman, Vol. II, pp. 277–8.   [124] Jean Baptiste Cadotte.
[125] Warren, 1885, pp. 210–11.   [126] *Idem*, p. 214.   [127] Keesing, 1939, p. 83.
[128] Kellogg, 1935, p. 270.   [129] Gilfillan, p. 74. See also Kohl, p. 270.

dealings with white traders and national officials and with their "presents" and bribes had taught the Indians how to drive a hard bargain. At least, the white man made them many far-reaching promises. Our federal government has not lived up to its side of these contracts with the Indians and has not paid them all the money to which they are entitled under the old treaties. This, of course, is one of the never forgotten grudges of the Chippewa.

We can see, therefore, how a continuity was established, leading from the early French trader down to the Indian agent of the present day. In both cases, the white man is the key figure in the political and social structure of the Indian community. He is the source of goods and rations, the promiser of gifts, the organizer and initiator of new schemes of social action. He is also the butt of complaints and grudges, the target of sarcastic jokes. Significantly, he is "the father."

THE TRADER AS A PARENTAL FIGURE

From an early period the Indians were accustomed to refer to all important white men as "father." Speaking of the American Commissioner of Indian Affairs, Kohl remarked, "The Indians call him their 'Great Father *from* Washington,' as they call the President their 'Great Father *in* Washington.' They call everybody at all connected with government, Father. . . . "[130] Malhiot, the Wisconsin trader, said " . . . they never call me anything but their 'Father'."[131]

The presence of French Catholic missionaries in the Indian region may perhaps have helped to confirm this usage of the parental kinship term, but I do not believe that this factor was responsible for the original application of the word "father" to the white man. Rather, I think that the custom of calling "everybody at all connected with government, Father" was a heritage of aboriginal times and may best be understood in the light of the earlier social order.

It has already been stressed that the trader in many ways fulfilled the political functions of a chief; he was sometimes even referred to as a chief.[132] Now chiefs were also addressed as "father" by the Indians, and this made the extension of the parental term to the trader a very natural process. Further light is thrown on this relationship by a passage in Denig's account of the Assineboines, whose social organization was intermediate between that of the Chippewa and the more centralized Plains tribes to the south.

. . . these bands are nothing more than large families, the chiefs resembling the old patriarchs, being intermarried and connected in such a way as to preclude the probability of clashing of interests or separation. . . . The chief is little more than the nominal father of all and addresses them as his children in a body. . . . Now, although

---

[130] Kohl, 1860, p. 13. See also Warren, 1880, p. 132.
[131] Malhiot, p. 185.   [132] See above, p. 46.

some of these children may be as brave as he, and have accomplished greater feats in war and the chase, yet they do not feel disposed to dispute his acknowledged authority.[133]

Such bands developed among the Chippewa as well, as we can see in a passage by Warren, who describes an outstanding chief addressed by the Indians of his band as "father." Warren writes:

In the words of one of the principal men of his band, "He was a father to our fathers, who looked upon him as a parent; his lightest wish was quickly obeyed; his lodge was ever hung with meat; and the traders vied with each other who should treat him best; his hand was open, and when he had plenty our fathers wanted not."[134]

So it is evident that an identification of some kind was established between father, chief, and trader. However, the psychological significance which may be inherent in this identification is yet to be determined. Many other Indian tribes across North America, including the neighboring Dakota,[135] called the government agent "father" as the Chippewa did; but the psychological attitudes of the Dakota toward the white man were very different from those of the Chippewa. In many cases, of course, the use of the term "Father" was a meaningless stereotype which embodied no particular mental conception of the white man. But it is my belief that in the case of the Chippewa, the use of this kinship term was more than an empty formula. In the Chippewa region, as we shall see, the trader played a significant parental role for many generations, and the attitudes of the Indians toward the trader paralleled in many ways the attitudes of children to fathers in Chippewa society. The trader occupied a functional position with regard to the different Chippewa families analogous to the position of the head of the family with regard to his dependent children.

In order to clarify this statement, it will first be necessary to say something about the role of the father in Chippewa society, for in order to know what the identification of the white man with the father might mean in any given context, it would be requisite to have some conception of the characteristic father-child relationship in the society. What was the stereotyped Chippewa conception of a father? Was he an affectionate, indulgent companion, as among the Manus or Trobrianders?[136] Or an authoritarian head-of-the-household as in the nineteenth century Europe? What was the structure of the Chippewa family, and what was the father's place in it?

---

[133] Denig, 1929, p. 431.

[134] Warren in Schoolcraft, 1851a, Vol. II, pp. 160–1. It seems possible to me that the above-mentioned chief was a half-breed, since his name was Big Curly-Head.

[135] MacGregor, 1946, Note 15, p. 42.

[136] Mead, 1930; Malinowski, 1927.

IV. THE CHILD-PARENT RELATIONSHIP IN CHIPPEWA SOCIETY AND ITS ROLE IN THE FORMATION OF ATTITUDES TOWARD THE "GREAT WHITE FATHER"

THE ISOLATED BIOLOGICAL FAMILY

IN ITS essential constitution the Chippewa family structure was like that of the western world. The patrilineal clan was of secondary importance, and the single biological family, consisting of husband, wife, and children with occasionally a grandparent or two, was the significant social unit. The kinship term for "father" was not extended, as among the tribes to the south of the Chippewa.[137]

When we turn to the Dakota, we find a very different situation. Here there were many men whom the individual called by the term "father"—i.e., brothers and cousins of the father—just as there were many women called "mother." Moreover, within the same generation, there was a large number of classificatory "sisters" and "brothers" who could be counted upon as allies. In such a situation one would not expect an "inflation" of the parental figure, such as we find in our own society.[138]

Among the Chippewa, however, where the family was small and often isolated, parental figures might assume a magnified importance to the child. Such a milieu could also foster the development of an Oedipus complex akin to that of the western world, inasmuch as parental figures assumed similar functions in the two societies. Indeed, Chippewa folklore is one of the world's collection of folktales in which Oedipus stories may be found.

AN OEDIPUS LEGEND

The story of Filcher-of-Meat, which may be described as an Oedipus story, is worth citing as a case in point. In this tale, a husband suspects that his wife and son are having a sexual relationship. (He has two wives and the boy's step-mother is the woman suspected.) Consequently, the father takes his son away and abandons him on an island. But a guardian snake transports the youth to shore and the boy heads for home again. When the boy's father hears that he is returning, he calls upon everyone to throw valuable goods in his son's way in order to distract him. But the angry youth kicks them aside and says, "Truly very far on the water did my father leave me. Pray, why should my feet become sore from having walked thus far? Only for the sake of my mother have I returned home." Then he continues on his way. To quote Jones' translation of the text:

When he beheld his mother nude as she lay, (he saw that) she was entirely without

---

[137] For an analysis of Chippewa family and social structure, see Landes, 1937a.
[138] See Erikson, 1939.

any eyes. It was so that the wife of Filcher-of-Meat was weeping. Into a certain place he had flung her; as hard as he could he had beaten his wife.[139]

The son takes care of his mother, bathes her, and breathes upon her eyes, restoring her sight. Then he angrily says to his father. "Don't you ever do that again!" Finally, in revenge against those who have rejoiced in his misfortune, the boy sets the whole village on fire.

A similar theme appears in Schoolcraft's version of the *Wenebojo* cycle. *Wenebojo's* grandmother tells him: "I have nourished you from your infancy, for your mother died in giving you birth, owing to the ill-treatment of your father." "He [*Wenebojo*] appeared to be rejoiced to hear that his father was living, for he had already thought in his heart to try and kill him."[140] When he finds his father, *Wenebojo* asks him if he had been the cause of his mother's death. The answer is "Yes!", whereupon *Wenebojo* takes up a rock and strikes his father with it. However, he does not kill his father, because the old man tells him that this is impossible; he has too much power. The father buys off his son by offering him a portion of the universe to rule and promises him as much power as his brothers, on condition that he first go to the earth and conquer some serpents and *windigos*. *Wenebojo* is pacified and returns to his grandmother's lodge.

In both of the foregoing tales the father escapes the son's revenge. He has too much power and cannot be touched. The son of Filcher-of-Meat expresses his hostility by burning up the village, while *Wenebojo* returns to his grandmother after an initial display of aggression. In both stories the old man tries to appease his son. Filcher-of-Meat strews costly presents in his son's path to distract his attention. *Wenebojo's* father offers him as much power as his brothers have, if he will continue to work and direct his aggressions elsewhere. The sons cannot forgive their fathers for the maltreatment of their mothers. Yet they have no choice but to restrain their hostility and accede to the situation.[141]

PARENTS AND GRANDPARENTS

Grandparents often played a significant role in the raising of Chippewa children, a pattern which slightly modifies, but does not essentially alter, the general picture of Chippewa family organization presented above. The reader who examines the life-history material in the Appendix will discover that all three informants—Jim Mink, John Thunderbird, and Julia Badger— were brought up by grandparents instead of by their parents. While not at all universal, this seems to be a fairly common pattern among the Chippewa. Judging from various accounts, the child sometimes learned to call the grand-

---

[139] Jones, William, 1917. Part I, p. 393.   [140] Schoolcraft, 1839, Vol. I, p. 139.

[141] There are also numerous Chippewa folktales about hostility between father-in-law and son-in-law. See Jones, William, 1917, Part II, p. 71. Also Skinner, 1912, pp. 90–2, 170–3.

parents "mother" and "father," which occasionally resulted in some confusion in the kinship terminology.

Mrs. H. S. said "I always stayed with my grandmother, my father's mother. . . . I stayed with my mother when I was small, but as soon as I could toddle, I stayed with my grandmother. . . . My grandmother taught me to call my father 'brother'." Mrs. E. I. remarked "My mother always had my son with her. He was her pet. He used to call me sister and George [his father] brother-in-law. George didn't like that." In her biography Julia Badger describes the confusion of learning the identity of her real mother after having become accustomed to thinking of her grandmother as her mother.[142]

At the present time many young couples who have children shift the responsibilities of baby-tending onto their own parents. In doing so, they are probably acting in accordance with Chippewa tradition.

In the old days of nomadic hunting, mobility was greatly prized, and an active young couple would not like to be held up on the march by the very old and the very young. While a baby was still in the cradleboard, it could be taken along without too much trouble and carried on the mother's back. But after the first year or two, the child became a handicap. It could no longer be carried easily and was unable to keep up with the others on foot. Consequently, during the hunting season, the child was often left with grandparents, either the mother's or the father's parents. Those too old and too young to hunt stayed behind in relatively settled communities, stocked with provisions, while the active, mature members of the group ranged through the woods in search of game. Staying with the grandparents did not constitute a complete break with the child's own parents, for they generally returned after a few weeks or months. But their visits were fitful, and often the grandparents, in a functional sense, became the real parents. That is why we have so many Chippewa tales beginning "So-and-so was living alone with his grandmother."[143]

Under present-day sedentary conditions there is less excuse for the shifting of parental responsibilities to grand-parents. Nevertheless, it is still done, particularly when a man or woman wants to go away in search of work off the reservation. Sometimes old people deliberately take their grandchildren

---

[142] See Appendix, p. 121.

[143] In many of the folktales, grandparents are endowed with magnified powers to harm or to bless. The grandmother is generally associated with the self-replenishing-kettle motif. The hero cannot believe that her tiny kettle will provide enough nourishment for him; but she magically causes it to pour forth endless quantities of food. In some folktales the grandmother also appears as an evil witch—for instance in the story of "Filcher-of-Meat." Here the hero encounters a series of old women who address him as "grandson." The first one cooks a meal for him in her self-renewing kettle. The second one tries to kill him with pus from her knee, until the hero calls on his pets, a mink and a wood-chuck, to save him and they kill her. After that he meets two blind old grandmothers, who try to kill him with their elbows; but instead they kill each other. (Jones, William, 1917, pp. 381–99).

from the children's parents, because they think that the youngsters are not being brought up properly. Since many families are characterized by excessive drinking and neglect of children, there is often some justification for such action.[144]

In some cases the transfer from the parents to grandparents (or vice versa) may well involve a traumatic experience for the child. Julia Badger seems to have suffered an unhappy childhood, living with her grandparents. She did not like her grandfather, "because he switched me so often," but she preferred him to her grandmother who switched her "for nothing at all." However, when Julia went to boarding school she began to value her grandfather's long-distance telephone calls. Finally, when she spoke to me about her grandfather's funeral, Julia gave a rhapsodic description of the old man, saying "My grandfather was the most wonderful thing that was created on the face of the earth." In reading Julia's biography one receives the impression that Julia lacked true parental affection in childhood, and that in later years she was still trying to find an acceptable father. It seems significant that of the three men Julia married before the age of twenty-three, two were elderly men in their sixties. Moreover, in her numerous phantasies, Julia attributes to various older men an enormous, cherishing concern for herself. She ascribes this parental devotion to various school teachers and to the school principal, as well as to her father and grandfather, who seem, for the most part, really to have been rather neglectful and callous toward her.

John Thunderbird was also brought up by grandparents after the death of his mother. His father continued to visit him, but evidently had little close contact with him. John said little about his father, but he did talk a good deal about his uncles and grandfathers, and particularly about his father's father whom he greatly admired. "I looked at him then and wished I could reach his age and be as smart as he was at talking and be wise the way he was. That's what I had in my mind whenever I took him around to different places."

John also admired some of his teachers at school and told stories about their admiration for him in a vein which is somewhat reminiscent of Julia Badger's more extravagant phantasies.[145]

Jim Mink preferred his mother's father to his father and his father's father. Of the latter two he remarked "They were *mean*. If I was hungry, I'd reach for some more bread; then they'd take it away from me." Like Julia Badger and John Thunderbird, Jim apparently harbored unsatisfied needs for dependency. When a father's uncle—and later an Indian agent—enacted a father role on a few occasions, the experiences evidently left a deep impression upon Jim Mink's mind.[146]

---

[144] See Appendix, p. 139.   [145] See Appendix, p. 101.   [146] See Appendix, pp. 81–87.

Unlike my other three informants, Tom Badger was raised by his own parents; but he said very little about them, although he seems to have been much attached to his mother. In speaking about his father, Tom emphasized the latter's aloofness and cold impersonality.

My mother said "My husband never says anything to his children." So one evening, when he came in from one of his hunting trips, she said to my father, "Why don't you say something to your children, and tell them a story?" He never said anything, just laid around and smoked his pipe. He was all tired out every night after he'd been out hunting during the day.

When Tom's father took him along to build a bear trap, he didn't explain what they were going to do, but merely told him to come along. "My father gave me no explanations," said Tom. "When he set out to build the house [trap], he didn't tell me what it was for." Similarly, when they went on a long trip to Flambeau, Tom Badger's father did not say where they were going or why. "I didn't know what it was all about, but I went along with him," said Tom.[147]

The quotations from Tom Badger and Jim Mink seem to echo something of the unfriendly father-image painted in the Chippewa folklore cited above. Of course, we need not therefore assume that the Chippewa male was always a forbidding parent. Kohl, who commented on the "ape-like affection" manifest by Chippewa parents for their children, observed that "Even fathers are very kind to their sons, and never treat them with severity."[148]

Be that as it may, our Chippewa biographies all seem to be characterized by unsatisfied needs for affection and dependence. We can detect a similar manifestation of such feelings in the Chippewa folklore and also, as we shall see later, in the characteristic Chippewa relationships with the white man.

DEPENDENCY AND THE APPEAL TO PITY

It is true that discussions of the Chippewa usually emphasize their independence, fostered and encouraged from the earliest years by parents.[149] Nevertheless, there is also a dependent attitude intermixed with this feeling of autonomy. Indeed, it would not be surprising if a desire for dependence should spring from a growing child's reaction to being pressed toward autonomy in a world characterized as dangerous and fearful.

One way in which the Chippewa child seems to have sought protection and gratification in aboriginal times was through the appeal to pity. The Chippewa often speak of pity. When fasting, they ask the spirits to pity them, which here means "to adopt" and "to take care of" as well as "to

---

[147] Compare Jim Mink s description of his father's uncle, who gave no explanations of their trip to town. Appendix, pp. 81–82.

[148] Kohl, 1860, p. 309.

[149] E.g., Benedict, 1938.

have compassion."[150] A fasting child is supposed to be addressed by his guardian spirits with the words, "My grandchild, I come to pity you."[151]

Sometimes the parents "took pity" on their own fasting children and gave them something to eat, although this lessened their chances of supernatural aid. John Thunderbird went home and begged for food while fasting. "My grandmother took pity on me," he said, "because I was so cute and small. She gave me some bread."[152] John remembered his grandmother with affection for this charity; but Tom Badger, the *Míde* priest, felt differently about his mother's comparable act of mercy.

I didn't fast long enough [said Tom]. I stopped at noon every time. If I'd kept it up longer, I'd have more power. My mother used to take pity on me and feed me at noon. She didn't want to see me go hungry. . . . That's why I never had a dream. Now I'm sorry. I don't know nothing now. But it was my mother's fault.

The following story, which appears in Schoolcraft's *Algic Researches*, gives a striking picture of the appeal-to-pity mechanism. A young boy fails to kill any birds and squirrels, although he goes out hunting in the cold wintry weather every day. Finally he meets a squirrel, who speaks to him as follows:

Listen to me. As soon as you get home, you must commence crying. You must throw away your bow and arrows in discontent. If your mother asks you what is the matter, you must not answer her, but continue crying and sobbing. If she offers you anything to eat, you must push it away with apparent discontent, and continue crying. In the evening, when your father returns from hunting, he will inquire of your mother what is the matter with you. She will answer that you came home crying and would not so much as mention the cause to her. All this while you must not leave off sobbing. At last your father will say, "My son, why is this unnecessary grief? Tell me the cause. You know I am a spirit, and that nothing is impossible for me to perform." You must then answer him, and say that you are sorry to see the snow continually on the ground, and ask him if he could not cause it to melt, so that we might have perpetual summer. Say it in a supplicating way, and tell him this is the cause of your grief. Your father will reply, "It is very hard to accomplish your request, but for your sake, and for my love for you, I will use my utmost endeavours." He will tell you to be still, and cease crying. He will try to bring summer with all its loveliness. You must then be quiet, and eat that which is set before you.

The boy does so, and "all was exactly fulfilled."[153]

In a long origin legend narrated to me by Tom Badger, the creation of the Indian race and the gift of the Medicine Dance from the supernaturals are attributed to a big sulking fit and temper tantrum on the part of *Wenebojo*.

---

[150] Landes, 1939, p. 6.   [151] Jones, William, 1917, Vol. II, p. 303.

[152] Consider the implicit appeal to pity in John Thunderbird's tirade against the whites. Supra, p. 38.

[153] Schoolcraft, 1837, Vol. I, p. 59.

In this case the *manidog* (spirits) appease *Wenebojo* not only out of pity but also because their security is at stake to some extent. *Wenebojo* utters vague and ominous threats against them, which cause them alarm.

One day when he [*Wenebojo*] was walking along by the ocean, he happened to remember the time when those *manidog* made him angry. Then *Wenebojo* just sat down by the beach with his feet nearly in the water, and he hollered and cried. He sat there crying, remembering the *manidog* who had made him angry, and thought of what he would like to do to those *manidog*. He spoke to the earth and said "Whoever is underneath the earth down there, I will pull them out and bring them up on top here. I can play with them and do whatever I want with them, because I own this earth where I am now."

Wenebojo then makes similar threats to the spirits of the sky and threatens to knock down the sky. The two main *manidog* of the universe—referred to as *Wenebojo's* "grandfathers"—nervously confer about this disturbance. *Gičimanido* (the Great Spirit) says to the god at the bottom of the earth, "He will do just what he said. I told you never to make him angry in any way."

Interestingly enough, the *manidog* pacify *Wenebojo* by presenting him with some parents. Out of clay they create a man and a woman, who become the first Indians, as well as the parents of Wenebojo. Then the *manidog* also give the Indians the *Midewiwin* or Medicine Dance.

SOME CONTRASTS

Solicitation for supernatural aid through the appeal to pity is known among other Indian tribes,[154] but by no means in all. Comanche attitudes toward supernatural power contrast strikingly with the submissive approach of the Chippewa.

The technique for solicitation is merely to express the wish to have it and to render oneself worthy of possessing it by a demonstration of strength, endurance, or determination. Not helplessness, but resourcefulness is a claim for power. The power, after it is achieved, is used *by the recipient, and not by the donor or deity.*[155]

Kardiner links this confident attitude toward supernatural resources with patterns of child care among the Comanche. The father-figure was not inflated or deferred to in this society. In fact, young men "regarded the old men rather contemptuously. The young actually played jokes on their elders."[156]

This would have been unthinkable among the Chippewa where old men were granted ceremonious respect. "No people reverence old age more than the Indians," wrote Peter Jones in his description of the Chippewa. "The advice of the *uhkewaihzee*, or long dweller upon the earth, is generally lis-

---

[154] See, for example, Lowie's description of Crow religious traditions. Lowie, 1935, Ch. 11.
[155] Kardiner, 1945, p. 92. The italics are Kardiner's.   [156] *Idem*, p. 55.

tened to with great attention."[157] Most respected of all, of course, were old Chippewa medicine men, for their power was believed to grow with age, rather than to weaken, as among the Comanche. In Comanche society, however, old medicine men were not feared, and very few individuals believed that they had ever been bewitched.

Cheyenne and Arapaho patterns of soliciting supernatural aid had more in common with the Chippewa, but here again there was a difference which, to my mind, reflects the greater self-reliance of the Plains character structure. Among the Arapaho and Cheyenne, youths fasted for a guardian spirit *after* puberty, not before. Chippewa children began to fast at the age of four or five, at a time when they were still seeking security and protection from adults; and they were encouraged by the latter to transfer some of this dependency to guardian spirits. Cheyenne youths, however, learned to develop their own strength and agility *before* turning to the supernatural realm for assistance. Guardian spirits usually did not appear to men before the age of twenty, and often not until the young men had been to war or gone through the Medicine Lodge.[158] Among the Arapaho, it was the same. "Few went on such a quest, and those who did usually went long after puberty."[159] These customs relating to the guardian spirit quest enable us to see that self-reliance and a sense of mastery were encouraged among the young warriors of the Plains, while among the Chippewa, children were implicitly encouraged to seek outside guidance and protection.

THE "GREAT WHITE FATHER" AND HIS "MILK"

Our discussion of the Chippewa father-child relationship has been necessary to help us interpret the Chippewas' identification of the white man with the father. An objection may be raised that this identification was merely a superficial matter of terminology, but the Chippewa themselves frequently insisted on the father-child parallel. Thus, in a speech to some United States government representatives in the 1820's, a Chippewa chieftain said: "Fathers —as such we look upon you; and we expect to receive from you such treatment as fathers give to their children." [160] And on the same occasion another Chippewa orator pleaded, "Fathers—you have many children. But your breasts drop yet. Give us a little milk, *Fathers*, that we may wet our lips."[161] As a footnote informs us, "milk" was a synonym for firewater. This term for whiskey and rum seems to have been current among the Wisconsin Indians.[162]

The expression of oral dependency symbolized in this curious metaphor draws attention to the trader's strategic importance as dispenser of liquor,

---

[157] Jones, Peter, 1861, p. 68.   [158] Grinnell, 1923, Vol. II, p. 113.
[159] Elkin in Linton, 1940, p. 218.   [160] McKenney, 1827, p. 467.
[161] *Idem*, p. 462.   [162] See also Keesing, 1939, p. 55.

tobacco, and food rations, commodities of the highest value among the Chippewa. A brief discussion of tobacco at this point will indicate something of its significance in religious and social affairs and consequently the importance of the trader as chief source of such supplies.

IMPORTANCE OF THE TRADER'S TOBACCO IN CHIPPEWA CULTURE

Even nowadays tobacco is carried from one household to another by a runner in invitation to any ceremonial or private gathering on the reservation. It still constitutes the entrance ticket of the guests, who offer their plugs of "Standard" to the *manidog*. The *Mide* priests at every ceremony make a speech about the food and tobacco presented to the spirits, and in some ceremonies a sacred pipe is passed around, from which the men (usually not the women) each take a puff. Tobacco is also used in payment to a medicine man for services rendered. Indeed, no activity of importance can safely be negotiated without it. Tobacco is sprinkled on the water before embarking on a canoe trip as an offering to the dangerous underwater creatures; and it is presented to the thunderbirds during a storm. When a hibernating bear is killed, a little cut-plug is inserted in his lair. When medicinal roots are cut, a pinch of tobacco serves as replacement for what the earth has lost. Tobacco always redresses the balance which man upsets. It placates the *manidog* and makes them favorably disposed toward those who remember them. When Tom Badger honored me with "sacred" information, he did so with the explanation, "I'm only telling you these things because you brought me tobacco."

Tobacco is both chewed and smoked. At present, every Chippewa home is provided with "spitting-cans"—the number depending upon the popularity of the hosts. Men sit around clearing their throats, spitting at intervals into the cans, which are shoved across the floor to a newcomer. Snuff is also chewed by the Indians. Their mouths seem to be seldom unoccupied.

The tobacco habit apparently began very early among the Chippewa. Gilfillan writes, "I have seen a boy of four beating his mother with his tiny fists to make her give him more tobacco. Every boy and girl thinks he must have tobacco, and plenty of it."[163]

We need not speculate on the unconscious emotional significance of this craving. It is enough for our immediate purpose to recognize the high valuation given to tobacco by the Indians, and to understand that the white man was the main source of this commodity, as he was the dispenser (and introducer) of liquor, which had so strong an attraction for the Chippewa. The white man also issued food rations to the hungry Indians, in connection with treaty obligations. Thus his function in the satisfaction of oral cravings was a very important one. If for no other reason than this, it appears that the title "Great White Father" possessed a certain functional validity.

---

[163] Gilfillan, 1898–1900, p. 87.

SOLICITING "PITY" FROM THE WHITE MAN

The trader was not only a source of food, liquor, tobacco, and valued trading goods; he was also, very frequently, a binder of wounds. Denig, a trader among the Assineboines, spoke from personal experience about such community services.

Traders are very much subject to calls on their charity, both by persons who really are in want and almost everyone else. All the roving tribes are great beggars, even if they do not actually stand in need. But viewing the question only in the light of an act of charity they are numerous indeed. Unskillful in the treatment of diseases, the different demands for medicines and attendance are great, which at all times it is not safe nor expedient to comply with. The forts are the depositions of all the old, lame, sick, poor, and feeble; in fact, every one who can not follow the camp, or is of no use there, is thrown on the hands of the traders, and his house has more often the appearance of a hospital than a trading establishment. For all this there is no pay, not even thanks nor kind words, but frequently reproach and revenge if they are told to move off after recovery.[164]

Whenever the Indian wanted something, he was apt to approach the white man, as he might have approached a parent or guardian spirit, with the appeal to pity. Schoolcraft says that a common expression of the Chippewa Indians to the agent was *"Kitte-mau-giz-ze sho-wain-e-min"* meaning "I am poor, show me pity [or rather] charity me."[165] Elsewhere the same author writes, "Metosh came in the office and said: 'My father I am very poor; I have nothing, not even an axe to cut wood. Show me pity.' "[166]

Denig reproduces in some detail the speech of an Assineboine Indian to his trader, which so markedly exhibits the attitudes ascribed to the Chippewa that I quote some selections in illustration.

When *Wakoñda* created man he made two sorts; one clothed, comfortable, rich, plenty to eat, and endowed with wisdom; these were the white men. The other he produced naked, in a cold climate, poor, ignorant, obliged to hunt for their meat, to labor, to starve, to suffer, to die; these were the red men. . . . When your Great Grandfather across the sea sent you to reside with Indians, what did he say? . . . Did he not tell you, you will behold a poor, naked, starved nation, have pity on them? . . .

I was told if you meet a white man give him your hand, take him to your lodge, give him to eat, let him have lodging, show him the road. I have done so.

If you meet him while on the warpath, do not steal his horse or rob him of his property. If others steal his horses, bring them back; if any of the fort property is damaged, pay for it. I have done so.

I know you are a chief and good father to your red children and will never refuse them what they ask. Remember our hardships, dangers, and exposures in hunting for

---

[164] Denig, 1929, p. 460. Assiniboine patterns of adjustment to the white man seem to have been similar to those of the Chippewa.

[165] Schoolcraft, 1851b, p. 472.

[166] *Idem*, p. 250. See also the appeal to pity in the quotation from Morse, 1856, above, p. 38.

you. Open your heart and lengthen your measure and reduce, if ever so little, on the prices of trade. Indians suffer for everything; even the tobacco chewed and spit out by the whites is picked up and smoked by them.[167]

The submissive and dependent attitude expressed in such speeches was, quite naturally, regarded by the traders as abject begging. Duncan Cameron wrote of the Canadian Chippewa: "They are the greatest and most shameless beggars on earth; give them ever so much, they will still continue to ask for more until they receive a decided refusal."[168] And Grant remarked, "These haughty people, though commonly reserved among themselves, are, with their traders, the meanest beggars and most abject flatterers on earth."[169]

The apparent need for dependence upon the white father illuminates the psychological importance of the annuity payments and rations for the Indians. Annuities were often scanty indeed, and yet many of the Chippewa went to a great deal of trouble to attend payments. The episode at Sandy Lake illustrates not only the cruel indifference of the white man, but also the tenacity of some of the Indians in waiting for long-delayed payments, despite the greatest hardships and discomfort. Gilfillan touches on this problem when he writes: "We would not spend the long time, and endure the sufferings for the amount, perhaps five dollars a head, which they get. Had they let the payment go, and gone hunting or working in a logging camp, they would have earned many times that amount."[170] Gilfillan also tells about a Chippewa chief who exhorted his fellow Indians not to raise crops, lest the rations be cut.[171]

INFLATED CONCEPTIONS OF THE WHITE MAN'S POWER

Long traditions of dependency on the white man led to some exaggerated notions of this benefactor's power. In his description of the Chippewa, Peter Jones wrote:

The ideas entertained by the Indians generally of the King of England, with regard to his power, riches, and knowledge, are most extravagant. They imagine his power to be absolute, and his authority unlimited; that his word is law, to which all his subjects bow with implicit obedience. . . . They also consider that his riches and benevolence are unbounded, the whole resources of the kingdom being at his command, a portion of which he grants to those of his subjects who are needy. With regard to his wisdom, they conceive that he knows everything that is going on in the world; that even the speech or talk of an Indian chief delivered to a Superintendent of Indian Affairs in the wilds of Canada is made known to him.[172]

To be sure, such fictions were fostered by the white officials themselves,

---

[167] Denig, 1929, pp. 600–602.   [168] Cameron, 1890, p. 249.

[169] Grant, 1890, p. 325. Schoolcraft and McKenney both speak of a "begging dance" being performed by the Indians. (Schoolcraft, 1851, p. 146; McKenney, 1827, p. 286.)

[170] Gilfillan, 1898–1900, p. 121. Elsewhere (p. 113) Gilfillan describes the Indian's habitual expectation of gifts—particularly tobacco—from the white man.

[171] *Idem*, p. 125.   [172] Jones, Peter, 1861, p. 207.

but the Chippewa seem to have accepted them much more readily than did groups such as the Dakota or Cheyenne. The Chippewa never dared to mal-treat an Indian agent, for example; but the Cheyennes sometimes locked their agent in his office, or out of it, and he had very little control over his "wards."[173]

A very different attitude toward the Indian Agent from that exhibited by the Cheyenne is expressed in the stories narrated by Jim Mink which appear in the Appendix. Jim turned to the Indian Agent as an almost magical source of support. In his stories he pictured this man as a powerful being who boasted proudly, "I'm a big man, that's what I am. I'm the Indian agent. I've got the whole United States government right back of me. I hold the Indians right in the palm of my hand." It seems very unlikely to me that such a por-trait of an agent would be drawn by a Dakota or Cheyenne Indian.

Incidentally, this inflated conception of the powerful white man seems to echo the earlier inflation of the medicine man in Chippewa society. In aborig-inal times the feared and respected shaman was a kind of omniscient father-figure, who was credited with the most extraordinary magical powers. It ap-pears that for the half-acculturated Jim Mink, the white official plays a comparable role.

VIOLENCE DURING INTOXICATION NOT DIRECTED AGAINST THE WHITE MAN

When we realize what the Chippewa identification of the white man with a powerful "father" meant to them, it becomes clearer why there were so few outbreaks against the whites. White men were even safe during the violent brawls which took place around the trading post when rum was distributed to the Indians. It was on such occasions that aggressive passions were unleashed and broke through the constricting armor established by fear of sorcery and by the other inhibitions of daily life. Under intoxication, murders were readily committed.

Writing of the Chippewa in the early nineteenth century, Duncan Cameron remarked,

They very seldom take revenge when sober, as few people disguise their minds with more art than they do, but, when in the least inebriate all they have in their mind is revealed and the most bloody revenge taken.[174]

In describing the effects of liquor among the Chippewa, Peter Jones wrote,

I have seen such scenes of degradation as would sicken the soul of a good man; such as husbands beating their wives, and dragging them by the hair of the head; children screaming with fright, the older ones running off with guns, tomahawks, spears, knives, and other deadly weapons, which they concealed in the woods to prevent the com-mission of murder by their enraged parents; yet, notwithstanding this precaution, death was not unfrequently the result.[175]

---

[173] McGillycuddy, 1941, p. 165.   [174] Cameron in Masson, 1890, Vol. 2, p. 248.
[175] Jones, Peter, 1861, p. 167. See also Tanner, 1830, pp. 163-64.

When we read the numerous traders' accounts of these occurrences, we notice that the victims were always Indians. The drunken Chippewa turned upon their own relatives, wives, and children, but not upon the white man.[176] Sometimes, according to Long, the Indians were beaten up by the trader for drunkenness, and they offered no resistance. What is more, they apologized to the trader for their disorderly conduct the next day, when they were sober. Long's reflections on this anomaly deserve quotation:

It seems to be the constant attention both of the male and female part of the Indians to instil ideas of heroism into the minds of the rising generation, and these impressions they carry far beyond the line of reason or of justice. Is it then surprising that every action of their lives should tend to satisfy their thirst for revenging offences committed against them, and that these sentiments should operate so powerfully in directing their future conduct? There is, nevertheless, one exception to these observations—their conduct to traders, who are obliged on some occasions, when intoxication runs high, to beat them very soundly; –to their credit, in these instances, I must confess I never knew them to resent this severity when sober. The only remark they have made has been—"Friend, you beat me very severely last night—but I do not mind, I suppose I deserved it—it was the liquor made me offend."[177]

This indicates how deeply ingrained was the Indian's submission to the white man's authority.

Another episode will illustrate this theme: It may be recalled that a Canadian *coureur de bois* was murdered by an Indian at Lac Court Oreilles.[178] Immediately on learning this news, Jean Baptiste Cadotte sent a messenger to Court Oreilles, demanding that the murderer be brought to Fond du Lac and delivered into his hands. If this were not done, he warned, no more traders would ever again visit Court Oreilles. In time, accordingly, the murderer was brought to Fond du Lac, and a large crowd of Indians assembled to observe how the case would be handled by the white man. The captive was judged guilty and executed in public. The Chippewa onlookers were apparently horrified by the brutality of the execution and there was much mourning among the women. Naturally, there was also some uneasiness within the fort and worried speculations about the possible reactions of the Indians. The story can be concluded in Warren's words:

Mons. Cadotte was himself so closely related to the tribe, and knew the strength of his influence so well, that he felt no apprehension of these general consequences; but, to satisfy his men, as well as to discover if the relatives of the executed Indian indulged revengeful feelings, he presented a quantity of *"eau de vie"* to the Indians, knowing that in their intoxication they would reveal any hard feelings or vengeful purposes for the late act, should they actually indulge them.

The Indian camp was that night drowned in a drunken revel, but not a word of displeasure or hatred did they utter against the traders.[179]

---

[176] For some accounts, see Long, pp. 86–87, 93, 122, 142.
[177] Long, pp. 114–116. See also p. 129.
[178] See above, p. 39.   [179] Warren, 1880, pp. 294–297.

V. WOODLAND AND PLAINS ACCULTURATION

TWO CONTRASTING AREAS

AT THIS point it may be well to point out that many of the differences which we have noted in the historical development of the Wisconsin Chippewa and the Dakota extend to broader regions than have been indicated so far. That is to say, the general patterns of adjustment made by the Wisconsin Chippewa to the trader and his culture were paralleled in other Algonkin-speaking Woodland tribes in the Canadian and Great Lakes area, such as the Saulteaux (Canadian Chippewa), Ottawa, Menomini, Forest Potawatomi, and Cree.[180] On the other hand, the general patterns in Dakota acculturation were found in other Plains tribes, such as the Arapaho and Cheyenne.

The members of the former group were all relatively atomistic hunting-fishing-gathering societies, some of which practiced a little horticulture, and some of which, like the Ottawa, became enterprising middlemen for the traders. In the Woodland area, adjustment to white contact was relatively easy. The Indians quickly entered into a dependent relationship with the trader. His goods became essential to them; while his status as a father-figure was psychologically acceptable. Economically, the Indians were bound to the trader by bonds of credit; psychologically by an undercurrent need for dependence.[181]

In the Woodland area, the trader did not effect any great change in social organization, except that he assumed some political responsibilities and appointed a number of "chiefs." Apart from this, the aboriginal network of social ties remained much the same, and the structure of the family, so similar to that of the western world, was unaltered. The dependent and symbiotic relationship which developed with the white trader proved to be sufficiently advantageous to both sides, and there were few rebellions against the whites. Indeed, the most outstanding rebellion in this area, Pontiac's conspiracy, was to a large extent instigated by French traders.

---

[180] I do not include the Central Algonkin tribes, such as the Sauk, Fox, and Kickapoo, whose reactions to white contact were in many ways more like those of the Plains societies. However, the Siouan-speaking Assineboines might perhaps be incorporated in this list, despite their somewhat better-integrated type of Plains social organization and their dependence on the buffalo.

[181] To illustrate the similarity of the Potawatomi to the Chippewa in this respect, consider the following speech made by a Potawatomi chief to a British official after the final defeat of the French: "We are no more than wild creatures to you, fathers, in understanding; therefore we request you to forgive the past follies of our young people, and receive us for your children. Since you have thrown down our former father on his back, we have been wandering in the dark, like blind people. Now you have dispersed all this darkness, which hung over the heads of the several tribes, and have accepted them for your children . . . we hope you, fathers, will have pity on our women and young men, who are in great want of necessaries, and not let us go home to our towns ashamed." (Parkman, 1907, Vol. II, pp. 310–311.)

For a recent discussion of dependency on a Menominee reservation, where the Indians insist upon retaining their status as "wards of the government," see Sady, 1947.

Among Plains tribes, such as the Dakota and Cheyenne, the situation was very different, the nature and tempo of acculturation differing in consequence. Each autonomous, integrated Plains society consisted of a large number of interacting, interdependent individuals, who in spite of individualistic values (expressed in such patterns as military rivalry, coup-counting, etc.) still possessed a strong community *esprit de corps* which was manifest in well-developed techniques for co-operation and group living. Although white traders established contact with such tribes and had sufficiently profitable dealings with them, they were seldom able to gain enough foothold to dominate the scene as they did in the Woodland area. Plains tribes were too mobile, independent, and self-sufficient for that. Even during the early half of the nineteenth century, when they were secure in resources of buffalo meat, the Indians of the Plains were still able to withdraw from the advancing white frontier, trading for western goods which they could utilize, but never surrendering their autonomy.

In 1794 M'Gillivray remarked,

The inhabitants of the Plains are so advantageously situated that they could live very happily independent of our assistance. They are surrounded with innumerable herds of various kinds of animals, whose flesh affords them excellent nourishment and whose skins defend them from the inclemency of the weather, and they have invented so many means for the destruction of animals that they stand in no need of ammunition to provide a sufficiency for their purposes.[182]

M'Gillivray concluded that luxuries, rather than necessities, attracted Plains tribesmen to the trader. But often the warriors of the Plains disapproved of such luxuries—particularly after brushes with the frontiersmen which aroused hostility toward the whites.

In the narrative of an Oglala, quoted by Wissler, we learn that

When the tribe first mingled with the whites, the braves would not sanction it because they did not wish to eat the white man's food and the white man would eat all their buffalo. If the braves discovered anyone going among the white people, they would intercept him and kill him and his horse. They were afraid that the smell of coffee and bacon (foreign smells) would scare the buffalo and make them stay away. However, they would allow the white traders to come in and bring merchandise but would not buy foods that created a peculiar smell. They did not want the *"wakpamini,"* the government issue, and did not want the white people coming in.[183]

A similar picture is painted in a United States Government Report of 1862:

With the exception of Bear's Rib, they [the Dakota] actually refused to receive presents with which Agent Latta was provided, and which he offered them. After much parley, Bear's Rib consented to receive that portion of the goods designed for his people, stating at the same time that he thereby endangered his own life and also the lives of

---

[182] M'Gillivray, 1794–95.   [183] Wissler, 1916, p. 9.

his followers. . . . A few days after this event . . . a party of Sioux came in from the prairies, assaulted and killed Bear's Rib and several of his followers . . . thus repressing every manifestation among their own people of friendly feeling for the government.[184]

Despite these difficulties, some traders were able to attain a position of considerable power and importance in some of the western tribes.[185] But by and large, the Plains tribes were by no means willing to enter into the kind of dependent relationship which the Woodland tribes soon developed with the white man. They were able to pursue an independent course, not only because of the nature of their subsistence economy, but also because they seem to have been more self-reliant and aggressive psychologically than were the Woodland peoples. The kinship structure and child training patterns of most Plains tribes did not foster an inflation of the father image or tend to the development of submissive attitudes toward authority; but rather, there was every encouragement of self-mastery and audacity, while the social bond between siblings was emphasized as a potential basis for co-operative action. Because of a complex of economic, cultural, and psychological reasons, therefore, the trader on the Plains was unable to assume the central position that his competitor occupied in the Woodland area. For the most part, the credit system current in the forest region could not be applied on the Plains. The trader had less hold over the individual, therefore, and he often had to carry on negotiations with a group rather than with individual hunters.[186]

Because of the long and stubbornly preserved autonomy of the Plains tribes, the full impact of acculturation came much later on the Plains than in the Woodland area; and then it came abruptly, at the point of a gun, all at once. When the press of white frontiersmen across the prairies, accompanied by United States Army forces, coincided with the vanishing of the buffalo herds, the Plains tribes found themselves for the first time with their backs to the wall.

The Plains Indians were crushed into submission, not gradually absorbed as the Woodland peoples were. In the Woodland area there was no great change in social organization; but on the Plains the whole fabric of the social order was altered. The camp circle was broken up, bands dispersed, and the Sun Dance forbidden by the government.

CHANGES IN CHARACTER STRUCTURE

This catastrophic change undoubtedly resulted in an alteration of the character structure in many Plains tribes. To my knowledge, there are no Rorschach records of Dakota old-timers; but records of Dakota children have been taken,[187] and these reveal a personality picture quite incompatible with what

---

[184] U. S. Government Report, 1862, p. 31. Quoted in Goldfrank, 1943, p. 75.
[185] See Hyde, 1937, p. 95.   [186] Denig, 1929, pp. 458, 459.
[187] MacGregor, 1946. See Chapter XIV.

we know of the old society. It is evident, therefore, that Dakota personality
structure has undergone a change. According to Dr. Bruno Klopfer, Dakota
children are remarkably lacking in vitality, spontaneity, and creative inner
resources, and appear more "washed out" than any of the other Indian groups
represented by Rorschach material.[188] The Thematic Apperception Test, also
given to Dakota children, revealed "a great deal of insecurity, lack of definite-
ness and recognized purpose, indecision, and passivity."[189] These traits were
hardly characteristic of the old culture!

MacGregor summarizes the evidence of these personality tests as follows:

> The picture of Dakota child personality which emerges from the tests is one of weak-
> ness of natural drives and spontaneity resulting from repressive forces set in action
> early in the child's life. This paucity of impulse and emotion appears to blight the
> creativity, imagination, and fantasy that are normal in a healthy mental life and to
> prohibit wholesome relationships with other people. Dakota child personality seems
> crippled and negative, as if it rejected life. The unfriendly environment, which offers so
> little opportunity or satisfaction, retards the growth of personality and prevents it
> from becoming positive, rich, and mature. Life is lived on the defensive.[190]

While Chippewa test materials do not paint a picture of strong self-confidence and security either, the situation is not as bad as this. Moreover, among
the Chippewa there does not appear to have been any marked shift in personality patterns from one generation to the next. More striking than any
sign of change is the continuity of personality characteristics.[191]

I would ascribe this to the fact that Chippewa acculturation resulted in
no disorganization of social structure, no change in the nature of interpersonal
relationships. The long apprenticeship with the trader, so to speak, served to
induct the Chippewa gradually into their present place in the western world.

THE *SHAWANO* CULT

We have seen that there were not only differences in the nature of Woodland and Plains acculturation, there was a difference in tempo as well. Partly
for obvious geographical reasons, the expression of anti-white hostility among
the Woodland tribes occurred much earlier than it did on the Plains. Resignation to the white man's domination also set in sooner. And the same is true
of the development of nativistic movements with an anti-white orientation.
The Ghost Dance, animated by hostility for the dominant whites, swept the

---

[188] Seminar notes at the Rorschach Workshop, Crafts, New York, 1946.
[189] MacGregor, 1946, p. 206.   [190] *Idem*, p. 209.
[191] This continuity is particularly striking in the Rorschach records of the women. Out of 70
female records from Court Oreilles and Lac du Flambeau, collected by Ernestine Friedl, Robert
Ritzenthaler, and myself, there was almost no variation in the group profile from one generation to
the next. (There were 20 over fifty-eight years of age; 30 between thirty and fifty-eight; and 20
below thirty.) Men showed more of a change from one generation to the next. See p. 20, fn. 41.

Plains tribes in 1890, but it failed to kindle the imaginations of the Wisconsin Chippewa. The latter had already experienced a nativistic movement over eighty years before, and even at that time the Chippewa essentially accepted the domination of the white man in their country.

Like the later Ghost Dance, the *Shawano* cult was based upon revelations received by an Indian prophet from the Great Spirit and was characterized by certain anti-white features, including the expectation of eventual deliverance from the white man. In the "program" of the *Shawano* cult there is also something reminiscent of the techniques of nonco-operation developed in the anti-British nationalist movement in India; in both areas the essential aim was to become independent of the white intruder.

The *Shawano* prophet called upon the Indians to return to their primitive ways and to give up the corrupting inventions introduced by the white man. Even flint and steel were to be discarded, and fire made by friction once again. Indian women living with white men were to return home, leaving the children with their fathers. Every attempt should be made to attain self-sufficiency along aboriginal Indian patterns. No white merchandise should be purchased, and all white men's clothing should be handed over to the whites. Skins and furs should not be offered for sale, although they might be traded for supplies in some instances. No Indian should eat any food cooked by a white person or the liquor or provisions raised by whites, including bread, beef, pork, fowls, etc. Nor should any Indian sell provisions to the white man. Even the white man's cats were to be turned out of the wigwam.[192] Certain aboriginal Indian patterns were also under the ban. Thus, medicine bags were to be thrown away, *Mide* songs forgotten, and sorcery abandoned.[193] In reward for obeying these regulations, the *Shawano* prophet proclaimed that a speedy deliverance from the white man was at hand, and he called upon all the Indians to come and meet him at Detroit.

There was much sound strategy in the provisions listed above. If the anti-white boycott had been followed with any consistency, the fur trade would have been completely crippled. The taboos on drinking, fighting, and lying and the restrictions against sorcery and medicine bags were also shrewd provisions, aimed at reducing the conflicts and mutual suspicions current among the Indians and establishing a greater solidarity *vis-à-vis* the white man.

However, by this time the Indians had formed by far too organic a union with the traders for such provisions to take effect. It was already too late. Even if the prophet and his brother, *Tecumseh*, had not been disastrously defeated in battle, it is doubtful if the drive for Indian autarchy would have succeeded for long. The Indians needed guns and traps, if nothing else; and they had become dependent upon the rest of the white man's stock in trade as well.

However, the *Shawano* cult did meet with some success for a brief period,

---

[192] Blair, 1912, Vol. 2, p. 277.   [193] Tanner, 1830, pp. 155–158.

and many converts were made in spite of the inconvenience of the numerous regulations. Abandonment of flint and steel constituted a particularly severe hardship in the northern woods; so it is quite understandable that Tanner complained, "Can it please the Great Spirit that we should make fire by rubbing two sticks [rather] than with a flint and a piece of steel?"[194]

Tanner had a white skin, and the anti-white features of the cult probably did not appeal to him.

. . . as was usual with me, in any emergency of this kind [wrote Tanner], I went to the traders, firmly believing that if the Deity had any communications to make to men, they would be given, in the first instance, to white men. The traders ridiculed and despised the idea of a new revelation of the Divine Will, and the thought that it should be given to a poor Shawnee.[195]

However, despite this scorn and despite the hardship of doing without flint and steel, Tanner finally went over to the cult. " . . . the serious enthusiasm which prevailed among them so far affected me that I threw away my flint and steel, laid aside my medicine bag, and, in many particulars complied with the new doctrines."[196]

As has been mentioned, the *Shawano* excitement was partly responsible for the plundering of a trader's storehouse at Court Oreilles and the escape of the frightened trader, Jean Baptiste Corbine.[197] But that this involved no real challenge to the white man's supremacy can be learned in a revealing anecdote related by Warren. Warren informs us that a party of 150 canoes set out from Court Oreilles to visit the *Shawano* prophet at Detroit. So great was their faith in the latter, that in one of the canoes there was a dead child, who was to be resuscitated by the prophet. This enthusiastic delegation of pilgrims was met on the way by the trader Michel Cadotte. Once more, the influence of this man over the Indians is demonstrated. Alone, Cadotte harangued the Indians, told them that they were making a mistake, that the prophet was misleading them, that they would all go hungry at Detroit, and that it would be best for them all to turn around and paddle back. And the Indians did so! The few who went on to Detroit were disillusioned by the prophet and spread discouraging stories about him on their return. So the *Shawano* cult rapidly fizzled out.[198]

Warren claims that the cult had one good result: it led to a diminution of sorcery, or "poisoning," as Warren calls it.[199] And Tanner also had some good things to say about it:

The influence of the Shawnee prophet was very sensibly and painfully felt by the remotest Ojibbeways of whom I had any knowledge; but it was not the common impression among them, that his doctrines had any tendency to unite them in the ac-

---

[194] *Ibid.*   [195] *Ibid.*   [196] *Ibid.*   [197] See above, p. 39.
[198] Warren, 1880, pp. 321–325.   [199] *Ibid.*

complishment of any human purpose. For two or three years drunkenness was much less frequent than formerly; war was less thought of, and the entire aspect of affairs among them was somewhat changed by the influence of one man. But gradually the impression was obliterated, medicine bags, flints, and steels, were resumed; dogs were raised, women and children were beaten as before, and the Shawnee prophet was despised. At this day he is looked upon by the Indians as an impostor and a bad man.[200]

Tanner says nothing about the consequences of the anti-white agitation inherent in the *Shawano* cult; but to my mind the last sentence of this quotation implies a sense of guilt on the part of the Indians. The *Shawano* prophet is blamed as a bad man for having misled them. A similar implication appears in Warren's account. " . . . the excitement gradually died away among the Ojibways, and the medicine men and chiefs who had become such ardent believers, hung their heads in shame whenever the Shawano was mentioned."[201]

I do not know whether reactions of shame and guilt are often found in the aftermath of other nativistic movements; but I found no similar descriptions of Dakota reactions to the subsidence of the Ghost Dance.

THE GHOST DANCE

The Ghost Dance, which violently agitated the Dakota, Cheyenne, Arapaho, Pawnee and other Plains tribes in 1890, was a much less practical and sober affair than the *Shawano* cult. Instead of promulgating measures of non-co-operation with the intruder, this nativistic movement relied upon a promised supernatural deliverance from the white man. Thus the Ghost Dance expressed not only the violence and hostility which Plains tribes felt for the white man, but also the hopeless desperation and dismay which they experienced after their defeat and loss of independence.

The most dramatic belief in the Dakota Ghost Dance was that a new world was approaching the earth, bearing with it the resurrected dead and all the buffalo and other game that had disappeared. It was said that the Indians would be transferred to this new earth, while the old one was destroyed. According to the Arapaho leader, Sitting Bull, the new world would be preceded by a wall of fire which would drive the whites across the water back to their original home, while the Indians would soar up to the other earth, where the buffalo were grazing in vast numbers. The Ghost Dance was meant to prepare the Indians for this great event.[202]

Enthusiasm for the new cult was very strong. Among the Cheyenne and the Arapaho the Ghost Dance practically superseded all other dances.[203] But among the Chippewa it never caught on.[204]

[200] Tanner, p. 113.   [201] Warren, 1880, p. 324.
[202] Mooney, 1896, p. 786.   [203] *Idem*, p. 901.
[204] In a rather vague passage, Gilfillan says that the "Sioux dance" spread like wildfire on the Chippewa White Earth Reservation in Minnesota. He seems to have reference to the Ghost Dance

This abstention from the Ghost Dance on the part of the Chippewa is rather striking, because the Chippewa have always been interested in religious matters. As an early traveler through their region remarked, "Of all the Natives, these people are the most superstitious, they may be accounted the religionists of the North."[205] Moreover, the Wisconsin Chippewa have accepted numerous religious importations, such as Catholicism, Presbyterianism, and even (at Flambeau) the peyote cult. Some fifteen years before the Ghost Dance craze, the Wisconsin Chippewa took over the Drum Dance from the Dakota, which shows that they were not averse to receiving religious novelties from their former enemy. Why did the Ghost Dance not exert an appeal for the Chippewa as the Drum Dance did?

The answer, I think, is simply this: While the Drum Dance may be labeled "nativistic" in the perpetuative sense, to use Linton's phrase,[206] it was not marked by any explicit hostility against the white man. On the contrary, the Drum Dance was organized to promote peace and harmony among all men, even though membership was confined to Indians. Nothing in its provisions ran strongly counter to Chippewa values.[207] But the Ghost Dance of 1890 was evidently much too violent in its expression of anti-white aggression to appeal to the Chippewa, particularly since it came at a time when conditions were improving considerably in northern Wisconsin. Indians were beginning to receive timber money and greater governmental assistance. There was probably less, rather than more anti-white hostility at the time; and many of the Chippewa were beginning to feel that their lot in life was changing for the better.

All the same, we do know that considerable resentment against the white man existed in 1890, as it still exists today in northern Wisconsin. Consequently, it might have been expected that some of the Chippewa would have welcomed the opportunity to express submerged aggressive feelings in the realm of phantasy and religious "projection" afforded by the Ghost Dance. Yet, as we have seen, submission to white authority was deep-seated indeed; and even under intoxication violence was not directed against the white man. Similarly, the world of phantasy was guarded with inhibitions.

In an analysis of Chippewa-Saulteaux Rorschach records, Hallowell remarks that the phantasy life of these Indians is lacking in genuine creativity and suffers from a certain amount of repression through fear. " . . . all

---

here, but Gilfillan may have confused the latter with the Drum Dance or with one of the other dances which the Chippewa took over from the Dakota. According to Mooney, the Chippewa were not receptive to the cult, and I have found no references to its existence in Wisconsin. See Mooney, 1896, p. 816. According to Landes, the Manitoba Ojibwa took over the Give-away and the Rabbit Dance from the Dakota; but she does not refer to the Ghost Dance. (Landes, 1937a, p. 113.)

[205] Thompson, 1916, p. 246.   [206] Linton, 1943.
[207] For a description of the Drum Dance, or Dream Dance, see Barrett, 1911.

phantasy is dangerous, more especially aggressive phantasy of which there is little evidence. Where aggression is mainly covert, hostile thoughts must be inhibited in the individual for fear of inviting the evil thoughts of others to attack him."[208]

Dakota phantasy and self-expression, on the other hand, seem to have been much more violent and extravagant.[209] Moreover, there seems to have been a greater general readiness among the Dakota to give expression to aggressive feelings, whether directed outwardly or against the self. Dakota religious ceremonies, as we know, involved elaborate public displays of self-torture, a pattern which was completely lacking among the Chippewa. Suicide, which was often resorted to among Plains tribes, was relatively rare among the Chippewa.[210] The Ghost Dance would therefore not have found the receptive soil that existed among the Dakota and Cheyenne, where the dance filled emotional needs which were either lacking among the Chippewa, or else were deeply inhibited.

[208] Hallowell, 1947, p. 224.

[209] For a sample of riotous Dakota phantasy, consult Black Elk's long description of his great vision. (Neihardt, 1932, pp. 24–47.)

[210] Gilfillan, p. 60.

VI. CONCLUSIONS

IN THE preceding pages we examined some features of Chippewa history, and some general reactions to the acculturation process on the part of the Wisconsin Chippewa. We related those features to certain widespread personality characteristics of the Indians and to the patterns of culture and social organization prevalent in aboriginal times.

In this study we chose to emphasize idiosyncratic aspects of Chippewa acculturation, the ways in which their adjustment to the impact of western civilization differed from the reactions of neighboring Plains groups. We might, instead, have chosen to stress the similarities of response in these Indian groups. We might have underlined the leveling tendencies at work in the acculturation process, which subjected such different Indian societies to so many of the same pressures, laws, and cultural dilemmas, for after all, the reservation cultures of the present-day "Antler," Dakota, and Chippewa do not differ very much. Many passages in the writings of Mead, MacGregor, and Erikson could be applied without alteration to the Chippewa.

However, we elected to emphasize differences rather than similarities because in this way we hoped to attain some insight into the nature of historical causation. In the beginning of our inquiry, therefore, we singled out some characteristic aspects of Chippewa acculturation for analysis.

The outstanding feature of Wisconsin Chippewa history seems to have been the ready compliance with which these Indians accepted white domination and control. They retained resentment for the "Great White Father" but never turned their guns upon him. Isolated outbursts of violence were rare indeed, and there was no organized resistance such as characterized the Fox, Dakota, and Cheyenne.

We also noted the absence of the Ghost Dance among the Chippewa—a feature evidently allied with the preceding.

Another distinguishing characteristic, manifesting a continuation of aboriginal patterns, was the failure of the Wisconsin Chippewa to develop co-operative ventures in recent times comparable to those of the Dakota and Arapaho.

Finally, we noted that not only were sociological patterns retained; personality characteristics and attitudes also appear to have persisted into the new setting. Since Chippewa acculturation was much less traumatic psychologically than that of the Dakota, the old personality structure seems to have survived without much change.

Further inquiry into these aspects of Chippewa acculturation showed that they were not limited to the Wisconsin Chippewa alone, but appear to have been characteristic, by and large, of a number of other Woodland peoples in the Canadian-Great Lakes region, such as the Saulteaux (Canadian Chippewa), the Ottawa, Menomini, Forest Potawatomi and Cree, all of whom shared roughly the same type of culture and social organization. This Woodland group was contrasted with the tribes of the Plains, particularly the Dakota, Cheyenne, and Arapaho, who had a much more violent history of acculturation.

Our Woodland-Plains dichotomy, however, does not envisage two watertight compartments, for there was naturally a great deal of overlapping in these neighboring culture areas. The Fox were originally a Woodland people, but their patterns of acculturation were more akin to those of the Plains. The Assineboines, on the other hand, possessed a type of culture approaching that of the Plains, but they reacted to white contact much as did the Chippewa and Menomini. To further confuse the picture, there were Chippewa, Cree, and Potawatomi groups which pushed out onto the Plains and adopted a Plains way of life. It is partly because of the ambiguity of this historical picture, but also because of a lack of adequate data about other Woodland peoples, such as the Ottawa, Potawatomi, and Cree, that it seemed preferable to limit our discussion to one particular group which has been studied in some detail: the Wisconsin Chippewa.

In our analysis of Wisconsin Chippewa acculturation, we first discussed the failure of co-operative ventures to develop during the reservation period and pointed out that this feature illustrated a persistence of aboriginal patterns, related to the former atomism of Chippewa social organization. It seems evident that the atomistic nature of this social structure was reinforced by certain attitudes of fear and suspicion engendered through the process of child training and continuing throughout adult life. Children were disciplined by scaring techniques and taught to be afraid of owls, bears, snakes, ghosts, white men, Indian enemies, menstruating women, medicine men, and people in mourning. Particularly significant was the widespread fear of sorcery, which multiplied mistrust and inhibited social interaction.

Fears springing from these sources are still current today, although belief in sorcery is no longer universal. There is still relatively little social interaction, in spite of the fact that there has been a concentration of population during the reservation period. The few co-operative undertakings which are occasionally organized for short periods of time are attended with continual bickering and criticism of superiors, which has the effect of inhibiting constructive social efforts.

This picture was contrasted with that of the Plains societies after their defeat by the whites. Here, the formerly unified camp circle was disbanded, and families were often scattered over wide areas. Naturally, an increase in individualistic behavior took place at this time; but in spite of the reassertion of individualistic tendencies such as those described by Goldfrank,[211] and in spite of the geographical dispersal of the Plains societies, co-operative techniques (cattle associations, mutual aid groups, etc.) are still in evidence. In the Plains area, therefore, as in the Chippewa region, we find some continuity of tradition and of social attitudes; but here the traditions and attitudes are different. Fear of sorcery, for instance, does not seem to have exerted the inhibitory social influence that it has among the Chippewa.

To be sure, the present younger generation of Dakota children is very different from the generation of old-timers. While they engage in co-operative action, they probably do not do so in the same spirit that once animated their grandfathers and great-grandfathers. The tradition exists, nevertheless.

When we turn to another characteristic feature of Chippewa acculturation, the absence of violence, we are again driven to consider group attitudes and personality variables. We indicated why it was not adequate to explain this contrast with the Plains solely in terms of the differing natures of the white frontier. Nor can we account for it merely by saying that the Chippewa had become familiar with the white man's strength. The atomistic nature of society among the Chippewa and their difficulty in organizing for warfare provide a partial solution, but not a final one; for they do not explain the rarity of isolated attacks on individual white men in the Chippewa region. Nor did social atomism prevent the Chippewa from ably waging war against better-organized Indian groups.

If the Chippewa had always liked the white man, there would be no problem for us to solve. But there was a great deal of hostility against the white man, expressed for example in the *Shawano* cult of 1808 and in the speeches of individual chiefs which have been recorded. There was a natural resentment at white exploitation of the Indians' resources. And we noted some additional reasons for such hostility, springing from temperamental differences, the friction of intermarriage with whites, etc. Yet anti-white sentiments were marked by a peculiar impotence among the Chippewa, as if it were admitted that nothing could be done about them.

In order to understand this phenomenon, it was necessary to analyze the relationship between the Indians and the fur trader, who played such a crucial role in their drama of acculturation. The trader was a dispenser of guns, traps, food, tobacco, liquor, clothing, pots and pans and other trading goods. Through the operations of the trading system, the extension of credit, and similar means he acquired considerable authority over the Indians and influenced the movements of Chippewa bands, leading a group from one hunting area to another, sometimes instigating war with other tribes, or negotiating peace, if

---

[211] Goldfrank, 1943, 1945.

this happened to be in the interests of the fur trade. He created "chiefs" and bestowed other privileges. By the Indians he was addressed as "father," which symbolized his dominant power and their submissive, dependent relationship to him. This relationship was a crucial one, because the attitudes toward the trader served as prototypes for later dealings with white government officials, who took over many of the trader's functions in the society, and who continued to deal with the Indians in much the same way.

But behind the prototype-relationship of Indian and trader lay the still more basic prototype-relationship of child to parent, which unconsciously influenced Indian dealings with the white man. Some discussion of this basic relationship was necessary. We saw that the Chippewa family unit was a small biological family unit like that of the western world, which often existed in a state of isolation from other groups. The parents and grandparents therefore played a role of magnified importance in the life of the child. Kinship terms for "mother" and "father" were not extended among the Chippewa as among the Dakota and other Plains tribes.

In the folklore father-figures are often depicted as malevolent, particularly in stories with an Oedipus theme. In these folktales the hero is overshadowed by his father, and although he struggles with his father, the hero never kills him. It seems to have been the pattern to repress hostile feelings against the father and to magnify the latter's magical powers to harm or to bless. Paradoxically, a dependent type of personality was fostered among the Chippewa, in spite of their high evaluation of self-sufficiency.

Parents probably failed to satisfy their children's needs for security and protection. Instead, every effort was made to make children independent at an extremely early age, although children were also frightened into obedience, and given a picture of the world which was dangerous and threatening. This may help to account for the undercurrent need for dependency which is illustrated by the biographical material in the Appendix. It is perhaps partly for such reasons, moreover, that fathers were described with resentment and why the folktales represent father-figures as inimical and frustrating persons.

One way in which children apparently learned to appeal to these powerful but stern adults was by evoking pity in their hearts. Folktales illustrate this mechanism, and some of my life-history material provides further illustration; while the relationship with guardian spirits again exemplifies the appeal to pity as a technique in dealing with powerful and potentially generous beings.

The trader naturally fitted into the latter category. As we have noted, he was addressed as "father" and he fulfilled paternal functions in providing security, guidance, and oral satisfaction through his stores of food and tobacco. The white man's liquor was referred to as "milk," which furnishes additional testimony to the symbolic role which the trader filled. It is not surprising, therefore, that the Chippewa utilized the appeal to pity in their efforts to tap the generosity of the trader.

Such mechanisms give us an insight into the psychological dependence of the Indians on the trader, a dependence which led some of them to place an excessively high valuation on government rations and annuities. The same emotional orientation may be responsible for the impotent quality of Chippewa resentment against the whites and for the inflated conceptions of the white man's power held by some of the Indians.

Hostility against the white man who was identified with the father-image could be expressed only in complaints, bickering, and denunciation. Beyond this, aggressive impulses were deeply inhibited. White men were hardly ever attacked in the Chippewa region, even when the Indians were badly intoxicated. Moreover, the white man's goods were seldom plundered, which provides another striking contrast with the situation on the Plains.

In the Plains area there is a long record of plunder, attacks on wagon trains, murders of settlers, and intermittent warfare with the white man. The white man was not held in any great veneration. Partly because of the self-sufficiency of Plains tribes, traders were often driven away, rather than welcomed; and government rations were regarded with indifference—at least while the buffalo held out. While the appeal to pity was employed with guardian spirits, it does not seem to have been used with the white man. "I was not born to eat out of the white man's hand," said Sitting Bull with scorn;[212] and in saying this, he summed up the resolutely independent attitude of the Plains.

The reservation system, however, is one which encourages attitudes of dependency in the long run. Erikson notes a development of such tendencies among the Dakota shortly after their defeat.[213] But in this respect the Chippewa had a head-start over the Dakota; for among the former the submissive and dependent relationship with the white man long preceded reservation life, originating with the trader, who established the pattern for later Indian-white relationships.

Once again, it may be noted that the tempo of Plains acculturation differed from that of the Chippewa, the latter accepting the domination of the white

---

[212] McGillycuddy, 1941, p. 263.
[213] Erikson, 1939, pp. 106, 112 (fn).
Among the Dakota, the traditions of independence did not die overnight, even after confinement on the reservation. This may be learned from the speech of a young man named Plenty Horses: "I am an Indian. Five years I attended Carlisle and was educated in the ways of the white man. When I returned to my people, I was an outcast among them. I was no longer an Indian. I was not a white man. I was lonely. I shot the lieutenant so I might make a place for myself among my people. Now I am one of them. I shall be hung and the Indians will bury me as a warrior. They will be proud of me. I am satisfied." (McGillycuddy, 1941, p. 272.)
A statement like this cannot be matched among the records bearing on the Chippewa.

man about a century before the forced submission of the Dakota. This partially helps us to understand the rejection of the Ghost Dance by the Chippewa. Yet even if the Ghost Dance had been introduced a hundred years before, one wonders if the Chippewa would have taken to the violently anti-white phantasy expressed in this cult, which ran counter to Chippewa patterns of inhibition and self-control, as well as to their habits of submissive dependency upon the white man.

Although some friction and irritation were unavoidable during the contact period, the Chippewa adjusted without any real protest to the new state of affairs, because the white man brought many gratifications which they valued highly. The atomism of their society favored a gradual and piecemeal type of acculturation. The Chippewa did not have to undergo the traumatic disorganization experienced by the Plains tribes, for in their case there was no marked change in the social order attendant on the white man's assumption of power over them. Patterns of interpersonal relationships did not significantly alter, and consequently there seems to have been no change in the personality structure of the Chippewa.

Among the Dakota, on the other hand, where the aboriginal social structure was swiftly disrupted, there is evidence that there has been a change in personality structure since the beginning of the reservation period.

To my mind, the preceding material warrants one important generalization of broader relevance. In the Introduction I suggested that the history of a given society might illuminate the "basic" personality structure characteristic of that society. I think that this assumption is warranted, in the light of the data presented above. I think we may also conclude that no analysis of historical causation can afford to leave personality variables out of the reckoning. Those differences which we observed in Chippewa and Dakota acculturation were not only the results of contrasting socio-economic conditions; they reflected as well emotional responses and attitudes characteristic of personality structures which had been moulded by different cultural environments.

APPENDIX: BIOGRAPHICAL MATERIAL

A WORD OF EXPLANATION

The Appendix is devoted to selections from the life-histories of three individuals, Jim Mink, John Thunderbird, and Julia Badger, chosen to illustrate some of the points made in the preceding pages. I have also included some interpretative comments. In the cases of John Thunderbird and Julia Badger I have incorporated Rorschach analyses made by Maud Hallowell and by Dr. Bruno Klopfer. In John Thunderbird's case, some of the Thematic Apperception Test is given. Dreams are included with the biographical material.

The information here presented was obtained from interviews in the homes of the informants. Their incentive for working with me was largely financial. (Rates were roughly forty cents an hour.) Since the work did not seem too demanding, my subjects were generally willing to talk; but after six or seven sessions they usually experienced some difficulty in producing material. This did not apply to Julia Badger, who talked compulsively and who did not really need a financial incentive. John Thunderbird often enjoyed orating to me, although he was afraid of possible repercussions from the supernatural world. Jim Mink, however, was seldom able to relax; and he did not care for this peculiar kind of work. He felt most at home when giving straight ethnological information—about the structure of a sugar-camp dwelling, or the rules of a game, etc. The subjects were somewhat mystified about my intentions in collecting so much pointless information. They were puzzled, and a little scornful, concerning the Rorschach test, not knowing what to make of it. Julia Badger, again, was an exception; since she enjoyed novelties and diversions. With the exception of Julia, there was considerable reluctance to discuss religion, particularly the Medicine Dance; although this does not hold true for all Chippewa informants. Jim Mink and John Thunderbird had mixed feelings about working with me. Sometimes they enjoyed talking. On other occasions they were worried about the adverse gossip of other people, or they felt guilty at having betrayed some information about the Medicine Dance. On many occasions they broke appointments; or rather, they would not be home at the appointed time. But if I met them later and asked whether they would care to continue the interviews, they generally assented. The interviews, whenever possible, were held alone with the informant. In Jim Mink's case this was generally impossible, since his large family made it difficult for him to get any privacy. Tom Badger was very often present in my interviews with Julia. John Thunderbird, however, usually worked with me alone. During the sessions I tried to maintain a friendly, informal atmosphere, although this was a little hampered by the necessity of taking notes in longhand. When religious matters were to be discussed, I generally brought some tobacco for the men; and this sometimes facilitated the disclosure of mysteries.

Before presenting my material, let me first give a word of explanation to readers who may be puzzled by the unevenness of acculturation manifest in these biographies. In Jim Mink's anecdotes, for example, we make the acquaintance of an old Chippewa Civil War veteran who owns a barn, a carriage and pair, and other trappings of western culture. We might assume, therefore, that acculturation set in very rapidly in northern Wisconsin after the 1860's. There is little in Jim Mink's account to contradict such an impression. But when we turn to John Thunderbird's life history, we get a very different picture. John's grandfather was of the same generation as the Civil War veteran, but this old man lived in a wigwam instead of a house, and wore leggings and breech clout instead of a military uniform. It is clear that he was an Indian of the conservative school, a visionary credited with having obtained a powerful fasting dream.

John Thunderbird's biography, in general, sounds more "Indian" in its ethnological details than Jim Mink's; and so does Julia Badger's. In Julia's account, however, we find the same unevenness of acculturation. We learn that both of her parents went to school, and that her grandfather owned a farm; and yet Julia spent thirty-two days in a seclusion hut at first menstruation, and was treated by most of the aboriginal methods of healing.

If John Thunderbird's and Julia Badger's life-history material sound more "Indian" than Jim Mink's, the discrepancy is partly to be explained by the fact that Jim Mink is from the Court Oreilles Reservation, while John Thunderbird and Julia Badger are from the Lac du Flambeau Reservation. Court Oreilles seems to have been about twenty years ahead of Flambeau in the process of acculturation, partly because of the greater isolation of Lac du Flambeau.

In 1832 a missionary who visited Lac du Flambeau commented that "glass, nails and all other foreign materials for building are imported as other foreign goods are. To this post they are brought more than 50 miles of the way *on men's backs.*"[214]

Such conditions seem to have persisted on both reservations into the 1870's.[215] But in his report to the Commissioner of Indian Affairs in Washington in 1874, the La Pointe Indian agent noted that some progress had been made at Court Oreilles, where a logging camp had started work.

Nothing has been done for these Indians, by way of civilization, previous to July, 1873 [he remarked]. Since then a teacher and a farmer have been provided; 65 acres have been cleared and 150 cultivated; a school-house, with rooms for the family of the teacher, a warehouse, a stable, and seven hewn-log houses for Indians, have been built; 8,000 feet of lumber sawed; 30,000 shingles made; 3,000 rails cut; and another school-house bought and fitted up in another part of the reserve. Roads have been cut, bridges built, and everything is organized and in readiness for vigorous work next season. The school has been attended by 110 children, and the progress made will compare very favorably with that of white schools for the same time. This has been accomplished through the wise and faithful labor of a Christian family, who have been intrusted with the expenditure of a portion of the funds received for sale of pine on this reservation.[216]

The agent painted a much gloomier picture of the Lac du Flambeau band, whose number he estimated at 629.

The Indians subsist entirely upon the proceeds of their hunting, fishing, and trapping. There is no white settlement within sixty miles of the reserve. There are no houses or agency buildings on this reserve; in fact they have nothing but the land and the timber, and such game and fish as the good God sends them. Poor, isolated, neglected, and forgotten people![217]

In his report for 1876, the agent wrote that the Flambeau Indians "have made no

---

[214] Nute, 1931, p. 190.   [215] See above, p. 35.
[216] Annual Report, 1874, pp. 28, 189.   [217] *Ibid.*

progress in civilization; they roam through the country, trapping, fishing, and hunting."[218] But he was much more optimistic about Court Oreilles.

Three years ago, when I first visited the Indians of these bands [wrote the agent in 1876], I found them dirty, ragged, and filthy; lazy and indolent to a degree beyond anything I had ever imagined. Their blankets, clothing, and hair perfectly alive with vermin; they had the woods covered with birch-bark wigwams. Today I find them generally dressed in civilized costumes; their hair combed, and their faces and clean white shirts show that some one has taught them the use of soap and water.[219]

In 1883 the agent guessed that less than half of the Indians at Flambeau wore "citizen's dress" (i.e. white men's clothes)—200 out of the total population of 480. Only five families were engaged in agriculture, and five in "civilized pursuits." There were no churches or missionaries at Lac du Flambeau. It was estimated that 43 Indians there could speak English, and that ten houses were occupied by Indians.[220] Court Oreilles, however, was credited with 102 houses in 1883 and 736 Indians wearing "citizen's dress" out of a total population of 841. Over half of the population could speak some English, and 161 families were engaged in agriculture, 21 in "civilized pursuits."[221] It is clear that Court Oreilles rapidly outstripped Lac du Flambeau in speed of acculturation after 1873. This acceleration was partly due to the fact that Court Oreilles was more accessible by road and by train; also because it had been prospected by logging companies before Lac du Flambeau was investigated, and because the government seems to have taken a greater interest in its development.

The difference between the two reservations should not be exaggerated, however. Actually, life is much the same at Court Oreilles and Lac du Flambeau at the present time. The same aboriginal patterns of religion and of social life can be found in both places. *Within* each reservation, moreover, there has been the same uneven pace of acculturation; which means that highly acculturated families will often be found living next to conservative "pagan" families. There is one fifteen-year-old boy at Court Oreilles, for example, who has had a traditional fasting dream; while there is a sixty-year-old lawyer at Lac du Flambeau who graduated from Yale. The uneven development of acculturation is a general characteristic of this region, probably related to the atomistic nature of Chippewa society.

While the biographical data that follow will illustrate various points made in the body of this paper, it may be noted that each section illustrates different kinds of material, because of the individual differences in personality and status among these informants. Thus, Mrs. Badger provides data on fear of sorcery, menstrual taboos, etc.; while John Thunderbird furnishes information about fasting, Indian oratory, etc. I am starting with Jim Mink's material; because although his biography is less satisfactory than the others, it provides the most striking picture of an Indian's attitudes towards the white man.

[218] Annual Report, 1876, pp. 148–149.   [219] *Ibid.*

[220] The latter must have been log houses put up by old voyageurs or else by loggers, who were beginning to appear in the neighborhood. No frame houses were erected until after Herrick's mill was started in 1893.

[221] Annual Report, 1883.

1. JIM MINK

INTRODUCTORY COMMENTS

Jim Mink is a thin, wiry half-breed, aged fifty-five. He is talkative, restless, short-tempered, and very burdened down by the problem of supporting his wife and six children on a meagre income. Jim went to school for nine years in his youth and then spent fourteen years away from the reservation "trying to become like a white man," to use his own words. This effort failed, and Jim returned to the reservation, where he married a girl of conservative Indian family. He has lived with her for the past twenty-one years, working at the random occupations followed by Chippewa men—guiding for tourists, picking beans, carpentry, house-painting, etc.

Ever since his return to the reservation, Jim Mink has been trying very hard to be like an Indian, despite his long estrangement from the old ways. He attends all religious ceremonies, War Dances, Drum Dances, as well as the *Midewiwin*. For the past eight years Jim has been understudy to the old *Mide* priest and some day will probably occupy the priestly office himself. It must be said that Jim Mink is very unlike the *Mide* priests I have met, all of whom possess a certain dignity. He is too nervous and insecure to be very impressive. Of all the Rorschach records I collected, his was one of the most disturbed. This might invalidate him as a representative spokesman for his group, were it not for the fact that many Chippewa men of his generation manifest similar insecurity.

Jim's childhood was apparently unhappy. He was afraid of his father's father and of his own father, a big 200-pound man, according to his statement, who used to beat him—a form of punishment relatively rare among the Chippewa.

That's why I stayed away from my father [Jim explained]. Oh, I sometimes use the stick on my own kids. But that's not being mean, the way they were. They were *mean*. If I was hungry, I'd reach over for some more bread; then they'd take it away from me.

Because of this maltreatment, Jim preferred to stay with his mother's father, whom he described as being a more kindly, wise old man, who had great prophetic gifts. Jim said nothing about his mother, except to describe how she once stitched a cut in his foot with sinew thread.

When Jim was sent out to fast, as a boy, he washed the charcoal off his face and went elsewhere to get food. He seems to have been more rebellious than the usual Chippewa child. This rebellious quality was also manifest at boarding school, where he went at the age of eleven. Jim hated school and often ran away. But oddly enough, he developed some affection for the disciplinarian who came to get him and take him back to school.[222] "He was a nice man," said Jim. "He was about the nicest man we had." This seems to be characteristic of Jim Mink—an attitude of respect, mixed with fear and resentment, for strong authoritarian older male figures, including the Indian agent. Jim's inflated conception of the latter is almost fantastic, as will be seen presently. Nevertheless, Jim Mink has frequently voiced the greatest antipathy for the white man. Just as he outdoes the real Indian old-timers in professions of loyalty to Indian ways (in spite of the fact that these are actually quite foreign to him), so Jim also ex-

---

[222] This man is a half-breed who looks and acts like a white man. He is relatively well to do and is not popular among the Indians.

presses more adverse criticism of the government than one normally hears from the older men. "Nobody in the government wants to help the Indian!" Jim exclaims bitterly. "They just want to rob him!"

One of the grievances Jim Mink has against the white man is the flooding of reservation land now known as the Flowage. This was done by the Wisconsin and Minnesota Light and Power Company, which sought to build a dam. Jim thinks that the Indians shouldn't have let them do it. One result of this inundation is that the home where Jim lived as a boy is now under water.

Another grievance that Jim Mink has against the whites is their despoiling of the forests. All of the white pine and birch was plundered by the lumber companies. How could the Indians make their canoes or birchbark containers now, even if they wanted to? They can't make things in the old ways nowadays, because the raw materials are gone. At the present time, the Indian is forbidden to cut down green timber. But who's to blame if there aren't any trees? The white man, not the Indian. Moreover, the Indian isn't allowed to shoot female deer. But who's to blame if there's no game in the woods, no fish in the streams? Once again, the white man.

Although Jim expressed opinions such as these readily enough, he was not a good informant. He seldom stuck to one subject, but nervously rambled and jumped from one topic to another. Toward the end of our sessions, however, he told me five long anecdotes, which all possessed a common basic theme. They seemed to have some inner relationship in Jim Mink's mind, because he told them one after the other, as if each story were suggested by the one preceding.

The common theme in these five stories is the benevolent despotic power of an older male figure. In three of these stories, this figure is a white man, the Indian agent or deputy agent. In the other two anecdotes (the first and last to be told) the comparable figure is an old man, the uncle of Jim's father. Somewhat abbreviated, these stories follow.

JIM MINK'S ANECDOTES

First Story

[In the first story Jim Mink described his father's uncle, a wealthy old Indian who had served in the American Civil War. One day Jim went hunting and borrowed this old man's gun. Unfortunately, the barrel of the gun cracked in the explosion. After the old man had pointed this out to Jim, he asked him to come back the next evening and stay overnight. We continue in Jim Mink's own words.]

So I came back the next evening. I got there about five o'clock. He said, "You go out in the pasture. There's some ponies in the pasture. Take them into the barn for the night." So I took them into the barn. I didn't know what was up. I stayed there that night. Along about three o'clock in the morning—it was just breaking daylight—he woke me up and said "Go and get the ponies some grain and hay and harness them up." Well, I done all that. While I was doing all that, his wife was cooking. Breakfast was about ready when I came in again. The old fellow was all dressed up in his Civil War uniform. I didn't know what was up at all; but I figured that something was wrong.

Right after breakfast he said, "You go into the barn and harness up the ponies to the buggy." He had one of those old-fashioned covered buggies. Well, I hooked them up and brought them in front of the house there, and went in. I told him "The ponies are all ready." Then I noticed that he had his uniform on, the uniform he had in the Civil War. He used to call me "grandson" in Chippewa. He said "Grandson, get the gun and put it in the buggy." Well, he went out, and I followed him. We got in the buggy. He said "You drive the ponies." I asked him "Where are we going?" I was wondering what was up. He said "Grandson, we're going to Hayward." I said "It ain't necessary for me to go to Hayward, I ain't got no money." He said "Well, I want you to go along with me."

Well, we was on the road a half a day, going to Hayward. Then I drove into town. I wanted to feed the horses at a barn next to the hotel there. He said "You leave the gun where it is." I was thinking he might take me to jail for spoiling that gun. He said "When you get through putting up the ponies, you come into the hotel. We'll eat dinner there." I told him again "I ain't got no money to pay for my dinner." He said "I ain't asking you for no money to pay for your dinner. I'll see that you get your dinner." I went in the hotel—used to be an expensive place then. He was sitting there in a rocking chair. I sat down opposite him on the other side of the door. He said "Grandson, come and sit next to me. Bring that chair up."

He used to have a big billfold with a big rubber band around it. He had his uniform coat and vest on. His clothes were all buttoned up. I was wondering what in the world the old man was bringing me there for. He opened his vest. I could see him reaching for that big billfold. He unwrapped it. He pulls out a ten dollar bill and puts in on his knee. Then he pulls out another one. Then a five dollar bill. Then he buttoned himself up again. He handed me the twenty-five dollars and said "Here, grandson. Here's what you made by driving me down here." He said "You buy your clothes with that money." Then he reaches and brings out another pocket book. He gave me a five dollar bill. He said "When you go out after dinner, you take that gun to the blacksmith's shop and get it sawed off where it's starting to crack." [Jim went on this errand, brought back the gun and the cash.] . . . I told the old man, "The gun is all ready." I reached into my pocket and took out the four silver dollars, fifty cents, a dime, and a nickel. I handed it over to him, and he said "I didn't tell you to bring that change back. You keep that change. You can buy a pretty good pair of shoes with that."

[Then the old man announced that he was going to a saloon. This, in fact, was why he had put on his Civil War uniform. At the saloon he said to the bartender "Do you know who I am?" The bartender said "No." The old man then pointed to his uniform and told him about "the tough time he had had in the Civil War." This apparently enabled him to be served with liquor. In fact, the old man even had the bartender fix up a drink for his "grandson" after the latter had bought some shoes and clothing. Then the two drove home.]

Second Story

[Jim Mink's father owned a little store. He gave credit to a man who didn't pay his bill. Consequently, he almost went broke and failed, in turn, to pay a bill owing to a storekeeper. The latter knew that Jim Mink's father had some money at the Indian Office. So he took a lawyer over to see him.]

My father's name was Mike. The storekeeper said to him, "Say, Mike, you've got money coming over at the office." "Well, yes. I've got money down there, but I can't get it. Let's go over to see the Farmer" [the deputy Agent]. "No, you don't have to see the Farmer. This lawyer can make out a paper. You just sign the paper." But my father was smart. He told him "I'm not signing any papers without seeing the Farmer first."

The storekeeper's lawyer told my father "You've got a horse and buggy and a harness. Now tomorrow, if you don't sign this paper, I'll have to get the sheriff after you, and the sheriff will have to take your horse and buggy and harness to pay for that store bill."

Then my father said, "Go ahead and take it. After you've taken it, I'm going to go and see the Farmer."

Just while they were arguing, they saw a team of ponies going by the window. My father looked and saw the government agent. That's a higher official than the Farmer. It just happened that the Agent was with the Wisconsin Light and Power attorney. So they had two lawyers there.

They came into the house. They were just looking around. My father had a lot of watermelons. He'd just happened to raise a lot of watermelons that year. This agent asked my father and said "I hear you've got a lot of watermelons. I'd like to buy one." Then my father said "Let's go outside. I'll get you a watermelon." He talked English pretty good. My father talked French and English both.

These other fellows didn't know who this man was that had come in. They didn't know he was a government man. While they were outside in the garden, the Agent asked "What do them fellows want here?" My father told them: "I've got a store bill over there in the store, and they're going to take my horse away from me to pay it." The Agent told him "Don't pay that bill. Don't pay any attention to those fellows." My father said "They're going to get a sheriff to get my horse." The Agent said "Let them take it. They're going to pay for it. They'll pay twice as much for that horse as you paid for it."

So then Mr. Agent came into the house with the watermelon and said "Hey, Mike, have you got a knife? I'm going to cut this up." And he cut the melon up into six pieces, one for the Agent, one for his lawyer, one for the storekeeper, one for his lawyer, and one each for my father and mother. While they were eating watermelon, the Agent asked those two felllows what they were doing there. But he knew what they were doing all right. These two fellows, they didn't know who they were talking to. The storekeeper said "This man hasn't paid his store bill, but he has money coming to him over at the Farmer's office. I want him to sign this paper, and if he doesn't sign it, we're going to get the sheriff to take his horse and buggy and harness to pay for the store bill."

"I see," said the Agent. Then that's where Mr. Agent spoke up, then. He said "Do you know who you're talking to? I'm the Indian agent, and I've got all the Indians in the palm of my hand. They're the wards of the government, and I'm responsible for them. And I've got all the power of the United States government right behind me. All right, you take that horse away tomorrow, if you want it. We'll give you a chance to take it. But just as soon as you take it, you're going to bring it right back, and you're going to pay for it twice as much as Mike paid for that horse." Then he said. "Mike's got money in my office at Hayward. Mike can't take that money, and I can't either, not for that kind of use. A United States marshal will take that horse, and he's supposed to get money before he takes that horse. Is your lawyer going to take up this case? If you're going to take it up, I'll take it up too. I have my lawyer here."

The lawyer spoke up: "I'm a lawyer. I'm attorney for the Wisconsin Light and Power Company. I'll help Mike. We'll give you a chance to take up your case. We're not going to take up this case on a County Court or a State Court or a Federal Court. We'll put it in the Supreme Court. I'll back Mike on a free charge as long as this case lasts." A free charge means he ain't going to charge anything.

The Agent asked him, "Well, what are you going to do? Are you going to charge him? I'd like to know before I go out of this house."

So Mr. Lawyer and Mr. Storekeeper, they got scared. The Supreme Court—that's supposed to be the highest court in the United States. He named a month that the court would be set in Washington—May or June—I don't know what month it was.

The Agent said "Before Mike run a credit with you, why didn't you come and see me? You've got a lawyer with you. You should have known that you have to see the Indian Agent for permission to run up a credit with an Indian. If you had come to see me about it, I'd have okayed the credit. Before you let an Indian run a credit again come and see me first. Before I go out here, I want to see you go. Don't you ever come back here again bothering Indians. You know where you're at. All the Indians on the reservation are on my hands, and I'm under the government."

Then those fellows pulled out.

Third Story

[This involved a traveling salesman who sold Jim Mink a blanket on the installment plan. Before Jim had finished his payments, the salesman came and took it away, on the grounds that he had not kept up with his installments. Jim ran, swearing, over to the Indian Farmer, a young white man, and told him the story. The two of them managed to corner the salesman at the local store.]

I waited till he got through his trading. Then I asked him, "Mister, I don't know your name, what are you going to do with that blanket? Do you want me to pay for it or not? The agreement we made, I paid $3.75 for that blanket, and you told me that I had a year's time, and I told you I'd pay you as much as I could each time. That's the agreement we made."

"No," he said. "I told you two weeks."

"No," I said. "You told me twelve months. I can understand some English. I want to know what you want to do—either give me back my money or else give me the blanket and let me pay for it. One of the two."

We had quite a argument there. While we were arguing, the Farmer was standing there by a show case, looking at a paper. I was ready to get into a fight with that man. He was bigger than I was, but I was ready to take him on, since the Farmer was there, and a policeman was outside too.

The Farmer spoke up "What are you boys arguing about?"

I told him "This man here sold me a blanket, and we agreed to pay on time. He gave me a year to pay for it, and I paid him $3.75 down. Now he wants to take it away from me after two weeks. I want him to let me pay for it or give me back my money; either one."

No, that salesman, he didn't want to do either one or the other. He didn't know who the Farmer was.

Then the Farmer said "Do you know who I am? I'm an Indian Government Farmer. That's who I am. Your company has to get a permit from the Government to make a sale to the Indians. The best thing for you to do is either give him the money or the blanket before you go out of here. If you don't give him that money back or else the blanket, I'll have that policeman put your car in my yard. That young man is willing to pay his agreements on time. You'll have to do what I said."

The young fellow turned red, just like the blood was going to pop out of his face. He was scared. So Mr. Man give me the $3.75 back.

The Farmer spoke up again. "Before you ever come in here again, you get permit from the Agent. When you get permit from the Agent, you bring that permit right in my office, and I'll okay it. But right now, as you get in that car, turn and get out of here just as fast as you can—and stay out—and stay away until you get a permit from the Agent."

That man left in a hurry.

Fourth Story

[This tale concerned the problem of hunting and fishing rights.]

There are no violations on the reservation, [said Jim Mink]. We're wards of the government. So we can hunt or do anything *inside* the reservation. But we don't do that. We try to conserve our meat for later on—for hard times, for winter-time, and like that. So we go outside and violate. We don't follow Wisconsin law.

I got my fish on the reservation—right off my father's boat landing—quite a ways off on the lake. I goes across to the other place and kills some more fish there. It was getting pretty late in the evening, getting dark. I told my brother-in-law I was going home. We got to their place. He asked me to fish some more the next morning. I said "All right." So we fished that morning. Coming back, off the reservation, we stopped, and the other fellow traded some fish for grub with a storekeeper. . . . Then some bugger squawked on us. He knew we had fish in our car.

We got to a farm where they made moonshine. We asked the farmer if he'd trade whiskey for fish. He said "Sure, bring in the fish." We brought it in, and he dumped the fish into a big pan. Just then there was a rap on the door, and Ernie Swift, the game warden, came in. He pulled his coat open and said "I'm the game warden." There were two more of them in the car. They counted the fish we brought outside. The game warden said "I got you fellows." I didn't say nothing. So they took us to Exland.

The Justice of the Peace sentenced us. He made out a warrant. I was unlucky enough to be the first they questioned. He asked me where I'd got the fish. I told him: at Chief Lake. I was getting pretty mad. If they wanted to pinch me, I didn't care. He asked me "Are you guilty or not guilty?" I knew what that meant all right, but I said "I don't know what that means." He said "All right. Twenty-five dollars fine or thirty days in jail." I said "If I did have money, I wouldn't pay it. I have a family to look after. I'll take thirty days." They asked the same questions of the other four fellows. They all took thirty days too. Then they took us to Hayward and locked us all up in separate cells. I got to thinking. I asked the under-sheriff if I could call the government Agent. He said "You can use the phone at noon tomorrow."

Next day I rang up Central and asked for the Indian Agent at Hayward. "Hello" [Jim imitated a dual phone conversation]. "Hello. Who's this?" "It's me." "Who's me?" "Jim Mink." "What do you want?" "I want to talk to the Agent." "This is the Agent speaking. Where are you?" "I'm in jail." "Where?" "The jail in Hayward." "What did they put you in there for?" "I don't know. For trading fish we got on the reservation." "You wait a little while. I'll be right there. I'll be there in an hour—at one o'clock."

After that the sheriff didn't lock us up separately. That man had been listening to our conversation.

Well, the agent came at five minutes before one. He drove up in his car. He was banging at the door, but the under-sheriff was downstairs. "Isn't there anybody to take care of this door? A man'll freeze on a day like this!" When he was let in, he asked "Who are those boys you brought in last night? . . . Bring them all down! I want them to come and sit down right here." So the sheriff went up and let them all out of the bull-pen. "All right," the Agent said, "now what's the story?" We all told him what had happened.

The Agent said "These boys have no right to be in here. I'm going to take them back with me."

The sheriff said "They've broken the law."

"What law?"

"They violated the game law."

"There ain't no violation on the reservation. You go by the state law. I don't pay any attention to that law. I stand by the old treaty law." Then the Agent said to the sheriff, "You're a pretty small man to be talking to me. Do you know who I am? I'm a big man, that's what I am. I'm the Indian Agent. I've got the whole United States government right back of me. I hold the Indians right in the palm of my hand. They're the wards of the government. I'm protecting them. I'm willing to carry this case to the Supreme Court; and if you want to keep these boys under arrest, I'll see to it that from this minute on you're going to have to pay all their expenses until the trial and the fare to Washington and back. That's going to cost you a lot of money."

[Here Jim went into a complex legal argument, showing how the Agent pointed out illegalities in the way in which the Indians were put in jail. The justice of the peace had no right to issue warrants having them confined to jail in another county, etc.]

Then the Agent picked up the telephone and said "Give me the number of the justice of the peace in Exland." When he got hold of him, he told him who he was and said, "I'm going to give the sheriff just five minutes to give me the warrants of those boys. They've violated no law."

The sheriff was scared. He didn't know what to do.

The Agent said, "Unlock that door."

Well, the sheriff unlocked it, and the Agent pushed us through one by one. "You go on out," he said. Then he said "Where are the fish those boys caught?" They had some of them over there, and he made them hand it all back to us.

Then he said "Where's their car?"

The car was in back, with a lot of snow around it. The Agent said to the sheriff, "You get a shovel and shovel all this snow away." He wouldn't let us do it. We just watched him. At first the car wouldn't go. We put a stick in the gasoline tank to see how much gas there was. It was dry. The Agent just put his hand in his pocket and pulled out a dollar bill. "Take it to the station and get it filled up," he said. Then he made the sheriff get his car and drag us out. He was pretty hard on that sheriff and made him work pretty hard.

So that's how we got out of jail. We're wards of the government. We live on reservation land, and there's no violation there. That's under the old treaty law, and its higher than Wisconsin State law.

Fifth Story

One day my father's uncle drove up and asked me if I'd like to go to Odanah. I was sitting with my wife, her mother, father, and her uncle. I told him, "I can't go. I've got no money." He said "I ain't asking if you've got any money. I'm asking you to go along with me." I told him, "I'll have to talk it over with my wife." He said, "All right. We'll only be gone three or four days." My wife said, "Go ahead, if you want." So I went and dressed up.

He seemed to be watching me to see how I was fixed up for clothes. I suppose my shoes didn't look too good to him. At Hayward, our first stop, he said, "Are your shoes any good? You'd better buy some new ones." He gave me the money, gave me a pretty good wad of money. I bought a shirt and underwear and other things too.

[They go to Odanah. There Jim gets drunk, for which the old man rebukes him.]

The third night we were there, they had a grand opening of the bridge built at the Bad River Reservation. They had a white man's dance on one side of the bridge and an Indian dance on the other side. That dance lasted only one night, but the Indian gathering lasted four days. That was really why the old man had gone to Odanah.

[I asked Jim, "Which side of the bridge did you go to?"]

Both sides. I didn't take part in the Indian dance. I joined in on the white side, though. They had an orchestra playing waltzes and fox-trots. I used to be able to do them dances in those days. But I've quit that stuff now—ever since I joined the *Midewiwin*. They've had a couple of orchestra dances over at the Community Hall here, but we don't go. I took my wife, once, but we didn't like it. I know that *she* didn't, anyway.

The bridge was partitioned off. In the middle of the bridge they had a soft drink stand. I kept crossing the bridge, going back and forth to both sides. It lasted pretty nearly all night. We came home the next morning. The old man brought me home and told me we'd make another trip soon somewhere, but it never come.

COMMENTARY

I think the reader will agree that there is a remarkable similarity of theme in these five anecdotes. The inflated father-image appears in each case, represented by the father's uncle in the first and last stories and by the Indian Agent or Farmer in the remaining three tales.

The father's uncle is represented as a laconic but very generous individual who provides Jim Mink with food and clothing. Like the father of Tom Badger, he does not tell Jim where they are going when they set out on a trip; nor does he explain the purpose of their journey. He just gives orders, which Jim obeys with some misgivings. However, Jim Mink is richly rewarded for his obedience in terms of material goods. He never seems to have had a warm, friendly relationship with the old man. The two were apparently strained and ill at ease with one another. But the old man was a good deal more generous and kindly than Jim's father and grandfather, of whom he remarked, "They were *mean*. If I was hungry, I'd reach over for some more bread; then they'd take it away from me."

The Indian Agent, like the father's uncle, is also represented as a generous and powerful person, who helps his wards in time of trouble. The picture which Jim Mink draws of this benevolent despot should be considered together with Jim's bitter verbal attacks upon the whites and his criticisms of the government. ("Nobody in the government wants to help the Indian! They just want to rob him!")

Actually, of course, the Agent or his deputy is the hero of these stories. In the second anecdote Jim Mink's father instinctively turns to his protection, and when presented with a bill, says to the storekeeper, "Let's go over to see the Farmer." It is the Indian Agent who saves him from his predicament and confounds the creditors, chasing them off the reservation.

The same theme appears in the next two stories. When Jim's blanket is taken, he runs to the white Farmer. When he finds himself in jail, he calls up the Agent by phone. In each case the government official comes to the rescue. All three tales end with white men being cowed and browbeaten by the Indian Agent or his deputy. Thus, both hostility toward the white man and dependence upon him are satisfied at the same time. The white men who attempt to exploit the Indian (the storekeeper, the blanket salesman, and the sheriff) are either driven away from the reservation and warned not to return, or else they are humiliated and frightened by legal threats, which render them powerless. But the hero who trounces these villains is not the Indian himself, but the protective white father, the government official, who "takes pity" upon his wards and defends them.

There is only one point where Jim Mink expresses readiness for open combat, and that is in a situation where Jim is safely under the protection of the white Farmer and police. "I was ready to get into a fight with that man. He was bigger than I was, but I was ready to take him on, since the Farmer was there, and a policeman was outside too."

A person who suppresses aggressive tendencies would be apt to derive vicarious satisfaction from the ruthless behavior of the government agent, as depicted by Jim Mink, with his enormous legal threats ("I'm willing to carry this case to the Supreme Court") and his stern warnings to delinquent white men. Jim must have felt some sadistic pleasure in describing the scene wherein the jail superintendent is ordered to shovel the snow away from the Indians' car, while the Indians stand around and watch.

In past times, the Chippewa sometimes attended conjuring lodge performances, where shamanistic duels between rival medicine men (in spirit form) took place. Nothing could be seen of these combats except the shaking of the tent in which a lone shaman was sitting; but the cries and thumps of the invisible contestants could be heard within the quivering structure. Bystanders at such "duels" must have derived the same kind of gratification as that experienced by Jim Mink in following the legal threats and counter-threats of the big white lawyers and government officials. Note the boasting of the Agent in the fourth story. "I'm a big man, that's what I am. I'm the Indian Agent.

I've got the whole United States government right back of me. I hold the Indians right in the palm of my hand."

Part of the drama of these tales lies in the fact that for a while this powerful individual keeps his identity a secret (as in the second and third anecdotes). In his telling of these stories, Jim follows some old Chippewa patterns. Just as, in various folktales, *Wenebojo* conceals his real identity from others and thereby misleads them, or as a *manido* acts with deceptive humility, so that his antagonists do not know of the supernatural resources of the individual with whom they are dealing, so, in the same way, the Indian Agent makes a secret of his status until the appropriate dramatic moment has arrived. Then he stuns his hearers with the shattering announcement: "Do you know who I am? I'm the Indian Agent."

The secrecy is one manifestation of the wariness and caution of Chippewa social relationships, which is also expressed in Jim Mink's pretense that he cannot speak English, when he is being cross-examined by a justice of the peace.

Part of the time Jim insists on his Indian status and wants to enjoy the rights and the security of reservation life. At other times he envies the powerful whites and would like to be like a white man. This uncertainty is depicted in symbolic fashion by the conclusion to his last story. There is a bridge across the river. On one side a white orchestra is playing waltzes and fox-trots. ("But I've quit that stuff now—ever since I joined the *Midewiwin*.") On the other side an Indian dance is in progress. When I asked Jim which side of the bridge he went to, he answered "Both sides," and added later, "I kept crossing the bridge, going back and forth to both sides." Here we see the dilemma of a person in a society which is undergoing the process of acculturation, caught between two worlds, in neither of which he is really at home. I have never seen Jim Mink at a "white man's dance," but I have seen him officiating at Indian ceremonies and know that he does not feel at ease there, in spite of his efforts to observe all the old-time traditions.

It is clear that Jim still has not completely abandoned his desire to be like a white man. And yet, although he is neither fish nor fowl, so to speak, Jim Mink's viewpoint remains a very Indian one after all, as these stories show.

2. JOHN THUNDERBIRD

INTRODUCTORY COMMENTS

Like Jim Mink, John Thunderbird is a thin fifty-five year old Indian who works at odd-jobs, carpentry, and occasional guiding. Like Jim, he is an acculturated individual, who spent several years in government boarding school. John also did some traveling away from home with a wild west show, as leader of an Indian brass band.

John Thunderbird is married to a woman who was a former school-mate of his. They have no children. John's relationship with his wife seems to be much more friendly than one finds in most Indian families. I never heard any scandal about them, except that they get drunk together on Saturday nights. John and his wife have only been married once, which is rather unusual on the reservation.

In giving his life-history, John didn't simply tell it to me; he lectured with a deep, slow, impressive voice, as if addressing a large audience. He particularly delighted in those passages which dealt with public gatherings, such as the feast for his first kill.

This afforded him the opportunity to give all the speeches of the four old chiefs. For similar reasons, John enjoyed talking about the Drum Dance, in spite of his fear of discussing religious matters. Although he is quite acculturated, John Thunderbird evidently fancies himself as an Indian orator who carries on the traditions of his forebears.

John comes from an important Indian family and does not often forget it. He has an unusually strong family sense, in which respect he seems rather atypical in his community. The ramification of clan and family ties are matters of relatively little interest to most people on the reservation, as far as I could judge; but John was very proud of his family connections. His grandfather was a highly respected chief. John's uncle was Mashos, the much-feared *Mide* priest and medicine man;[223] and among his uncles and grandfathers there were still other prominent individuals. John wants to be like these old-timers, and yet he occasionally makes disparaging remarks about them. On one occasion John amusingly compared a chorus of men saying "Anh!" to the croaking of frogs in a pond. Another time, he spoke with irritation about a long speech made by one of his uncles: "But that's how those old-timers are. Give them a small question, and they'll make a long answer. He talked too long."

If these are indications of ambivalence, such are more evident in John's attitudes toward the white man. John Thunderbird was the author of the long and eloquent tirade against the whites quoted above.[224] Yet, John likes and respects individual white men. It is interesting that after he had got through with this harangue, John was particularly friendly and cheerful with me.[225]

While a boy at school John resented interference with his freedom; but dislike of authoritarianism was combined with a desire to remain in the good graces of the authorities. John never ran away from school; and he is still proud of his good scholastic record.[226]

John Thunderbird used to be a sort of secretary and interpreter for the association of old chiefs. This group was the nearest approximation to a nucleus of political power on the reservation in the old days, and it still retained some authority until the passing of the Reorganization Act, which attempted to set up democratically elected self-governing bodies on Indian reservations.

As a result of this act, a Tribal Council was set up to deal with matters pertaining to the reservation, and the more ambitious acculturated half-breeds—who were often the more unscrupulous men at Flambeau—managed to get themselves elected to it. The setting up of this new organization seemed like a deliberate affront to the old-timers, who now felt the last crumbs of authority slipping out of their hands. "We have

---

[223] See pp. 26, 131.   [224] P. 38.   [225] *Ibid*. See also p. 111.

[226] It is characteristic that when I asked John how he felt about being turned down by the Army ("Were you glad or sorry?") John angrily retorted: "I can't say things like that. If what you write down gets printed, the government will see it. I can't say something against the government. You're not just writing this down to keep it to yourself. Put down that I was sorry. I wanted to join. I was mad I couldn't join."

John expressed the same fear of publicity in connection with liquor. In one reference to liquor, he said, "Don't put that down. I don't want it on record that I've drunk liquor." John didn't want to work with me at the hotel, "because they'd hear me talking and think I was getting drunk."

a name for the Reorganization Act," said John. "We call it the Flop-over-backwards Act. It knocked us out."[227]

As scribe and interpreter for the group of old Indians, John Thunderbird identified himself with the old-timers and their ways. He often expresses his dislike for Bill St. Croix, a half-breed older than himself, who went to Carlisle and then to Yale, and who came back to Flambeau with a law degree, to become an important member of the Tribal Council. It may be added that John's dislike of Bill is mixed with envy, because John wanted to be a lawyer too. He fancies himself as something of an authority on tribal law and politics, and has a whole trunk full of legal documents, printed Congressional speeches which have been sent to him, etc. I don't think that John can understand them, and I don't believe that he ever reads them, but he keeps them all nevertheless. "I could have been a lawyer if I'd been to a different school," says John. However, he also says that a man who goes away to study gets out of touch with his people—as Bill St. Croix did; and when he comes back, he's a fish out of water.

While I was at Flambeau, John suffered a loss of face, which made him even more touchy than usual. John is one of the organizers of pageants and pow-wows for tourists and he was arranging with some of the other Indians to put on a two day pow-wow to be held on the main highway two miles out of town. When the pow-wow was given, it was a complete failure, and nobody showed up. So plans were made to advertise the next show ahead of time. Colorful hand-bills were printed and distributed, local papers mentioned the pow-wow, and a considerable buildup ensured success. However, John sulked like Achilles in his tent, because his name had not been mentioned in the hand-bill. What was more, Bill St. Croix was going to be the announcer and interpreter, a job which John felt he was best qualified to fill. "Did you see they left me out of the poster?" John said. "I was one of the main ones to get the pow-wow started, and they left me out. I don't see how Bill is going to announce those dances. He don't know the dances. He can't tell one from another. He's been away to school all his life. How is he going to explain anything about those dances to the people? I could tell them all about it. I can tell what they mean and give the history of them. Bill don't know anything about it."

When the pow-wow was given, John Thunderbird didn't show up. I asked one of the women why he wasn't there. "Oh, John wants to run everything," she said. "He always wants to be the boss."

John is very emotional and cannot bottle his feelings very well. The very mention of the Reorganization Act can start his eyes smoldering. But his passions are not always gloomy ones. He can be a genuinely friendly person, and his solemn long face often lights up with a charming horse-tooth smile.

AUTOBIOGRAPHICAL MATERIAL

I was born in 1890 near where Ben C. Gauthier's insurance place is now. When my mother was carrying me, we were all out in the sugar-bush, getting maple sugar. We were just getting ready to leave, when my mother got sick. The snow used to get very

---

[227] Despite his great opposition to the Tribal Council, John accepted a position on it so that he could push through the building of his own house. Once it was built, however, John dropped out and is once more free to condemn the council.

deep in those days. Then it'd melt, and the ground would be all wet. We didn't have
shoes then, like you have now. My mother caught pneumonia out in the sugar-bush.
As soon as we got back to our wigwam, she gave birth to me. Three days later she died.

A day or two after I was born, I got my name. They had a big feast then. My *weʔe*
Mashos, was there. He was married to one of my father's sisters. My uncles all lived
together at my grandfather's place; a collection of wigwams.

When a child is coming, everybody knows about it in advance. They had prepared
the feast. As soon as I was born, Mashos was told that he was going to be my *weʔe*. And
that night my father went off to get the deer. They were waiting for us at my grandfather's place.

When I got my name that time, Mashos told me—so my parents said later—that I
must try to remember that feast given in my honor. It cost them one plug of tobacco,
a package of Standard, a handful of *kinnikinnick* and some eats to get me my name.
Also a piece of garment, a pair of mocassins or leggings, maybe a blanket or two. My
grandfolks paid all that to Mashos, my *weʔe*. At the feast he told about his dream, how
many days he had fasted to earn the dream, and how he got the name from his dream.
He had dreamt about buffalo. We call buffalo *biziki*. So that's my Indian name: *Biziki*.

My *weʔe* also gave me a costume to wear: a piece of cow tail one and a half inches
long hung down the back, fastened on behind. There was a shoulder bead bag as long
as my hand, covered with beadwork and fancy trimmings. The bag hung down the side;
strap went over my shoulder. I used to wear that costume whenever I went any place.
I don't have it any more. My step-mother was the last to have it; she kept it for me.
Then when she died, I don't know where it went to. I wore it whenever I went out of
town, went traveling, or went to dances. It had a picture of a buffalo in bead work on it.
My namesake used to wear a real buffalo horn in the war dances. He painted up in war
paint; wore nothing but a breech-clout. No leggings, vest, or anything.

My mother was thirty-five years old when she died. After my mother died, my
mother's sister took care of me, and my mother's father's parents asked for me. They
were the ones who raised me. My great grandparents lived in a wigwam near where
Mill's resort is now. My grandfather (paternal) lived on the highland by the lake, where
the big rock is. I used to stay with them too, every other week in summer. I stayed with
my great grandfolks in winter. I had an older brother then. He was with me. . . .[228]

When I lived around the big point, before I went to school my grandparents wanted
me to fast. My grandfather told me "You must fast, my child, to get something you
can remember and live with—something that can protect you in your life." He often
talked to me like that. My grandmother just sat there and listened when he advised
me. We lived in a wigwam then. He pointed to the fireplace. "Take a piece of charcoal
in the morning when you wake up, put that on your face, and go without a meal in the
morning."

I was pretty small then. I had to listen to him. He was a gray headed old man.
"Now child, listen to what I'm advising you now. The only thing you can do now is fast
—fast. Earn a living for yourself. *Manido* will give you life, if you fast long enough. He'll
tell you what you're going to be ahead of time. I fasted for fifteen days. I went fifteen
days without food."

---

[228] This brother died not long thereafter.

My grandfather was a wise man. If he wanted to know something, he pulled a blanket over his head and sat there a while. Then he'd take the blanket off and give an answer. He knew things that were going to happen—see things far off—just because he fasted. The old Indians could read your mind. That's how those Indians made treaties with the white men in Washington. They knew what the white man wanted. They could read his mind and knew what he was going to say before he said it.

So I tried to fast. In the morning I picked up the charcoal and put it on my face. My grandfather reached back of his pillow and found a bow and arrow. He must have made it during the night while I was sleeping. I didn't know about it and hadn't seen it before.

He said "Now go out and see if you can't shoot some birds and chipmunks. I've given you this bow and arrow for something to amuse yourself with. Don't think about eating anything you shoot. If you do this every day you'll soon be dreaming something which will be good for your life. In years to come, you'll make good use of it. Some day you'll be a medicine man, a speaker, a spokesman for the tribe. You'll be wise, and people will look up to you, and you'll be famous. If you take my word, my grandchild, you'll do well and live long."

When I went out I wore my costume that I'd got from my *weʔe*. When I was fasting, I was only three or four years old. I couldn't talk much yet. While I was out fasting I was watching the sun coming up until it got overhead. I was getting hungry. I ran home to get something to eat. My grandfather was sitting there smoking his long pipe and heard me begging for something to eat. He never said anything. My grandmother took pity on me, because I was so cute and small. She gave me some bread. I was satisfied with that. I ran out again and played by myself with my bow and arrow. I didn't come back until pretty near sundown. Then I ran home, and my grandfather asked me, "My son, where have you been?" "I've been out hunting in the woods—birds, squirrels, and everything." "Did you get anything?" "No." "Well, try it again tomorrow. Fast some more tomorrow."

I always came back about noon. I knew when it was time to come back too. I watched the sun. I came running into the wigwam. I never walked. I always ran. I asked my grandmother for a piece of bread. She gave it to me. Grandfather just sat smoking his big long pipe. That's all he did all day long, smoked *kinnikinnick* in a big red stone pipe. I don't remember how many days I tried it that way, but I didn't fast long enough to get a dream.

When I was a little older I tried it again; I fasted a half a day then. But then they took me to boarding school, and I stopped fasting. I had to take up white man's ways and had to drop my grandfather's ways. I had to learn how to read and write. . . .

When I was about four years old, my father was still living. My father married about two years after my mother died. I couldn't get along with my step-mother. She didn't lick me, but she was mean and scolded me. So I stayed with my grandparents. In the winter time I was the only kid around the house. I used to go and visit neighbors and relatives and play with other kids.

I was quiet. I wasn't noisy like some kids. The only time I spoke was when they asked me questions. If nobody talked to me I'd sit in a wigwam like a stump, if I had no kids to play with. The old people used to tease me a lot for being so quiet. One of the old fellows said "I wonder what kind of a visitor we got. I never hear him talk.

You know what I'm going to do with this young fellow?" He took a cane—a long cane—and poked me from behind. I didn't see him. I was sitting next to the stove. It was in winter time. We were in a house then. He shouted at me, "Hey! Why don't you say something? Talk! I want you to talk!" I didn't say nothing. I just let him talk to me. He and his wife kept talking about me afterwards. That was my uncle, my father's father's sister's son. . . .

My great-grandfather was living at that time, my father's mother's father. He must have been about ninety years old. He was blind and couldn't go around without a leader. I still remember him. I used to ask my grandfolks to let me go and visit him. His wife was living too. . . . My great-grandfolks stayed with my mother's sister in a log house near here. One day I went to visit them. I wanted to see them. I was about four years old at that time. When I got over there, my auntie was glad to see me. She started to run toward me, grabbed me, kissed me, and told the old people I was there. She brought me over to them, so that they could feel me and know how big I was. The old man grabbed me and felt me over. They were glad I'd come to see them. Grandparents are as close to you as parents are, maybe closer.[229] When my grandfather was feeling me over, he said, "You're a good boy. You're going to be a big boy." My grandmother felt me over too. They said they had been missing me and getting lonesome, waiting for me to come and see them. I stayed there a few days.

My father went back and forth while I was there. He'd stop in to see me when I visited my great grandparents too. I only saw them in winter time, when I crossed the ice. There were lots of Indians along the road then—wigwams all the way. There were a lot of dogs here too. I was afraid of them. . . .

My father's father was spokesman on one of the drums. When I was about eleven my grandfather took me along. I was the only child there. We went all along the road around the lake. He was getting old. We used to sit down and rest half way. He'd smoke his long pipe and rest. He wore leggings then and breech-clout. You could see his hips. But he wore a home-made shirt hanging down and a red yarn sash too. He had a woolen cloth cap made for himself. He wore ear-rings. His ears were pierced. He carried a blanket around himself. He had braids. His head was just snow-white. I looked at him then and wished I could reach his age and be as smart as he was at talking and be wise the way he was. That's what I had in my mind whenever I took him around to different places.

They had a dance ring up on the hill, where the dance hall is now. It had a wall with four windows in it; but no roof. They had two doors, east and west. You go in the west door and come out the east. They had an old fellow as door man and caretaker. He keeps the kids out. That place was just crowded with people. Lots of fancy beadwork. Big shoulder bags with fringes. They wore feathers too. I was the only child allowed in there. They let me in because I was with my grandfather.

I watched all those people dance all day long—speeches after speeches—about their lives way back. Those warriors had heavy paint on, men who had fought with the Sioux. They told about their battle experiences, whenever a special song was played. Only they could get up to dance when that song was played. They had about seven

---

[229] This statement was in answer to an interjected question concerning the relative closeness of parents and grandparents.

drums then, I guess. A lot of people in those days. They sometimes had a dance from a week to ten days. On the third day it's the hardest. You can't get up or leave the hall, unless you present your tobacco. But you can join a leader on one of the drums when he gets up to go out. That's how you can get out to go to the toilet. If you don't go with that leader, you're out of luck and have to wait until the next leader gets up to lead a bunch out.

The old men were heavily painted. They meant business in those days. Nobody was allowed in there drunk. They'd bunch up and throw a drunk man out. When a man gets up and talks about religion, everything is just quiet. Many times my grandfather would get up and talk about religion. Those old people knew their business. They didn't have to be coaxed. They didn't say to each other, "Hey, you do this for me; say this for me." No, they'd get right up and say what was in their minds. The ladies weren't allowed to get up and talk. They have to get a speaker to talk for them if they have anything to say. Nowadays the younger generation can't talk in public like I can. I don't have to get anyone else to speak for me. I learned by listening to the old-timers. That's why I know how to speak before the public and say whatever I have in my mind.

When I was about eight or nine I started going to school. There were no children for me to play with, and I was afraid of the dogs over at the Old Indian Village. They were mean. My great grandparents died when I was about seven. I had nothing to do. Older boys who were going to school told me about it and made me want to go. So I dropped my grandfather's ways and went to school and learned to speak English.

I didn't fast any more. If I'd done that, if it wasn't for the white people coming in and changing everything, I'd be a medicine man now. I could look at the sky and tell if it's going to rain. I'd be a wise man. But I didn't fast long enough. I don't know nothing now. I didn't dream enough. You have to have that dream three or four times.

One day, while I was at school, when I was around nine years old, I got sick of pneumonia. They took me to the hospital. I was laid up there for about a year. My grandfolks heard about me. They talked a lot about me and said "What can we do for him?" My grandmother said to my grandfather "Can't you use your dreams to help him somehow?" I was helpless in the hospital. I didn't know myself there. I just lay and looked around.

My grandfather started, put some *kinnikinnick* in front of him, while my grandmother watched him. He put a blanket over himself. There was a mat before him. My grandfather started to talk to the spirits from west, north, east, and south. He said to the spirits "I've put tobacco here as an offering to you. I do this for my grandchild who is suffering in the hospital." That man talked there all day and smoked tobacco. He did that part of the night too and had very little sleep. He talked four days and four nights. That's how he saved me from dying. The spirits took his word for him. The next morning after he presented that tobacco, he heard that I was dead.

I lay there still—no sign of life. But he was still working on the spirits, saying "Bring my grandchild back. That's why I fasted so many days, so that you'd help me, when I call on you."

I had a nurse. She had no hopes for me. That woman is still living—Harley Veddeneck. She'll tell you the same story. I was all out of wind. I wasn't breathing at all. They covered me up with a white sheet. They thought I was done. Then the nurse spoke to the head nurse at the hospital. "Have you got any alcohol on hand?" The head nurse said "Yes." I wasn't cold yet. I was still warm. Harley says "Can I get a glassfull of alcohol?" "Yes." "I'm going to try this on Johnny." So she used a spoon and poured the alcohol—maybe it was mixed with something—down my throat. She watched it going down. Both nurses watched. I wasn't breathing at all. At the same time the old man was working on his spirits, night and day. After they saw the alcohol going down my throat, a drop at a time, they saw my eyes open up slowly. I couldn't speak. I just looked at them. Pretty soon I got my wind and started to breathe.

Everybody had heard I'd died—even some of my school friends. My wife was going to school then. She's two years older than I am. She'd heard that I'd died too. They never expected me to live again. When I got wind enough, I finally spoke and said something. I don't know how long I was out of consciousness, maybe a night or a day and a night; I couldn't say. After I came to, the word went around "Johnny's come to life." All of my relatives heard of it. They were anxious to hear how it had come out, since my grandfather started working on the spirits.

So that's why I believe in my Indian customs as well as in the white man's customs. The white man has his customs. So has the Indian his customs. When I came to life again, my grandfather had already worked two days and two nights over his spirits. He put in two more days. That made four days without sleep, without eats. That's what made me come to. The spirits listened to this grandfather of mine and took his word and made me come to. So today I believe in the Indian customs. I wouldn't go to church. The church wouldn't save me. The reason I believe that is that God has given a different religion to every nation. God gave us all his religions to go by and stand by. White man, he got religion from God to go by and stand by. We are all serving one God in all religions sticking up on this earth. . . .

In the spring, about April that same year, I was able to walk around. I was weak. I could hardly hold myself up, I'd stayed so long in bed. My superintendent came to see how I was coming along. He came there every other day to see me. His name was Finn Reuben Perry. He ordered clothes for me—new clothes, shoes, shirts, hat, everything new to dress me up. I dressed up in those new clothes. I was proud of them, and I was glad to be on my feet again. I was out of the hospital the first of May—healthy again.

Around August, I found a shell on the ground. I took it to my grandmother and said "See what I've found." She handed it to my grandfather. "Look what our grandchild found."

He pointed to me and said "You are going to join the Medicine Dance. That thing has brought you good luck. The spirit has given that to you to find it. First we'll put up a feast for you to notify the Indians."

They put up a big feast the next day—all old fellows. My grandfather was spokesman for me and explained everything and said "I want my grandchild to join the *Midewiwin* in one year's time."

Then they began to collect articles to be used.

That feast was a big feast. I don't remember everything they said. I was tired of listening to them. All those fellows said "Anh!" like a bunch of frogs in a pond. It sounded good, though.

After that feast they pinned a *megis* under my shirt. They didn't let it hang in plain sight, because I was going to school, and they were afraid that one of the employees would jerk it away. They were trying to break down all the old ways in the school. They said that I'd have to wear that until I joined, and that I'd be in good health all that time. I was healthy all that time.

That spring, after sugar-making, in May, I came home from school. They were just waiting for me to come back on vacation. When I got home, they put up another feast. They gave the people so many days to prepare the *Mide* lodge. I was the first person to be fixed up. Others had a chance to come in then too.

I got my teachings the first day in the *Mide* lodge. They made some drawings in the heap of dirt and told me how I'd go around the lodge. When I got to have the shells shot into me, my father told me not to fall over on my face; just making a motion of going forward, so I wouldn't get a bloody nose by falling down. My father sat right behind me and whispered to me what to do when they shot the *megis*. . . . But I don't want to tell you about these things. I'd be giving my life away. I'd be hurting the feelings of the spirits. But this is how my life was saved. Those old-timers knew their business.

My wife was saved that way, after we got married. She'd gone before then through the *Midewiwin*, but she went through again after we were married and it saved her life. The Medicine Dance helps you more than the War Dance or the Drum Dance. You have to give more goods too. I don't want to tell you about these things. . . .

[V. B.: "Why do you tell me them then?"]

[Angrily] Because we have to amuse the white man. He asks us how we do this thing and that thing. We have to tell him what he wants to know. . . .

I remember how there were pine trees all over here in the old days and lots of fish and lots of game. Up to 1904 there were lots of pines. Nothing but a wagon road. No autos in those days.

I didn't mind going to school. It didn't take me long to pick it up either. Took me three years to learn English. I was smart at school and passed my grades every year. My father died when I was about ten; but my grandfolks were still living, and I went to visit them. Mashos and his wife were still living, and so were Sam Thunderbird, my uncle, and my mother's sister. They were all still there.

I commenced to realize about sports at this time. I took up baseball. There is a man today that could speak for me on the baseball: Dr. Minocqua. He remembers me when I was a baseball player. I got so I could be a good ball-player when I was fifteen. I played against men twenty-five to thirty years old when I was fifteen. I outplayed them on all positions. I was a good batter, good pitcher, good infield, good everything. I didn't take up much pitching, though.

When I was around sixteen years old, my uncle, Sam Thunderbird, taught me how to handle a gun and hunt deer, bear, and moose. My uncle was the one who was supposed to take care of me after my father died. He took me away from my father's funeral, took me walking on the road, and talked to me, telling me to forget my father. "You'll never see him. Don't think about him. When you see me, take me for your father. I'll take care of you. I'll raise you."

I often went hunting with Sam Thunderbird and my other uncles. One day, I finally shot a deer, and killed it. When we'd dragged it home, my *we?e*, Mashos, came out. He started to laugh when he saw the deer. *"Niewę?ę* [my *wę?ę*] killed deer," he said. "We'll soon have a feast." That was my feast for the first kill. My aunt went into the house and told the people I'd killed a deer. The news spread among all the neighbors. They started to prepare the feast. *Niewę?ę* went around and told the neighbors there'd be a feast at his place that evening. They notified people over here too at this side of the lake. Not just my own relatives came; everybody who could come was there.

When the feast was ready to serve, the house was just packed with people—all old-timers who couldn't speak English. No young people. I could speak English, because I was going to school then. I could hardly speak to my own people then. But I was the only one there who could speak English. They had four speakers at that feast.

My grandmother handed me some plug tobacco and said in Chippewa, "Give this to your *niewę?ę.*" I took it over to him. He was smoking there. I said "Here is some tobacco." Then I pointed to the food and said "This is my first deer." He nodded seriously and said "Anh!" and took the tobacco, whittled the plug tobacco down with a knife, and mixed it with his *kinnikinnick.* Then he filled his pipe again and started to speak. The room was full of old-timers; they all listened. This wasn't in a wigwam. It was in a house. But they all sat on mats on the floor, around the wall. After I gave him the tobacco, Mashos smoked a while. You could hear a pin drop; it was so quiet. Then he started to talk. My friends, my *niewę?ę* has just killed a deer and asked me to talk for him. If anyone else wants to talk for him, let him do so. I'm wishing my *niewę?ę* to have good luck all the rest of his life, so that he'll get deer whenever he goes out to look for it. By our customs, when any of our young people gets a deer, he puts up a feast like we have here today. I'm proud of my *niewę?ę* to do all these things, following up our religion and our customs, and I hope he will have hunting luck the rest of his life, and I advise you people that you help me out to say something for our *niewę?ę* here and talk to our spirits." Then everybody said "Anh!"

My father's father was sitting right next to me and said. "Let me say a few words. I am glad that my own grandchild is putting up a feast, his first deer in his life. He is starting a new life for himself, and I hope that he will be a success in years to come. He is a young man and has a long life ahead of him. I wish him luck! I am raising this grandchild of mine. I teach him what to do, and he listens to me. I am glad he does. It is our custom to teach our children what to do ahead of time—how to live. Now white people are here now, and we must drop our fasting; and the only way we can teach our children is to talk to them day and night. They need all our teaching to learn the old Indian customs."

That's all he said. Then an old man on my other side, Giwédno, (North Wind), got up to speak. He was my grandfather's cousin and called me "grandson." He said "I'm next to speak up for my grandchild. I'm glad that my grandson put up this feast and surprised to see him do it. That's the right way—to follow our religion. I am glad he listens to his grandfather. Now we can see that he listens to his grandfather's teachings of what to do in life. He's put up a feast right before us, and I wish him to have luck the rest of his life. I'm not going to say too much and take time off from our feast. I just bring this out before you to tell you what I have in my mind." The old fellows said "Anh!" each time he stopped. "That's all I have to say. If anybody else wishes to speak for my grandchild, let him start."

Another old fellow spoke up. "I am the next to speak." His name was Meméngwa

(Butterfly). He's married to my father's father's sister. "Yes, I am also very glad to have this feast here today in honor of our grandchild. He has done the right thing to present his tobacco to his *niewę?ę*. That's our Indian custom—the right way to do it. Our grandchild will be in luck in his lifetime. I'm not going to say very much myself and take up any time. But in years to come we may have a feast again like this; and I hope we all gather again when he gets ready to put up a feast. And I wish him luck all of his lifetime, whenever he goes out in the woods again—that he may see the deer he's looking for. Good luck to him! That's all I have to say. We'll have our feast now. *Manido* has taken our tobacco. He also knows what our idea is in having this feast. He reads our minds. He knows what we are here for today. Now then, we'll have our feast. Let everybody come forward to the middle of the floor and begin."

They had a big dishpan with that meat in it. My grandmother gave me a plate to fill up for my grandfather. I filled it up for him and handed it to him. The other man next to me got up and sat down over there and started to eat. My grandfather asked me if I was eating, and I said "No." My grandfather said "Go ahead and eat. Don't just sit there." Well, I saw a piece of meat in that big kettle. I saw a piece of the heart. It looked pretty good to me, so I reached over and took it. Giwédno was sitting there looking at me. He said "IIey, wait! Put that back! You're not supposed to eat. You're the one that's giving this feast. All the rest of us are supposed to eat, but not you. You're just supposed to offer tobacco to the Manido. You'd better put that back."

Well, I put the meat right back. Then he started to laugh. "I was just saying that," he said. "You go ahead and eat." Everybody was laughing all around, and I felt pretty foolish. I started to eat again.

After dinner everyone thanked me. My grandfather said "Auh!" for me. I was too young to answer for myself.

The other old-timers there didn't like the way that Giwédno had kidded me. They thought that he shouldn't have said that. Kidding is out of place in a feast like that. But nobody said anything. When they don't like someone, they just keep quiet. But when they get home they tell their wives what they think.

After that I didn't do no more hunting. I went to school, did farming there, and took care of cattle and horses. We had three months vacation from June 10 to September 10. Fellows took turns getting vacation. There were always students at school. I used to go hunting with my uncles when I came home on vacation.

I went to school eleven years, up to 1908. I got up to the eighth grade. But we had to work half the time, so that slowed us up. I was sick a half a year. That knocked me out. I could have graduated a year before that. I had a chance to go to college, but my grandparents didn't want me to go, and I didn't want to leave. If I'd gone away to school I'd learn a lot about law, but I wouldn't know anything about Indian life. I'd be away now working in town, earning my living some place. I'd forget all about my relatives. It's a good thing to stay with your relatives, know who's living and who's dead, and keep up with them. When I got out of school I could hardly speak any Indian. It took me a long time to pick it up again. They used to beat me with a rawhide whip if I spoke Chippewa in school. If they didn't do that, they wouldn't let me go home on Sunday, when my turn came. Up to thirteen I didn't have to work in school, but after that I worked in the field half the time.

In school we had board fences eight feet high all around the yard. There were four foot wide sidewalks made of planks. You had to walk on the sidewalks all the time. You weren't allowed to walk on the grass. If they caught you on the grass, you'd get punished.

We took up all kinds of trades—carpenter, blacksmith, engineer, farmer. I took in. every one of them—one year for each one.

The most I did was carpentry. I worked at that for four years. Then I took up painting in 1906. Charley Parkhurst, an Oneida Indian, who was disciplinarian, taught painting; and I took that until I was graduated. He taught music too. He put me on the slide trombone. That's how I got some experience in music.

I was pretty fair in baseball. It's funny I never tried the leagues. It all came easy to me. I had a good arm. They tried me on pitcher, but I couldn't control myself. So they put me on outfield.

We had good teachers in the school. I always got a hundred on my examinations— all of them. We had a good farmer. He raised good crops. We always had enough to eat. The superintendent, Mr. Perry, gave me this name I have now. I was just a little fellow. It was the first day at school. I was standing in the hallway. I was a stranger, didn't know my way around. Mr. Perry came out of his office. He looked at me. He said "Well, we'll have to give you a name, my boy. Hereafter they're going to call you John Thunderbird." All the other boys around repeated that name. That's how I got my name John. I didn't get it through the church.

Mr. Perry's wife taught the primary classes. That's where I started. She told her husband, "That's a nice boy. He studies hard and learns quick." Mr. Perry was glad I was learning fast. . . . After I was fourteen, he left the school, and another superintendent came in. His name was Henry Phillips. He was an old football star. He taught us how to play football. He was a good band leader too. Then we had a disciplinarian from Odanah—John Marksman. He organized the band and also the baseball team: the Flambeau Indians. They had letters on their shirts: F. I. S. But pretty soon Marksman retired, and also the chief engineer, Lockhart, and Phillips. The band broke down. They had nobody to lead them. Another superintendent came: John Flint, an old soldier. Charley Parkhurst came as disciplinarian. I had been practicing the horn by that time.

Parkhurst heard me playing by myself. Pretty soon I was blowing pretty good. He thought he'd try me out in the band. He called me and said "You're practicing pretty good. I heard you play." Ever since then I played in the band. We used to go out and play in celebrations at Woodruff, Minocqua, Rhinelander. We had sixteen pieces—all Indians. No mixed bloods.

One Fourth of July we went to Minocqua in our khaki uniforms. We had big cowboy hats on. That was our band uniform. We had a tie around the neck too. The superintendent ordered these suits for us and ordered some more instruments—clarinets. He was glad we had a good band. They had no band in Minocqua then, so we played there and got so much money a day to play. We spent that money for baseball and football clothes. Our football team averaged 140 pounds.

That same summer we made a trip to Rhinelander. There was a circus band and a military band of about forty pieces. We played in a stand while the baseball leagues were playing: Rhinelander against some other team. All three bands played. People there said that our band was the best, because we were all Indians. Even the band leader was an Indian—an Oneida. They applauded our music. Some of our pieces surprised the big bands. The circus band wanted to play along with us to see which was the best. We took turns. After they got through playing, we played. After a while we asked the circus band to play together with us—all at once. They couldn't read our music. It was too fast for them. Then we played with their music. We picked it up right away. We played like one big band. They shook hands with us and said "You're good players. We like to have you play with us." We *were* good players. We were well trained. We had one good cornet player—Bill Sky. We had a good band leader too. If anybody played a wrong note, he'd stop the whole works. He'd make you get it right. I like a band leader like that.

I used to take part in shadow pictures too. They put on big programs on national holidays. They had recitations and dialogues. I had to put on an act in a shadow play. My shadow was thrown on a big screen, and everybody on the other side of the screen could see it. They had a light behind me. I had to go and make motions like I was going to take out a man's tooth. I was supposed to be a dentist. The other boy sat with his mouth open. I walked up to him holding a big pair of tongs. When the audience saw those tongs, they laughed. I put the tongs right on the side of his head. It looked as if they'd gone right into his mouth. Then I got hold of a piece of wood with the tongs and pulled it out. Everyone was laughing and applauding then. I was good at that shadow play.

I graduated that year. We made up our own program. The band played. We had recitations, dialogues, and plays. You had to make a speech about what you'd learned, what trade you'd followed, and what you hoped to do. I wrote it all out—about how the paints should be mixed—what kind of oil and turpentine should be used. I wrote it all out and took it to my teacher. It was a real book. He read it. "Very good. Did you get Charley Parkhurst to help you out?" "No." "Where did you get all those long words?" "I picked it up and learned it." "I'll bet you Charley Parkhurst helped you out. I'm going to ask him." "Go ahead," I said. "Ask him if you don't believe me." He went to Charley Parkhurst. "Did you help John write this out?" Charley Parkhurst laughed and said "No. Didn't you know that John was that smart? He's the best painter I've got."

Everybody had to make speeches about what they'd learned. The government furnished our graduating suits nice clothes. I was scared of making a mistake while I was talking. I was afraid if I made one mistake, people would say "That man hasn't graduated. He has no education." I was about fifth or sixth on the program. I was sitting there thinking. One of the employees was reading out the names. "The next man to talk is a practical painter, John Thunderbird." I was shaking. I got up to walk to the front. I had the paper in my hand. Everybody clapped. I started to talk. I took it easy. I said "Practical painter. I've written this book to explain how this is done." I never looked up. I was nervous. "In mixing the paints we have different oils for different purposes: inside work and outside work. You must learn how to mix paints and where you're going to use them. For inside work you put in more turpentine and less oil. Two oils are used: linseed oil and boiled oil. Boiled oil is used for outside purposes. For outside painting you must use more linseed oil, less turpentine. Never mix paints with any other oil, when you have to paint outside. This is what I have learned at school—what I am telling you tonight." Then I repeated it all over again. When I was through, everybody applauded. I made a hit. Then we got our diplomas. I've still got mine, but I don't know where it could be.

About twelve of us graduated. Flint handed out the diplomas himself. I made a lot of friends there in town—white people too.

I was an officer at school—a second lieutenant, then a first lieutenant. A second lieutenant has one stripe; a first lieutenant has two gold stripes. After a while I got promotion to first sergeant (sic); then captain. That's what I was when I graduated. I didn't go any higher than that. I used to drill the boys in the evenings on the ball field. Lester Chapman, a half breed, was the only major. He played slide trombone. I could have been a major if I'd stayed another year. I was promoted every two months. I liked drilling the boys in the open. I learned that from the disciplinarian. We had inspection every Sunday morning. John Flint inspected us. We wore uniforms. We marched off to Sunday school right after inspection. We wore brownish gray uniforms with a red stripe down the side of the trousers. We wore dark or black caps. The girls wore uniforms too—navy collars with white trimmings. They had no caps; just dresses. We didn't have uniforms long, because the government was getting stingy with the cloth.

[V. B.: "Did you ever run away?"]

No, I had a good record. All the records are in the office. That's how the superintendent knows about my good record. The last year I was going to school the disciplinarian used to line us up for two hours before dinner and lecture to us. He was a smart man, Charley Parkhurst. We had to stand all the time. He talked all the two hours. When we heard the dinnerbell, we'd march out.

One Sunday he advised us to be sure to go to church on Sunday morning. One Sunday they caught three of us for not going to church. He asked how many of us had gone to church. Everybody raised their hands, except three of us.

I was an officer then, a second lieutenant. Two privates also didn't put up their hands. I made a bad name for myself then. He said "All right. The rest of you march into the dining room. I want to talk to these three fellows." Everybody marched out. John Bluebird, Joe St. Croix, and I were the three—the three oldest boys in the school. Then he asked us "Boys, why didn't you go to church this morning?"

We didn't say anything. He asked us more questions. We said "We didn't go; that's all." He said "All right, you boys will go without dinner today."

I was angry that day. We had to starve it out until supper. We couldn't go home. You know, I was strong on my religion. That's why I didn't go to church. I'd joined the *Midewiwin* four or five years before that. It was the same with the other boys. Not many of us ran away. William Frog was expelled from school for running away from school too much and coming home drunk.

I never forgot that time when they punished us. I told my grandparents about it when I got home. My grandfather said that I'd done the right thing in not going to church. "They can't stop you from following your religion. Nobody can. *Manido* gave the Indian his religion."

I got out of school that spring. Commencement was in May. They let us go home the day after commencement.

I went to see my grandfolks. My *niewę, ʔę*, my aunties, my uncle, were all living yet.

They were glad to see me get out of school. I'd been there long enough—eleven years. I could have been a lawyer if I'd been to a different school. But I was glad I'd learned some music. John Flint retired soon after we graduated; then Balmer came. It didn't take me long to get acquainted with Balmer. He knew I was a musician and a ball-player and he got after me to organize the band. But after I'd played in the band a couple of years, I left for Phelps to work for a lumber company.

I was married in 1912. My wife was in my class; graduated the same year I did. We were married legally; not in the Indian way. There was no church wedding.

In 1916 I had trachoma. Things began to look blurry. I went to the doctor who belonged to the reservation. A good doctor. He gave me some eye-water to use. I used it every day once a day. It didn't help me at all. I tried it a whole week. Then I tried another doctor: a doctor from Ironwood. I used to go down there on the early train and stay all day until nine o'clock P.M. He gave me some dark eye-glasses. My eyes were just red. He gave me eye-water and told me how to use it. He was a doctor of three different diseases: eyes, nose, and throat. I tried his eye-water, and it fixed my eyes all right: cured me.

Next year I had to register for the government when the war opened up in England. I couldn't pass the Army exams on account of my poor eye-sight. That's what the eye-water did to my eyes. It was too strong. Otherwise I was all healthy. My heart was good. My hearing was good.

[V. B.: "How did you feel about being turned down by the Army? Were you glad or sorry?"]

[Angrily] I can't say things like that. If what you write down gets printed, the government will see it. I can't say something against the government. You're not just writing this down to keep it to yourself. Put down that I was sorry. I wanted to join. I was mad I couldn't join.

In May 1916 I went on a trip with the band. We rehearsed the band once a week all through the winter, so we knew the pieces without looking at them. I was leader of the band. A wildwest show came by here that spring—the Bar G Ranch. It was a small show—about eight people in it.

The manager asked for the band leader here. He wanted to take a band along. Someone told him where I lived. He asked me if I'd take a band out. He said "I'll pay you good wages, and you'll have a good time on the trip."

We traveled through Michigan with the show. But after a while the rest of the boys began to leave. I was all alone, by July and August. I was the only one left. The boss said "You're the best man in the show. You stay with us. I'll get you a band to lead. I'll pay you good wages. I'll pay you more than the rest of the boys." But I was getting lonesome for home. I said to my boss, "My wife is sick. She's in the hospital. I have to go home." Her blood wasn't circulating so good. She had to go to the Sister's Hospital in Rhinelander. I showed the letter to my boss so that he'd believe me.

The show people all liked me and were sorry to see me go. When the boss paid me off, he said, "This is all the money I've got, but it isn't enough." So he took the men out in the streets and gave a show on the street to get up some more money for me. The next day I left. I found my wife at Rhinelander, and we took the train back to Flambeau. She got better and wasn't sick any more.

When I got home, I went to visit my grandfather. He was glad to see me back. He'd missed me all that time. He asked me how my trip was. I told him I'd had a very good trip. He says to me, "I heard they were taking you boys overseas. We all believed that, because you never came back. We never heard anything all that time." I laughed and said, "No, we crossed Lake Michigan twice—that's all. We remembered you while we were away. We'll never forget the old people."

My wife had a brother. I taught him how to play the slide trombone. He certainly picked it up quick. I used him a lot in the band. He was a better player than I am. She also had a cousin who played a slide trombone. My brother-in-law died in the first world war of some disease; I don't know what it was. My wife's cousin died too. He got shot hunting: an accident. So two good trombone players were lost. They were young, stout; could have been living now, if that hadn't happened.

We had a good band. One time, at a small town, there was a military band right behind us, on a big parade a half a mile long. The military band dropped out. Too much heat. They couldn't stand it. We redskins kept right on going.[230] We played by heart, didn't need to look at the music. Some of the selections took an hour to play. The school kids can't play that well now; it's too hard for them.

I used to guide for white people. I had a nice motor boat; had room for fifteen passengers. People from Chicago used to come. I got $7.00 a day. We had a team of ponies too. My wife had money from her allotment, from selling timber. She got the ponies and the boat. We were well off in those days, but we spent money foolishly. We should have put it in the bank. That's how an Indian is—crazy with money. He spends it all. The old timers say: The Indian wasn't meant for money. That's for white men. Before the white man came, he didn't have money. We didn't have groceries. Them groceries are for white men. The Great Spirit gave us meat: deer, bear, moose, elk, rabbits. We weren't meant to eat garden stuff or groceries.

I worked at Phelps for six years. Then I came home and stayed uptown (at Flambeau) for two years. I came here with $150.00 in my pocket. It didn't last three weeks. Groceries were too high. Then I stayed in Phelps for another year. I worked at Eagle River for five years. Then I came back to Flambeau, and I've been here ever since. In 1931 I bought a one-room house. After Reorganization came in, I put in application for a $300 loan for a home. Other people had applications way ahead of me. I was way behind. After a while I talked so much I joined the Tribal Council. I was in there for two years. That's where I had a better chance to get after them about building my home. Then they dropped other homes and started on mine. This is it: a three room house with parlor, kitchen, and bedroom. Cost $332.00. I'm paying $5 a month for five years. When that's come, I've got to extend my loan.

My mother's sister married a big chief, Jim Otter, the main chief of the Flambeau Reservation. I used to interpret for him at the councils when I was about twenty-three years old. He'd call up an agent to come and listen. Then I'd get up and interpret. My uncle did that before me, so that's why they picked on me. Also I could write and

---

[230] In a story which I have omitted, John tells about going hunting with a white man. The main point of the story is that the white man was lost and didn't know his whereabouts in the woods. John emphasizes that he knew exactly where they were all the time.

interpret good. Not only that[231]—*Jim Otter put me on the big drum to be a speaker in place of my uncle! In 1928 he put me on the drum!* My uncle, Sam Thunderbird, was still living then, so he was able to see me do all those things for him that he had done in the past. He was real proud of me for taking his place. Sam Thunderbird used to talk to me when he was old and blind. "Keep up your speeches. People will look up to you, be proud of you, if you work with them and work with them all the time. I'm glad that someone has taken my place, for I may not live very much longer. I'm glad that someone has taken my place, who will represent me as a speaker." Then he ended. That's what he said to me. He used to call me "son." He'd lost his son when he was about my age.

In 1928 the old Indians started a pageant. I was away at Eagle River at the time. One day the old chief sent a letter to me; told me that a pageant was going on at Flambeau. He wanted me to run it for him, announcing and interpreting for the people that were dancing. That's where I got my start making speeches and writing for the chief, keeping records, counting the money that comes in through the gate, and keeping time for the people taking part. Now I'm also one of the leaders in getting up pow wows for the tourists, and taking Indian parties to places out of town.

When I first joined the drum in 1928, I was shaking all over. I couldn't speak. I couldn't talk for myself. I wasn't used to being in public. Jim Otter was the owner of the drum and the leader. He led me over to the place where I had to sit. He put a blanket there. Then he got up to speak. Before he spoke, they sang one song. Then he came over and pointed to me. He called me "nephew"—*du·š.* "I'm glad you're taking my word," he said. "These people you see sitting around the drum are the ones who appointed you to be in that position. These people see you in your ways. They've seen you dancing. You dance good and hard. You take your religion good and hard. That's why they want you to belong and help us out every time we dance. You're a smart man, and I know you're a good speaker. You ain't afraid to talk. This is the kind of man we want—a man who will speak for himself at the dance. The people like your ways. You're kind-hearted. You never try to make trouble with anybody. You're quiet. You just live peacefully all of your lifetime. Now you're a headman. That's why we've chosen you. We want you to help us out and lead our dances hereafter. All you four headmen are just one. You're all in one. Neither one of you is the leader. All you have to do is meet together, talk things over, and arrange things nicely. Then everything will go well. Now I think I've explained everything to you about how to handle your position. If I leave anything off, I have a man here to tell you." Then he sat down. They were all proud of me after that. I was at Phelps working in the saw mill then. After a while I came home. Now I'm head man on one drum and king (*ogima*) on Eddy Mitchell's drum.

My mother's father's father was a chief. My father's father was a chief too. My father was a quiet man. He'd have made a good chief. My uncle took my grandfather's place as a speaker. Now I'm taking his place.

One time some white people from Chicago were watching a Drum Dance here. We

---

[231] Here John spoke in a ringing, impressive voice, and the rest of the sentence was spoken in a most reverent, dramatic way.

didn't charge them anything for watching. We paid no attention to them. I had a whole outfit on—leggings, beaded shirt, long belt, and head-dress. . . . I went outside after a while, while we were dancing. Then three ladies from Chicago came up to me. They wanted to take a picture of me and my partner with them. We let them photograph us. After that I went back into the hall.

I lit up a pipe before dancing and passed it around. I wasn't allowed to take a puff until I'd passed it all around. First I point it to the four directions. The head chief takes the first puff; then the others.

While I was puffing on the pipe, those white women came up behind me and nudged me and asked if they could have a puff of the pipe. I said, "I'll have to ask the chief." I went to ask him. He said "No! Only members can do this." So I had to tell the women I wasn't allowed to let them have a puff.

We'd make fools of ourselves if we'd let them have a puff. We're not even supposed to talk about our religion. We're afraid of *Manido*. That's why we don't talk. He wouldn't like it. That's why we keep these things secret. A lot of people make a mistake when they join this religion. They don't run it right. Those people don't live long afterwards. You don't know what *Manido* will do. If you talk about it or make things up, *Manido* won't like it.

There was a half-breed Frenchman, a Catholic I used to know. He was talking to a heavy religious man in our tribe. He told that man lots of things against the religion. He said "You Indians are crazy. You don't know what you're doing." The Indian said nothing. That's another thing we do. If a man talks out of the way like that, we just keep quiet. That man died inside of a year. He was an Indian. He talked against his own religion. Look what happened to him. We often think of him. That's why we're afraid of telling you these things. . . .

The headman can do almost anything on the drum. There's one thing he can't do; he can't touch the drum. The only time he can do that is when we're fixing up a woman or a man in mourning. Then after one of the chiefs has painted the man's face with blue paint, he touches the drum with his finger, which has the paint still left on it. He touches it on the blue side of the drum head. That's painting the drum's face. He also touches each of the feathers that hang down on the four stakes of the drum. The number of spots on the feathers shows how many people you've fixed up.

One time they had a dance here, and a lot of old fellows were talking. They said that a head chief could do anything: plan when the dances would be held, give instructions, drum and sing if they want—anything. I just sat there. I didn't say anything. When there were all through, I got up. "You say that the head chiefs can do anything on the drum—is that right?" "Yes, that's right." Then I said, "Well, let me ask you one question. Can the head chief lift down that drum over there and put it on the floor?" [John smiles triumphantly.] Those old fellows couldn't say a word. They said "You're right. We didn't learn it all right when we took over the drum. Yes, you're right! You're right!"

The old-timers called me over one day to see if I couldn't get rid of Mr. Owl, the Deputy Agent.[232] I went into his office all by myself to see him. I asked him, "What's

---

[232] An educated Cherokee who is more like a white man than an Indian.

your occupation here on the reservation, Mr. Owl?" He said "I'm community worker."

I said, "All right, Mr. Owl, then why is it you run around catching Indians who are getting licker? Is that part of your work?"

"Yes," he said. "I'm working for the government."

I said, "All right. You know what I can do with you, Mr. Owl. I can call up the Council and tell the people to put you off the reservation in no time. I'm telling you who I am, and I'm telling you what I can do. I'm head clerk for the chiefs here. You're doing no good for the Indians. . . . Don't go around getting Indians into trouble. They ain't going to let you do things to them. We have chiefs, speakers, and members—twenty-five to thirty members of the Council—all old-timers. I'm the only young man with them. Whatever they say goes. They know their business. If they make a trip to Washington, to ask for something, they'll get it. We stand by the treaties. We're going to stand by them forever. [John speaks in a ringing voice.] I don't want to hear any more about this work you're doing." [John looks furious.]

So I left him and came home. I was mad. I might have hit him. [He is almost trembling, as he tells me this.]

I was a leader of the band at that time. Owl knew about that. So one day he called me into his office to talk to me about the band and see if I couldn't get up a new Indian band. I said "I'll see what I can do." He said "If you can get up a band, I'll play with you. You can play concerts in the summertime when the tourists come and earn a little money." So I said "All right, I'll see what I can do."

After I got up a band—seventeen pieces—I went to Mr. Owl's office and said, "Here's a band right here." All those fellows lived in Flambeau, except for one from Ashland. We used to give concerts here, but it stopped, because the fellows kept leaving and dropping out.

[I asked John if he could tell me some of his dreams. John looked very serious and said warningly, "That's going to cost you an awful lot of money. I'm not going to tell you any of my true dreams for nothing. I have dreams that are true."

I said "Well, you don't have to tell me the true ones, if they're too sacred, although I'd like to hear them. But just tell me any old dreams."

John furrowed his brow and finally said, "Well, I'll tell you a short dream I had about a month ago."

In spite of his reluctance to tell something sacred, the following dreams are all what John calls "true dreams." V. B.]

I dreamt I was in a strange town I'd never seen before. I wanted to go home and find my way home. I had no money. The train was due in a few minutes. I had to rustle to get my expenses some way. I was walking around the streets. Then I ran into some of my friends from Flambeau. I thought I'd come along with them.

I met some more strangers after that—Indians from Reserve. I didn't recognize them. They were all dressed in Indian costume. I knew there was going to be a dance somewhere. So I thought of my costume. I went to get it, so I could go to the dance. While I was in the street, I met my wife. I said to her, "There's a dance going on here somewhere. We'll stay for the dance and go home afterwards." This was a religious dance, not a pageant or a show.

So I went. My friends and wife went along with me to look for the place where they'd have the dance. I saw some people going in and out of a little house. I went over there to see what was going on. Sure enough, there was a big drum in the middle of the floor; lots of people sitting around; big doings there.

I told my friends: "This is where the dance is." I got on my Indian costume. I wanted to take in the dance too. That was one good dance there. There were lots of lively dancers. I was right in there with them. But there were no speeches made during the dance. So between times I walked in the middle of the floor. I wanted to make a speech for this dance. All the people were looking at me, wanting to hear what I had to say. I said "Friends, I'm glad to meet you here. I am glad that you are dancing today; and the rest of my people are also glad to see you here. I have some friends from Flambeau who have come to see you dancing. I hope we'll have a good time together. We don't see each other very often. We are true Americans. We are glad to see each other whenever we meet. We ought to be proud that we are true Americans. No mixed blood with us. We are following our ancestors—what they did years ago, before we were born; and I hope that we will keep it up as long as we live. I have heard the old Indians years ago. They used to keep up their religion like this. That's what we are doing today. This is all I have to tell you people. I thank you for listening to me. I thank you." Then I sat down.

Some day, two or three years from now, it's going to come out that way. I don't dream for nothing, when I dream about religion. Your soul dreams those dreams: not your body, not your mind. Those dreams come true. All full-blood Indians believe that. The Indian believes that the soul (*ničag*) is for living, for your life. It keeps you alive. The soul will tell you about your life ahead of time through dreams. Then it will happen some day. Some of them don't happen; but I know that this last dream will happen.

That's how Indians know about things that are going to happen: dances, accidents, deaths, sickness. A man has a *manido* (spirit) and a soul (*ničag*). The soul travels all over the world when you dream. You go along. The *manido* is all over. You don't go along. It knows about everything. It tells your soul—not you. Your soul is your interpreter to your body. If you heard *manido* talk, you couldn't understand. But your soul can.

I've seen lots of old men shake the wigwam. It's the spirits in there talking, but you can't understand them.

Nobody knows what *Manido* is like. When Indians talk about *Manido*, we don't ask each other, "What are you talking about? What is he like?" We don't know. That's foolish. The only time anybody ever saw *Manido* was when Christ was on earth. The Devil is *Manido—mačimanido* (bad spirit). He took the wrong religion. The spirits had a meeting about the different nations—where to put them. This is *adizokan* (legend) I'm telling you now. White people were put in one country. Redskins were put in another. They all talked different languages. They decided to put the red men in North America and said "We'll have the white people in the Old Country." The white people had their own religion and churches; all kinds of churches to go by. Now we want to protect our redskins from the white people, so they won't get too near the redskins. We'll let them have dreams through fasting. They'll get their living that way. We will give them the *Manido* to go by. Their souls will be their interpreters. Every person has a soul. These spirits will tell their souls what to do ahead of time, how they will live. We'll give them a religion to go by too—the *Midewiwin* (Medicine Dance), the Drum Dance, and the War Dance. That's what *Manido* arranged for all the nations. That's part of Indian history. . . .

I'll tell you some dreams I had about my guardian spirit, the buffalo, the animal I was named after.

Three years ago I dreamt about buffalo. I dreamt that he (the buffalo) was good to me. He didn't want to hurt me. I dreamt that I was lying flat, helpless, on the ground when he come along, seeing me lying there. He knew that I was helpless. I was awful scared of him—coming right straight for me, where I was lying. I wanted to run away from him, but I was helpless and couldn't move. Pretty soon he was near by me. He stopped where I was laying and looked down at me. He started to blow his nose at me. I dreamt this more than once—maybe three times; so I understood his ways in my dream.

The way I understood his ways and actions is that he knew I was helpless and couldn't move; and he wanted to cure me by blowing that stuff—the disease—away from me. I wasn't sick then, but he knew I was going to be sick a couple of years later. I was a married man then. I knew that the buffalo wanted to blow that disease away from me, so that I couldn't catch it.

The second dream I had was the same. This time he was chasing me. I was really scared. I ran for the fence—a meshed fence. I ran into it. I saw a hole underneath it big enough for me to get through, so I could escape that animal that was chasing me. He wasn't really chasing me, because he's my guardian. But I crawled through that hole. Then I got away from the buffalo. As soon as I got through the fence, he went away. That was the end of my dream.

He didn't want to hurt me. That wasn't a bad dream. That's a dream I can be proud of. There's just one more dream. This has been dreamt two or three times too. About snakes—poisoned snakes—this time.

I dreamt I was walking on land somewhere and come to a prairie country. I looked ahead of me and seen all kinds of snakes—big six foot and seven foot long snakes— all colors. I looked around. I couldn't pass them. They were all around me. I wasn't afraid. The only thing I can do is take a chance and go right across them. All the snakes are all stretched out. I started to step over them—step over every one of them. They never moved, just lay there, and I had to go quite a ways before I could get over them all—stepping over every one of them.

I often think about that dream, why I dreamt that way. About a year after that I found out what the dream meant. I was walking on a sand road like this. It rained that night, good and heavy, and the ground was still damp. When I looked down on the ground, there were angle-worms. I was stepping over them angle-worms. I didn't step on any of them. They were behind me, in front of me, all around. I had to step over them. I didn't want to hurt them.

That was the meaning of that dream. I was going to step over those things—not the real snakes, but something representing a snake.

COMMENTARY

Judging from his Rorschach record, John Thunderbird seems to undergo a good deal of anxiety in connection with social relationships.[233] He has evidently suffered some

---

[233] The following paragraphs are based upon a Rorschach analysis made by Maud Hallowell. John Thunderbird's Rorschach record was also analyzed independently by Dr. Bruno Klopfer and by Pauline Vorhaus. Their analyses had many points in common with the foregoing interpretation; but I chose Mrs. Hallowell's analysis because of her familiarity with the Chippewa material and also because of the greater detail in her interpretation of John Thunderbird's record.

unfortunate emotional experiences, which have forced him into the introversive patterns characteristic of the Chippewa. But John is not able to live comfortably within his inner world, as many Chippewa old-timers (like Tom Badger) are able to do. He still feels a great longing for warmth and affection.

However, John also feels suspicious and bitter about people. He regards the world as dangerous and threatening, and is not willing to stick his neck out any more. Alert and ready to turn against potential enemies, John can be defensively aggressive and negativistic.

The Rorschach record also implies that John is—or was at one time—a very ambitious person. But these ambitions have soured. John must now feel a great lack in his life, accentuated by the frustration of these ambitions, and he seems to feel that he is no longer living up to his full capacities. John is very depressed by life.

But there are positive features in the record which modify this rather gloomy picture. John Thunderbird is intelligent and fairly practical; and he possesses some insight into his own difficulties. He is certainly much better adjusted than Jim Mink and many other Chippewa males of his generation.[234] John probably met with particularly affectionate treatment in childhood and can therefore retreat into the memory of early days. Some of his Rorschach responses have a childish, regressive quality to them. Jim Mink, by contrast, has no happy area in the past to regress to, and is much more destitute, with no emotional basis of support.

The Thematic Apperception Test seems to corroborate the general picture elicited from the Rorschach. John told stories which stressed themes of loneliness, bereavement, and death of parents (particularly with pictures 3 BM, 7 BM, and 13 B), of anxiety, fear of spirits and of sickness (in 12 M, 18 BM, 19); but he also told long stories about family lines, outlining events extending over three generations, in which John laid stress on the continuity of family relationships (in 7 BM and 12 F). The theme of ambition appeared in 4, 7 BM, and 17 BM.

The first story which John narrated is a particularly interesting one, for various reasons. It is reminiscent of aboriginal folktales concerning the orphan boy who goes forth in search of his parents. It also has a very personal meaning for him. After telling this story, John concluded with an outburst of anger and a denunciation of the white man similar to the earlier one quoted above. The stimulus picture which elicited the following fantasy represents a little boy sitting in the doorway of a log cabin. Somewhat abbreviated, John's story follows:

"He's wondering where his parents are. And he wonders how he come to be alone. He's going to try to locate them. There are no neighbors around. The only thing he can do is get out and hunt up some neighbors. Then he can find out what's happened to his parents, whether they're murdered or what happened to them. . . . On the way he hears a noise. So he knows that somebody is around. He goes right straight for the noise. There he finds people living—a family. The people there were surprised to see him alone, barefooted, no shoes, no hat, nothing on his head. The people asked him, 'Where do you come from?' He said, 'I come from a long ways by myself. I was alone in a log house, wondering how I come to be alone there without parents. Now I want to know what's become of my parents.'

---

[234] See above, p. 20, fn. 41.

"We'll call him Johnson. The people there were thinking if there was anybody by that name, Johnson. Somebody said, 'So that was your father? The Indians captured your father and mother, when you were sleeping. They never came back. They might have been burned up at the stake. I've never heard of them since. So we are glad to see you. You have come here for shelter. We are glad to take you in and take care of you. I know you have no parents now. So you must stay with us. We'll take care of you as long as you live with us. We never can find your father and mother. They might have been staked up and burned up, because the Indians are wild. They like to get a white man. That's the last we've heard of them. So, little boy, you're going to live with us.'"

I congratulated John upon this story.

"That one story here is worth $1,000.00. You're getting that from a true American Indian. I'm not mixed blood. If you want me to tell stories, you'll have to pay a lot more money. You're going to distribute these stories all over the United States. The United States is going to hear every word I say. Take the city of Chicago alone. There'll be over a thousand sheets there alone. That'll cost a dime for each one. The white people will make money on it. You'll make more than a thousand dollars out of this. I'm not going to tell you any more stories. That's why the Indians are mad at the white man. He comes and makes a profit out of the Indian. There's all that money owing us on the treaties. We can't get it back. You couldn't help us get it back. Now if you print these stories, you'll get a dime for each one you sell. I won't get anything out of it."

I denied that I would profit from these stories, but it was no use arguing with John. He was too angry. I gave him some money and said good-bye. A day or two later I ran into John on the street. He was very affable, and when I asked him if he would like to continue the test, he readily agreed to do so.

When the Thematic Apperception Test was finished, John explained that taking such tests might shorten his life. It might be all right for white people to do such things, but Indians are different. *Manido* laid down certain rules for the Indians to go by; and it is very dangerous to do otherwise. "I pretty near died last spring," said John. "That's why I don't want to do anything that might be out of the way. When I was a little fellow this high, I used to listen to my grandfather, and he told me how I should live my life. I try to do what he said. That's why I don't like to take these tests. I don't want to do anything wrong. I want to live to be seventy-five; so I've got to be careful in all my actions."

After taking the test, however, and defying the fates, John was in a very good humor. He reminisced about his life-history, as he had told it to me, and was very pleased at my recollection of small details in the account. As I got up to leave (this was our last interview), John said he hoped I would live to be as old as he was; and we parted on very friendly terms.

If it were not for their value as a check and corroboration, I might have spared John the uneasiness aroused by the Thematic Apperception Test for there is little in the projective test material which does not also appear in the biographical data. John vividly describes his own loneliness as a child, and refers to early anxieties, such as fear of the dogs in the Old Indian Village. John's dreams of the buffalo are sufficient evidence of the anxiety which he still experiences. His occasional outbursts of anger give testimony to the hostility and suspicion with which John regards the world. But in his life-history as well as in the projective tests we also discover the compensation of warm family ties and childhood memories concerning the grandparents and uncles who raised him and whom John desires to emulate. In these close family loyalties John differs greatly from Jim Mink and from many other Chippewa. His emotions are strong but still unsatisfied, so that in his bitterness and anger John is always in danger of losing self-control.

Even though John was blessed by substitute parents in infancy, we can still detect in John's life history the same undercurrent theme which characterized Jim Mink's anecdotes, the frustration of childhood needs for dependency, and we can also see how this frustration affects his attitudes towards the white man, whom John alternately denounces and seeks to please.

When we turn to Julia Badger's biography, we shall see that her childhood frustrations were even more severe, and that her personality structure was considerably more damaged as a result.

3. JULIA BADGER

INTRODUCTORY COMMENTS

Julia Badger, wife of Tom Badger, is a fat, bulky woman of thirty-four, who has gone through a great deal of sickness and misfortune in her life. Her father and mother were classmates at the Flambeau government school. Her father died when she was only five years old, but even before that time Julia had been transferred to her grandparents (father's parents), who brought her up. Julia always thought of her grandparents as her real parents and claims that she did not know who her real mother was until she was fourteen years old.

Julia's grandfather, "Big Bill," was evidently the most influential person in her life. He was of huge stature, sometimes described on tourist postcards as "The Biggest Indian Alive." "Big Bill" had spent four years in jail for killing a white man in a brawl. In jail he made considerable progress in self-education along western lines. After he got out, he bought a farm with his "timber money," according to Julia. There is agreement that in spite of the murder he committed, "Big Bill" was more popular with white people than among the Indians.

Julia Badger has always been very sickly. She is "wall-eyed," suffers from eye trouble, has a bad gall bladder, and gets terrific headaches quite frequently. In infancy Mrs. Badger contracted some kind of paralysis, so that she was unable to walk until she was two and a half years old. After that she wore a brace on one leg for several years. There is a possibility that some of these disturbances may be hereditary, for her mother and grandmother had eye trouble as well; and her daughter suffered attacks of paralysis in childhood.[235]

There is no doubt that these frequent illnesses have had a marked effect upon Julia and on her attitude toward life. They probably contributed a great deal to the remarkable passivity which characterizes her. Throughout her life-history Mrs. Badger seems to have played a most inert, inactive role; she is acted upon by others, but seldom

---

[235] Dr. Milton Sapirstein suggests the possibility of congenital lues or syphilis.

takes any initiative herself. Julia readily adjusts to the new scenes in which she happens to find herself and never questions or tries to change things.

In compensation for this passivity, however, Julia Badger has developed an inner activity—a ceaseless phantasy life, which is always transforming the colorless outer world in which she moves. Daydreams continually bubble up to the surface of her mind. For this reason, Julia greatly enjoyed working with me; it provided an opportunity for her to produce phantasies aloud—and get paid for them.

Most of the Indians I worked with talked to me only because of the money involved, but Mrs. Badger talked for sheer pleasure or inner need. In fact, it was generally hard to get away at the end of the day's work; for she hung on, sometimes for two or three hours after being paid, generally repeating old anecdotes which had already been told. "Talking is right in my mitten," Julia used to say. She really needed someone to unburden herself to about her gall bladder, her former marriages, and her ever-welling phantasies.[236]

It would be impossible to disentangle truth from fiction in Mrs. Badger's autobiography. No doubt much of her account was invented on the spur of the moment. One evidence of this is the over-exactness of Julia's memory. For instance, she describes a very improbable five-day trip which she claims to have taken with her "kid" brother when she was seven years old. "We started that morning—the tenth of August at eight o'clock." She remembers every item of the alleged journey in the row-boat down the river. Apart from the over-specificity, it seems unlikely that a grandmother would send two children—aged five and seven—for a five day trip alone down a river. One's suspicion of the story is heightened by the "cuteness" of the story, its sentimental details. ("After a while my brother asked if we could get out and pick flowers on the bank. We picked flowers for a half an hour. He said, 'Did God put these flowers here for us to play with?' ")

Another illustration of over-specificity is Mrs. Badger's penchant for exact numbers. For instance, she remarks, "There were 357 boys and girls at school." What arouses one's doubt about her statistical items is the fact that the numbers 56 and 57 seem to come up so frequently. When I asked her how many people were in the tipi at the peyote meeting she attended, the answer was 56. Julia's dormitory room at school allegedly had 57 beds. There were 357 boys and girls at school. There were 156 cows. 856 loaves of bread were made every day. The above statistics applied to the school at Flambeau, but Julia also went to school at Pipestone, where the situation seemed to be much the same. At Pipestone there were 357 students. 456 loaves of bread were baked every day.

Another manifestation of fantasy-making is Mrs. Badger's "literary" style. Sometimes she talked in a perfectly normal way, like anyone else. At other times, she suddenly swung into a literary manner of speech. Then she would say things like "Amid all my sorrow and pain I told him I needed his advice." Then she talked as if she were dictating a novel. Her voice changed too, becoming less matter-of-fact and more

---

[236] I have omitted Mrs. Badger's most interesting phantasies, which I hope to publish separately later on. The most striking is a lengthy "recollection" of a trip to the other world which Julia took when she was only two months old. This phantasy incorporates many old Chippewa motifs. See footnote, Bibliography.

poetic, and her face would take on a dreamy appearance. I have preserved this style when it appears in her biography and have recorded the material as much as possible in the way she told it. I have made some alterations in arranging and cutting the material, for publication. But Mrs. Badger's words remain unchanged.

Autobiographical Material

When I was about two months old I fell very sick. A woman who had lost a child stepped on my bonnet. It must have been laying around. Then I became paralyzed and got sick, so that I could hardly see out of my eyes. . . .

I never wore glasses. I went through school without glasses. I can read all right, and I can do beadwork like the rest of them. But I never really did see well. The doctor says I have "inverted squint." I think that's what he called it. My eyes see out each way— not straight ahead.

My mother and her mother could hardly see. I guess I take after them. The last few years before she died my mother was just beginning to feel what she was doing. She couldn't see her last baby, my youngest step-brother, very well. . . .

One time my father came home from St. Mary's Hospital. He was sick a great deal, had trouble with his appendix. He came home after an operation and said to my mother, "You'll have to divide the children among the old people. I can't take care of them any more. There'll be just enough money for three of us. I've asked my father and mother to do this favor for me. When the children grow up, they can come back to us because children never forget their parents."

So I was raised by my grandparents. I didn't get along very well with my grandfather at first, but after a little while we got along all right. But my grandmother was mean. She used to whip us often, sometimes for nothing at all. My grandfather scolded her for it too. He said "When I whip them, I tell them why I'm doing it, but you just hit them without explaining what it's for." My grandmother didn't talk much, but my grandfather was always preaching to us.

They used to scare us at night, so that we wouldn't go out to play, by drawing a face with chalk on a frying-pan and sticking it in the window. Also, if we were playing while it was getting dark, they'd say. "Oh, you don't see who you're playing with." They'd make us think there was a ghost playing with us, and we'd get frightened. . . .

When I was about seven they put up a shaking tipi one day to find out about some-one else's sickness—some woman. I don't remember who the doctor was, but I think that it was old man Whitefeather. I gave him a bottle of whiskey and a big piece of tobacco. They wanted me to give this to him to find out why I cried so much and why I didn't get along with my grandfather. I didn't like him, but I always got along well with old Sedemo, who used to visit me and bring me games like the bowl game. The bowl game had two miniature men made of tin. You'd try to make both of the men stand up when you shook the bowl. Sometimes he'd bring a little drum over and sing three or four songs. Then he made things out of wood for me too—dolls, miniature animals.

The last thing he did was tell me he was going to bring something to show to me. "People hardly ever see it on me," he said. He brought over his "hat." It was made of hair. It came down below his shoulders. He told me he'd had that since he was a boy.

At that time my grandfather called me to come into the other room. He gave me a pint of whiskey and tobacco. He told me to give that to him. That was how we thanked him for doing so many things for me and for showing me that head-dress which so few people ever saw. Old Man Sedemo took the pint of whiskey and the tobacco, but first he told my grandmother and grandfather that he was going to sing a song. He sang a song and I sat right in front of him. He said "Those people I sang about—those are the ones that will accept your whiskey and tobacco. They like your whiskey just as much as they like your tobacco." Those were the *Manidog* he must have seen when he was a boy, when he fasted. They were the "Holy Frenchmen," the white men who live behind the northern lights. Their light is just like the northern lights. They cause the northern lights to come into the sky. Those were the men he sang about. That was the first time I had heard him sing. He said "I hardly ever sing any place."

When they put up the shaking tipi that time, the spirits said "That man (Sedemo) should be the *weʔe* of this girl." Then they said to him "She likes you and the thing you showed her. You should give her a name. Then she'll be happier." We had a hard time understanding the *Manidog* (spirits), but that's what they said. This was in May. On June 15th old man Sedemo gave a feast to give me a name. He prepared everything himself. My parents didn't have to do anything. He gave me a dress, shoes, and stockings. The dress was a kind of silky dress that changed colors. His old lady made a pink slip with it. It was a full dress that came way down to my feet. It had puffed sleeves. I had hair way down to here (her buttocks); so he gave me some great big wide ribbons for my hair. This was the first thing he did—give me those things; and then he made a speech, saying that that was how that woman looked that he dreamed about in the days when he fasted. I guess he told his wife how to make that dress. There were a lot of people at the feast. He called them all himself—twenty-five of them. They weren't only relatives or *dodem* members; just so that they had 25. He had everything nice to eat—things that a white man eats—cake and pie. They had it all on a table with a nice white table cloth. They even had whiskey in little glasses like sherbet glasses. And there were flowers on the table and a ribbon doubled up to make a bow.

Before we ate, old man Sedemo said "I guess you all wonder why the table is set like this." Then he went on to tell about the dream he'd had years ago. He'd dreamt that he'd had a feast and invited 25 white men and women—"Holy Frenchmen." He went and invited them all himself. Then they'd had a feast at tables spread just like this. The women had been dressed in clothes just like the ones he'd given to me. Then he gave me the name of Adawewininkwe, Store Lady. He also gave me two kinds of ribbons to wear all the time—a light blue and a white one; but he told me to pin it right here (on the lapel, upper left side of her chest). He said that I could wear them on my head if I wanted to, but the ladies had worn them right there. The ribbons had to be made into a bow. They were long. He cut them at the end into a W. That man was laughing and joking all the time this feast was going on. It was a good feast. You couldn't have got drunk on the whiskey in those glasses, though. They were too small. I guess the people who came to that feast were laughing and joking all the time (in his dream) the way he was. When the feast was over, everybody went home.

After everybody had left, he said "Now I'm going to tell you what to do. Have some tobacco and whiskey ready for me once in a while. Get your grandfather to explain to you what I'm going to tell you. If you don't understand, ask him to tell you what it means." But my grandfather didn't have to explain anything . I understood it all right. My grandfather was there, listening to everything that was said.

The tobacco and whiskey were for those 25 people. He said "When you give me that whiskey and tobacco, you're giving it to those 25. If I'm not there, go right ahead with it anyhow. If you do what I tell you, you'll get to look like those people." So I always used to give him that whiskey and tobacco while he was still alive. He told me what I should do later on in life. "In years to come," he said, "you will always see plenty of people like that, like those Frenchmen. They will like to be around with you and you will like to be around with them also. They will even teach you their language. You will speak real good English and learn to mingle with them. Wherever you go among them, they will always be your friends. If you do what I'm telling you, you will never have a hard time living among them."

That's been so. I can go among the white people, and I'm always welcome there. I went to school and spoke their language and did everything they wanted me to do. I never had a hard time at school, and my life among them was full of joy and happiness. They're always glad to meet me wherever I am—anybody. It makes no difference. I get along with them good.

About a year later, when I was about 9 or 10, I was sick all summer with different things—mostly my legs, which were useless. I couldn't walk. I couldn't use either of my legs. My grandfather always carried me from place to place. That's how my paralysis is—it comes and goes. Sometimes I'm all right. At other times I can't walk at all.

My ears, my legs, everything was wrong. My skin was just yellow—no color at all. I was like that all summer. I wasn't able to go to school until April, after Easter. My hair kept falling off. They didn't cut my hair, though. I didn't want anybody to do that.

My grandfather called my *weʔe*, old Sedemo. Sedemo told me and my grandfather to get a white ribbon and a quart of whiskey. "After you've done that," he said, "call me again."

When he doctored me, I don't know what he did, because I had my eyes closed all the time. I could hear the beating of the drum. My grandfather beat the drum. I was laying on my left side. Before my *weʔe* started, he said "Don't get scared, now. I'm just trying to see what I can do for you." Then he put the bones at my neck, behind my ear, where it was a little swollen. He began to suck and spat the stuff into the dish beside him. The stuff he got out of there was three clots of dark black stuff about the size of a silver dollar. He told my grandparents that he'd never doctored anybody before.

Toward the end of the doctoring, he got out a long piece of stuff that looked like hair and a long one like a shoe string. He spat them into the dish beside him. It had to be a dish without any marks on it. When he coughed out those clots, they didn't even spread out—just stayed clumped the way they were. He showed me the stuff when he was through, and then he threw it into the stove. He said, "Those little clots would have become pus bags, if they'd stayed much longer. That's why she can't open her eyes. That stuff was making her sick." . . .

When I was young, I never knew who my mother was. I thought of my grandmother as my mother; but she told me that I had a real mother somewhere. She didn't tell me where. I used to see my mother all that time, off and on, but I never knew that this woman was my mother until after 1923. Around then, one day, someone told me that this woman was my mother.

One day this woman gave me some things to take to my grandmother. I took them along. I didn't know why she sent those things. That was my mother, but I didn't know it then. After I knew who my mother was, I used to visit her. I remembered who my father was, but I didn't know who my mother was. My father died in 1915. My mother married the second time in 1916 or 1917. I didn't like my step-father. He was mean.

I started going to school in 1918. I didn't like it at first. I was taken to school by an Indian interpreter, Charley Gauthier. They took me to the main office. They asked me what my name was, where I was born, and who my mother and father were. My grandfather had given a paper to Charley Gauthier with all those facts on it. He answered the questions. After they were through with all that, I went to the matron. She made out a slip just like the one they'd made out in the office. From there they took me around the different parts of the building. The last thing they showed me was my bed in the great dormitory room full of beds—about 56. We had 357 boys and girls at that time. . . .

We didn't have much to eat at school. The rules were kind of strict too. The girl's matron was strict. Not the boys', though. They could come and go as they pleased. All our teachers and instructors were good. We had plenty to do. My mind was always occupied.

We wore blue and red uniforms and chambray dresses. The boys wore dark brown, heavy uniforms. I didn't mind sleeping in that big dormitory. We had plenty of light and fresh air. I had four or five special friends. When we went to a show it was all paid for. They had movies for us every Friday night. We had basketball games, an orchestra all our own, a baseball team, a football team. But the only enjoyment I got out of school was to run and play. That's what I was supposed to do for my paralysis. But I sat around most of the time. We put out a paper all our own every month. It included the doings and life of the school. It was called "Flying Arrows." They had a literary society. There were big boys and girls going to school there. In the literary society they'd get up and make speeches about what they'd do in later years after they'd finished school. They had school at night too from nine to ten. That was Study Hour. After Study Hour we had music. Everybody was supposed to learn how to sing. The boys liked Study Hour. You can sit with anyone you want to sit with. We had 156 cows at that time. Plenty of milk and cream. But there was never enough on the table. They had pigs too. They had their own butcher shop, so we could have fresh meat. We had a big school garden too. But there was never enough to eat. Boys and girls worked in the garden to keep it up. I used to play around in the field, stand and give orders. 856 loaves of bread were baked in the oven every day.

A year later they gave us lunches in between meals, when the supervisor, Mr. Carter advised that we should get more to eat. He said, "There's money set aside for everybody to get plenty to eat."

We had a special day to go to town and a special day to visit our parents: every Saturday. We had to be back Sunday evening before six o'clock. The only thing we weren't allowed to do was play with boys—I don't know why. [She laughs and covers her mouth.] Boys and girls often ran away from school; but I never did. I got to like it after a while, when I got the swing of it. . . .

One evening we put on a play called "Indians of Long Ago." There were about 35 of us in that play. Two of the boys made a big drum for it. We had to make our own costumes. They gave us the materials for it. No one was boss. We all worked on that play. The main purpose of the play was to show that if the Indians ever stopped speaking their own language, they'd soon forget it and lose it. We were punished at school if we spoke Chippewa. They used a razor strop on the girls sometimes, but not for speaking Chippewa. We were often punished. I was whipped about four times for doing different things. Those that swore had their mouths washed with soap and water.

[V. B.: What did they whip you for?]

I was walking where I wasn't supposed to—way over by the boys' building. I was just looking around. The matron lifted up my skirts and whipped me.

The school authorities didn't know what our play was going to be about. It took us six months to get it ready. The whole student body knew about it. No employees were allowed in there when we met in the Assembly room to plan our play. The whole student body met in there to talk about the play. This was about two or three years after I got to school. We talked in Indian in that Assembly room.

The play showed how the Indians lived long ago. The speaker in the play said that we should live just like our ancestors did. "But if we are not allowed to speak our language," he said, "we are going to lose the songs that our grandmothers and grandfathers used to sing to us when we were babies. We will go so far as to lose our rights to go to the Indian dances. We will not be able to talk about the things our grandfathers did, because we won't be able to speak that language. We will just stare at the person who is speaking to us in those years to come; and we will not understand our grandfathers and our fathers and mothers. Maybe some of us will try to sing in Indian but be unable to, because they don't let us speak our Indian language."

While he was talking, the play was going on. You could hear the drum beating. "Let us all pull together and work so that we can get our language back. Let us ask our grandmothers and grandfathers what we should do." There were two kids there dressed up to look like old people with gray wigs. These two old people started talking. They said to their grandchildren, "If you lose that language that God gave you when he first put you on earth, how in the world is he going to understand when you talk to him. Please listen to me when I speak to you."

The principal, superintendent, teachers, and all the employees were there; but they couldn't understand what the play was all about, because we spoke in Chippewa. . . .

I missed a lot of school at Flambeau, because I got sick often, and I had that paralysis; so my grandfather kept me out of school. I used to have awful headaches and dizzy spells. So I stayed home.

When I was thirteen I fasted for thirty-two days, a half a day every day, and stayed in a hut (a dome-shaped wigwam) specially built for that. My grandmother said that if I did that, I'd live to be an old lady. My grandmother cooked my food and brought it to me—right on the dot at noon every day. The sun was shining then. It never rained all that time. This was across the lake at the Indian Village. The hut was a birch-bark covered wigwam. It was fixed up real nice—with reed mats and everything. Just like a home. They had an extra place there for somebody to stay. Other women came to stay there with me—my girl-friend, my cousin, and others. . . .

I wasn't allowed to wear my watch when I went into the hut. I had to leave it at home. The food I got was good food—everything nice. And my grandmother brought me a pail of water too. She didn't get it from the lake either; she got it from the pump. I wasn't allowed to eat anything that comes from the ground—no vegetables, potatoes, or anything. My grandmother baked her own bread. She saved the rest for my next meal. Gave me oranges and candy too. She gave me canned corn. That's all right, since it comes from the can. But she couldn't give me fresh corn. I could have had canned salmon and canned sardines too. My grandmother gave me a teaspoon out of wood for me to eat with, and a wooden cup and bowl.[237] She had all that ready ahead of time. [She laughs.] They had to use a new pail in the hut. They used ashes to clean it out afterwards.

The first day I was there I felt kind of lonesome, because I didn't understand why I was doing it. But later I understood. Girls don't do that now. That's why you don't see berries on the trees now. My uncle's son—my mother's brother's son—was touched by a girl who didn't do that. It was the first time she was that way, and she hadn't gone out into the hut. When she touched that boy, he became paralyzed. Later on, he died. It's true. I always tell young people about these things. The more you hide, the worse it is. . . .

While I was in that hut I fasted and put charcoal on my face. I only got one meal a day. Then I had a dream. I couldn't tell you that dream. It's only told on very special occasions. I told it one time a few years ago, when Tom's sister was very sick. I wanted to help her, and I didn't know what else I could do. I got someone there to give me some plug tobacco. Then I sat by her bed and told her about my dream.

When my thirty-two days in the hut were over, my grandmother picked cedar boughs and gave me a tiny plug of tobacco and put them down where I was supposed to step. I had to put tobacco wherever I stepped on that cedar. She said "Don't forget to put the tobacco down there before you step each time." There were cedar boughs stretched out from the hut to the house. Then she put some tobacco in the fire, and she said "I've brought my grand-daughter home to live among her relatives and friends." After that she told my grandfather "Now you have to look for something for her to eat" —like fish, garden stuff, berries. All of my girl friends were picking berries. They brought flowers. I couldn't pick flowers. If I touched them, they'd just wither and die. That's why my grandmother and my girl friends picked berries. I couldn't touch any berries or flowers for two months. After they'd gathered all the stuff they gave a feast, telling God that I was ready to eat stuff that grows from the ground, but that I still couldn't pick berries and flowers from the roadside. That would be too soon. I couldn't go berry-picking that summer. But I could eat them all right, and they used to bring them to me. I waited at least two months anyway.

The other girls I went with were supposed to do this too, but they didn't do it. That's why there are no berries now. That's why the birds pick everything dry. I know one girl; we didn't even know she was that way until her mother got after her.

That's what God put before the woman to do. But now they don't do it. My mother's mother was a heavy believer. She made me do these things. My own daughter wouldn't do it, though. I couldn't get her to go and stay with her grandmother. She wouldn't stay in the hut either. The young people won't listen to their parents any more.

When they had the feast, my father's father's brother got a deer for me. It only

---

[237] Grandmother is Mrs. Badger's mother's mother.

took him a half an hour to get it. He got it over by the big rock in the lake. He paddled as fast as he could go over there, since he'd seen signs of deer around there the night before. He brought it home, skinned it, and told the women to cook it. Everybody was surprised at him. They all laughed: "You sure got that deer in a hurry." They all said that that deer was given to me to use. . . .

My brother wasn't allowed to go around the house barefoot for two months after I came back from the hut.

When a man or woman loses a child or a husband or wife, it's just as bad. When you touch a small baby then, it becomes paralyzed. I've seen lots of cases like that with my own eyes. That happened to me and a lot of my relatives. That's why the Indian priest tells the widow or parent of a dead child at the funeral about all the things they mustn't do for four days. After that you can touch them a little bit, but you have to go slow. You mustn't pick them up or fondle them.

I was a great one for getting in a rowboat too. I didn't get into the water until I'd put my tobacco in the water. One day I wanted to go out on the lake, when I was between 13 and 14. You're not supposed to go out on the lake until you've put tobacco in the lake. It was my mother's mother who held the string, while I lowered it. The big tobacco plug was tied in the middle by a piece of string. She held it above first. Then I took the string lower down and lowered the plug into the water. She said, "My granddaughter is telling me that she wants to ride in a boat and play around in the water." I was a great one for playing in the water among the water-lilies.

My grandmother never talked. The only time she spoke was when she wanted to give us a licking. But my grandfather talked all the time. He'd sit in front of us and lecture us—me and my brother and my cousin. We'd sit in front of him in three chairs. This was over here, at this side of the lake, when I was thirteen or fourteen. He used to say to me, "You should set an example to the other two (my brother and cousin). Sitting before me are two women and one man. You will be men and women some day. At the age you are right now, you don't know anything. When you get to be men and women you will want to have a home of your own. But who wants a husband that's worth nothing? It's your place to pick out a man for yourselves, not mine. Maybe you'll want to live with one man, and then maybe another. Then maybe a third man. Maybe there's something you'll be looking for. You'll have nothing. All you'll have is your elbows for a pillow. You'll be no good. You won't know enough to get up in the morning early. You'll just lay there and think it's an honor to sleep with a man. And there'll be times when you'll want to drink. You'll be telling everybody what you know and what you're made of. You'll tell everybody "I know lots." I'll thank the man who'll throw himself away to marry you. Some man will do that. You'll be fighting and quarreling. Pretty soon you'll get into a great big fight." Then he said to my brother "You're just at the age when you should listen to me. You will have children by this woman and then some more by another woman. I don't know what woman will throw herself away to live with you. When I was young I heard all this preaching. You may think that I'm scolding you; but I'm not. I'm only telling you how to live. Now is the time to preach—before it's too late. Keep your ears open and listen to us. When you grow to be a man, you will go to another part of this country. Maybe while you're there you'll find a girl you'll want to make your wife. Then that's where the work begins. You'll work for that woman. Maybe after about one or two years of living with this woman, you'll have your first child. Maybe after that first year, I will be dead and gone. This voice of mine will be silent forever. There'll be no one to tell you what to do. You'll be saying "I wish my grandfather was there to tell me what to do." So you'd better listen to me now."

My cousin later ran around with a lot of men, but my brother and I didn't run around like that. She had no home, but we did.

While my grandfather talked, he'd grab our ears and shake us. He pointed to our mouths and said "You own this. Nobody else does. If something comes out of there, you're the one that said it. Nobody else said it."

I didn't get along so well with him when I was young, because he switched me so often. But later I got along with him better. My brother and I used to think he was scolding us, and we used to cry.

It was while I was at the Flambeau school that I was first introduced to my mother. This was in 1924. When I was introduced to her, I didn't know what to say. But she told me the little that she knew of what had happened in past years. She told me that she was my mother and that my father died when I was a little girl. Then I started to ask her questions. I said, "Why did I have to live with my grandfather then?"

"He's your father's father," she said. "The old lady is your father's mother. They took you when you were able to sit up."

[V. B.: Didn't you know all this?]

No, she (mother) never bothered us when she visited us. We were afraid of her. She kept out of the way when she visited us.

[V. B.: Didn't you know that your grandfather was your father's father?]

Yes, but I listened to what my mother said then anyway. Then I told my mother that I'd thought that my grandmother was my mother. I knew that my grandfather was my father's father, because I knew that my father had died. But I thought that my grandmother was my mother.

My grandparents met us, and my grandfather told me that this woman was my mother. "Why didn't I see her before?" I asked him.

He said, "You never noticed her. She was around, but you only paid attention to the kids."

My mother said to him, "I want to thank you for all the help you've given me. And I want to thank you for introducing me to my own daughter."

[V. B.: How did your mother get along with your grandfather?]

All right. But my grandmother was mean to her. Nobody can get along with her. She's mean to everyone. When everybody had finished speaking, my grandmother said, "Now that you know who your mother is, I guess you'll be running away from us now and then to go and visit her." That's just what I did. I often got all dressed up on a nice summer day and ran off to visit her.

One time, on the 11th of June, I remember I ran away. My grandfather was down by the lake, fixing his nets. I went down there and said I wanted to visit my mother. My grandfather looked at me without saying anything. He looked at me for half an hour. Finally he said, "If I let you go, will you promise to come back?"

I said, "I'll be gone four days. Then I'll be back."

He waited a long while. Then he said, "All right. You can go."

Then I went to see my grandmother and told her I wanted to go and visit my mother.

She said "What for?" I said, "There are some things I want to hear from her. And besides, she asked me to visit her on my birthday." That was the next day—the 12th of June. My grandmother said I couldn't go, at first. But finally she let me go.

My uncle—my mother's brother—was going by then, so I ran up to him and asked him to wait for me. Then I ran to get ready. My grandmother was kind of slamming things around, while I got dressed. She didn't like me to be going. I packed a little suitcase, and ran down the hill. My grandmother shouted at me to come back. My grandfather said "Go ahead. Don't listen to her."

At my mother's home, everybody was cooking, including my mother. She had brought her parents to stay there too for four days. Then I asked why they were all cooking and why everyone was so busy. She said that they were cooking, because it was my birthday. It was my fourteenth birthday. She said they were going to call all the people they could. They also called Tom Badger in to say a few words, because it was my birthday.

People kept saying to me, "Who is that lady over there?" Everybody knew that I hadn't known who my mother was. I'd say, "That's my mother." Then they'd laugh.

[V. B.: Why didn't your grandfather ever tell you who your mother was?]

He said that I'd find out for myself in later years.

[V. B.: Why didn't your mother tell you?]

Because I was afraid of her. I don't know why. But I always kept away from her. She couldn't get up courage to speak to me about it until that time she came to school.

At the feast, when Tom spoke, he said to me, "That woman is the best friend you've got with you today. She's the one that brought you into this world. When you're down and out and don't know which way to turn, she's the one who will know what to do. She can help you more than anybody else. She gave you your milk. That's why you're living today. You're the first one that was born to her. She's giving you this feast today as a birthday party and also in remembrance of the naming feast in which you got your name. You are giving your tobacco to the birds, because you are named after the big bird from the south (he's about four feet high). Fourteen years ago you came into the world." This feast was like an introduction to all of my relatives that I didn't know. After this I went to see my mother often.

School at Flambeau only went as far as the sixth grade. My grandfather asked me if I would like to go to Pipestone. I always liked to go to school; and I knew the superintendent, Mr. Balmer. He had been the superintendent at Flambeau, but he left there to go to Pipestone. Everybody liked Mr. Balmer. When kids saw him coming down the street, they'd all run up to him, and he'd take them in his arms. He'd say, "My heart is big enough for everybody." Even the Indians liked him. When he left Flambeau the Indians built him a bonfire. He said that he hated to go, but he had to. They had a big dance at that time. I was fourteen or fifteen then. I told him, "When I leave here I'm coming to Pipestone where you are." He said, "I'll save a place for you." Two years after I got through here at Flambeau, I went to Pipestone. I was sixteen then. I filled out my application and wrote and told Mr. Balmer I was coming on the 26th of August. Mr. Balmer used to write to me once in a while.

My grandfather asked me if I would like to go to Pipestone. He said, "You don't have to go there if you don't want; but you can if you want to." He planned to send me to another place, if I didn't like it there. My grandfather believed that we should all get a good education. He could read and write too.

Then my grandfather asked my uncle to come to the house. My uncle brought the paper that he had to fill out. We sat face to face and filled it out. When he came to the question that said "How many years do you want to go to Pipestone?" I asked him, "How many years do you think I should go?" He said, "The required number is three years." So I said, "Well, put down three years then."

That school has put a lot of memories into my head in past years. There are a lot of things I remember about that time. Sometimes I regret that I didn't go to school longer, so that I could do the things that I wanted to do.

[V. B.: What were the things that you wanted to do?]

I wanted to study the Indians and the life of men and women—women especially. I wanted to write a book about the people of America and their progress. I didn't talk much at school. I did a lot of thinking all the three years I was there. I wanted the American Indian to get the best out of his life.

At the home economics course I studied the relationship between men and women and how to take care of my own body. This book was called "The Greatest Creation on Earth" and it told about the relationship between men and women. Every chance I had I used to go to the library and read this book. It was a big fat book. When I came to things I couldn't understand, I asked questions of the doctor at the school.

The doctor was a great big tall man. His name was Dr. Jerry McKewn. After a while he became my greatest pal at Pipestone. He liked the way I was always reading that book. He said "That's the greatest subject of all the books in the building, but nobody ever bothers to look at it; but since you've taken such an interest in it, I'll help you all I can."

That's what he did. He took eight questions from the book, wrote them on a piece of paper, and told me to put my answers alongside of them. I did just as I was told.

I worked in the other departments too. I worked in the laundry, the sewing room. I learned how to clean house. I made eight beds a day. I worked in the hospital about a month, waiting on the patients, taking temperatures, and trying to make them comfortable. At the Indian office I didn't do much except clean up and talk to Mr. Balmer and the chief clerk, a Sioux, and the stenographer, who was a Cherokee Indian. At mail time I put the mail in the mail boxes. I took the Pipestone paper around to the people whose names I had on my list. This was the most interesting part of the work I had to do, because I came into contact with some of the employees and white people on the campus. Everyone seemed to like me.

When I got through my work, I'd go to the girls' building and sat around until I had to distribute the evening mail. I studied in the evenings. I had classes in the mornings; sometimes in the afternoon. I went to night school until ten o'clock, about four times a week, sometimes three. We went to YMCA and YWCA meetings. We had a singing class all our own, a glee club all our own, and an orchestra all our own of boys and girls. On Sundays we went to church in the auditorium. On Easter Sundays we went to any church in town that we wished to go to. We went to shows down town about once a week. We also had a day to go shopping. The bus took us to wherever we wanted to go.

Your mind was occupied all day long. I don't think I ever had an idle moment. The only idle moment I had was during the half hour when we waited for our names to be called out when they distributed mail before dinner-time. It was a joy to get a letter from home. I heard from my grandfather mostly, and from my uncle who made out my application and from some of the students I went to school with at Flambeau. Sometimes I would get a letter with some money in it.

Twice a year I'd get a long distance call from home from my grandfather, asking me how I was making out. That meant most to me of all. I had to answer the call at the Indian Office. Another great experience was getting a package from home. Sometimes they sent you clothes or canned blueberries or maple sugar. In the fall of the year you might get a little package of Indian rice.

Visiting day was the greatest day of my life then. It always came on the 20th of every month. On that day I had a chance to meet the friend I had met on the train.[238] Mr. Balmer told the students at Flandreau that they could visit Pipestone on the 20th. Their own bus brought them down. They'd start off after breakfast and stay all day until ten o'clock at night. You could go to town or to a movie if you wanted to. A lot of us used to eat at the "OK Cafe." A lot of them would go and dance in the Candy Kitchen, which was in a basement. Others went to the show. But we had to be back at ten o'clock at night. The faithful old bus-driver used to take us back to school. He'd wait for us at the Drug Store.

It was a good old sound when we heard the dinner bell at school. Everybody was hungry. At Thanksgiving everybody ate a lot. The employees waited on the tables. At Christmas we had another time everybody looked forward to. Every student in the whole school got a package from one of the employees. The next day we had our Christmas dinner. We got big candy bags. The student body would put on their Christmas play. In the fall, when they had a football banquet, everybody was invited. We had our own football team. We had our own baseball team. Our basketball team traveled to play in different parts of South Dakota. All the cars and buses were used when we went. Sometimes we went to visit the Sioux Falls packing company. It was the biggest packing company I'd ever seen. We went to a show there. We also visited the Sioux Falls penitentiary. We heard the prison choir sing. They had a half-breed Indian prisoner there. They had their own band in the prison.

We also went to a canning factory and to a big farm where we saw all kinds of domesticated animals. You had to take a notebook and a pencil along on those trips. When we came back to Pipestone we had to write about all the things that we had seen and done on that trip. Study Hour was another exciting time. Boys and girls studied together. After Study Hour we would sing for a little while. Sometimes people made speeches then. They were always welcome to make a speech at that time. Sometimes I got up before the student body and spoke about the American Indian of today. Everybody was glad to hear what I had to say.

In summer time there were 35 students there all summer long. They had their vacation at school. I stayed at school the first two summers. Mr. Balmer sent 50 students out to work. You had to have a good reputation before you were sent out to work. Some went to South Dakota, some to Wisconsin, some to Detroit. All the rest went

---

[238] I have omitted a long romantic phantasy about Mrs. Badger's train-ride to Pipestone, during which she and her girl-friend picked up a pair of devoted Flandreau boys, one of whom fell profoundly in love with her. At St. Paul, according to this yarn, they went to the circus, went dancing in the YWCA to Paul Whiteman's orchestra, played tennis in the gymnasium, and went to the movies. At the end of this busy day, before boarding the train again, Julia's boy-friend bought her a complete outfit of clothing—dress, shoes, etc.

home. In 1929 I went to Minneapolis to work for four months. It was too big a city; too much excitement going on. It pretty nearly pulled me down.

After I left Minneapolis, I went back to Pipestone. Then Mr. Balmer sent me home. All of my expenses were paid going both ways by the government. When I left, all of my classmates—twenty of them—were there to see me off on the train. Before the train came in, everybody was talking to me at once. I couldn't understand one from the other. I said "One at a time!" "How about two of us talking at once?" I said, "No, then I can't hear what the other has to say." We sang the class songs that we sang at the last day of school. They even had the class colors there—purple and gold. When the train came in the station, they all had different ways of bidding me goodbye. Some were crying, some were laughing, and some were singing our class song. Then Mr. Balmer came up and made a speech before my classmates. He said that he knew me when I was a little girl. He said that he was sorry I had to leave so soon, just when we were starting to know each other. Then he gave me a little verse to remember the student body as a whole. "We, the student body as a whole, hate to see our dear and faithful friend depart at this time. There will be one voice that we will miss in our midst for a while, that voice that we all liked to hear. We did everything that we could to please you, and you always got along with everybody so well. When you go along the pathway of life, may the torch of knowledge light your way."

Then they all sang the song "God be with you till we meet again." That's what they were singing when the train pulled out of Pipestone. It pulled out at 11:45 at night. My boy friend got on the train then too, along with me. He was going back to Ashland. When I stepped onto the train, Mr. Balmer came and handed me a white envelope with my name on it. After the train had been going a ways, I opened the envelope. There were $25 from Mr. Balmer's wife.

I rode on the train as far as Ashland. I stayed there overnight and got on again at six in the morning and then came back to Flambeau. The only persons who came to meet me at the station were my brother and Frank Wildcat. It was early in the morning. My brother said "I'll take you to your mother's. This evening you can go to your grandmother's."

When I got to my mother's, the door wasn't open. I knocked at the door, and my mother came to open it. I didn't like the welcome that she gave me, because all she could do was cry for a half an hour. She couldn't talk. My brothers and sisters tried to find out what was wrong. "What's the matter?" they asked. "You shouldn't do that. You should be glad that she's come back." After a while she said she was so glad to see me after all these years. "You went against my consent," she said "I didn't make out an application for you to go to school. But I'm glad that you're back anyway." She asked me to lie down and have some sleep, but I couldn't because my brothers and sisters kept bothering me and talking to me. After a while I got up to eat lunch.

About 6:30 I hired Mike Elliot to go in his car and get my trunk at the station and then take me to my grandfather's house at the Village. Halfway to the Village, we met my grandfather and grandmother walking in to town. My brother had told them that I was home, so they were walking in to see me.

Mike Elliot stopped the car. He told them that I was in the car; but I was sleeping, so I didn't see them. My grandfather woke me up. He wept just as my mother had done. I told him that nothing was wrong. "All the years I spent there were nice. I always had a good time, and people were nice to me. The only time I wasn't well was when I had my tonsils taken out, and then I was in the hospital for two months." I didn't tell them about the time I'd had eye trouble in Minneapolis.

My grandfather kept on sobbing until my grandmother said "Now, that's enough!" I told him "All the rest of the time I was all right, and I was happy."

When we got home we had the biggest meal I've ever had. My grandfather started to sing that little song he always used to sing when I was a little girl. He asked me if I would dance, but I told him that I didn't want to. He asked me if I'd received the money he'd sent a week before I'd come. I told him "Yes, I got it." Then he asked me how his old friend Mr. Balmer was. I said "He's the same as when he left here. He hasn't grown old. He still has a big heart for children. He said to me 'Tell my old pal to take care of himself and say hello for me.' "

My grandfather said to me, "Next week you can go to work if you want to. They've been inquiring for girls who will go to work. But you don't have to go if you don't want to." I wanted to work. I worked for one month at a resort at Fence Lake, but my mother objected to my going to work so soon so I quit. I came back and stayed around here and went around with different young people. My mother said, "Didn't you get enough of work when you went to school?" I said, "Yes, I did too much work." "Then stay around home for a while." So I didn't go to work any more.

I kept going back and forth all the time to my mother's and grandmother's, dividing my time amongst them. In July, shortly after I came home, I went to the Indian wedding of my cousin in Rhinelander. Her husband was half Potawatomi and half Chippewa. Everybody had a good time at the wedding. It was there that I met my first husband, a Winnebago Indian.

About a week later this man came up. He came up to ask my mother if he could live with me. I was sitting there. My mother made no objections. She said, "Yes, if you will take good care of her, because she arrived here only about a month ago. She hasn't spent the best part of her life yet." Then he told me to go with him to Woodruff. He hired a car to take us down there.

He was the age Tom is now when I married him [i.e. in his late sixties]. He was just like that when I married him. He talked all the way going to this town twelve miles away. When we got there we went to a place to eat. Then he told me that I had to go to the clothing store there. He asked me which clothes I wanted, so I told him. Then he bought them for me. Then we came back to Flambeau. On the way back he gave me some money. He said he was going to visit my parents for two days. After those two days were over, we went to Rhinelander and visited his brothers and sisters. He introduced me to all of them but one—his oldest brother. We stayed in a house that was paid for for about two months. He was working for the paper mill then, and they arranged this for him. "After those two months is up," he said "I have to go back to work." But he didn't. He asked for a leave, and we traveled around visiting different relatives of his.

My first husband was a leader in the peyote religion. We went to about four or five peyote meetings while I was down there with him. My husband worked in the factory, sometimes on the day shift, sometimes on the night shift. I didn't see very much of him. He used to ask to get off on Fridays. Then he'd have all day Saturday and Sunday free. At these times they'd have the peyote meetings, which started in the evening and

lasted all night. He and his older brother were in charge of them, and they were held
in a great big tipi, which must have held about 56 people. Two rows of people sat
around the tipi; one circle around the edge of the tipi, another circle inside that one.
They sang and played all evening. I didn't see anybody act crazy or get sick from the
peyote. They were just busy singing and praying all night. My husband shook his gourd
rattle, holding it close to his head. They were also beating little drums. Some of the
songs were Indian songs; some were Christian hymns, and some were in between. The
singing sounded good. I liked it and fell asleep where I was sitting by the wall of the
tipi. My husband didn't fall asleep, though. I don't know how my husband and his
older brother became leaders of the peyote group. But his older brother used to tell
how his life had been changed by taking peyote and joining the group. After that he
didn't sin any more—didn't lie and talk about people and things like that. My husband never tried to win me over to the peyote religion. He never talked about it to me.
But he sure loved to sing those songs and shake his rattle. When we traveled in his car,
he put the gourd rattle over the windshield-wiper. Sometimes he'd stop the car and
shake his rattle and sing. Sometimes he'd just sing as he was driving. One time we
drove all the way to Walt Hill, Nebraska, about eight or nine miles from the capitol,
where they had the biggest Indian pow-wow I ever saw—the Walt Hill and Omaha,
Nebraska Pow-wow. They had Indians from all over—Sioux, Winnebagos, Sacs and
Fox from Iowa.

We drove there in a big Nash sedan belonging to one of the two couples we drove
with—all Winnebagos. We left our car at their place and we all drove in this one
instead. My husband was at the wheel, and he drove all the way there and back. We
drove all day and all night, all day and all night. We spent one day there, and then came
back and drove the same way; so that we were gone five days. On the way there some
people came and met us half way and drove with us the rest of the way, so that they
could show us the way to the pow-wow.

When we got there it was the last day of the pow-wow. There was a lot of excitement
going on. We went to one or two dances but I was so tired when we got there that about
all I did was eat and sleep.

I only lived with my first husband about three weeks. Then my grandmother
(father's mother) and my aunt (father's sister) came down after me. They wanted me
to leave him. They objected to his taking that herb (peyote). I don't know if it's bad
for you to take peyote or not. I never took it. [Mrs. Badger took peyote later in life.]
But that religion is all right. We all worship the same god. It's all the same.

[V. B.: How did you get along with the Winnebagos?]

I got along with them all right. They're all right—same as here. Their language is
different, though, and when I wanted to speak with my husband we always talked in
English. Now with Tom I can speak either Chippewa or English, but with my first
husband I had to talk in English. But I got along all right with him. I had nothing
against him. After I left him, he died the same year. They say someone must have
done something to his hat [sorcery].

[V. B.: How did your grandmother and aunt get you to leave him?]

They came down to Rhinelander to get me. They told me that if I didn't come back
home with them within 24 hours, they'd get out a warrant for my husband.

[V. B.: Why? What had he done? Run away with you?]

No, he hadn't done anything.

[V. B.: But they couldn't do that.]

I guess they had no right to.

[V. B.: Did you have a chance to talk it over with your husband?]

Yes, he and I went to a nearby town and talked a long time.

[V. B.: What did he say about it?]

He didn't say nothing.

[V. B.: Was he willing to let you go back?]

Yes

[V. B.: Didn't he talk it over with your grandmother and your aunt?]

No, he never saw them. I just went back home with them. Later he came up to visit me, but they were so mean to him, that he didn't like to come.

[V. B.: Why did you let your grandmother and your aunt influence you so?]

I was young. I didn't know anything. They said they could get a warrant on him for using that peyote bean; but they had nothing on him. I was afraid of my aunt. She had a sharp tongue, and she was mean. She felt that because she was my father's sister she had a right to boss his children around. Later on they were sorry they had done it. Now I don't have any heirship money.

[V. B.: Why did you marry him in the first place? You weren't in love with him, were you?]

No. I guess I wanted to get away from home. I wanted to see other places.

In November of the same year, my grandmother and my aunt got me to marry another man—Joe Bluebird. This is the time when I should have married my old boy-friend, the one who saw me off at the station when I first went to Pipestone. But he'd got married while I was at Pipestone. Later on he said to me, "That's where I made my big mistake." When I came home, he planned to meet me at the train, but he wasn't able to. I couldn't marry him, because he was already married. But he said to me afterwards, "Why didn't you say anything then? That's the time we should have got married." Instead, I married his best friend, Bluebird. Those two were good friends. Bluebird was kind of small, but he wasn't a bad-looking fellow. My boy-friend is in the Army now. He's supposed to get a furlough next month. He said he'd come to see me. Two days before he left for the Army, he took me to a show at Minocqua. We had a long talk that night. He told some people he wouldn't mind taking me away from that old man [Tom Badger]. He said he'd do it. But I guess I'll have to wait until Uncle Sam gets through using him. His wife knew that we were going to the show together. But she didn't mind. I told Tom too. He didn't care. It made no difference to him. He said, "It's all right so long as you don't come home drunk."

I didn't care much for Bluebird, but my people wanted me to marry him. He was a lot older than I was. I'd gone around with him a couple of years before that; so when he came and asked my mother if he could marry me, I didn't mind. I wasn't anxious to marry him, but I didn't care about it. So I said I'd marry him. My folks all wanted me to do it. Before then, when we were going around together, he'd once said something about living together or getting married, and I said "Live with you? I wouldn't go along with you to a dog-fight, if there was a dog-fight in town." Later on, after we got married, he threw that all back at me, but I told him I'd never said it. You know, you have to say things like that. He treated me well, though. He was always good to me. He worked hard—guiding and different jobs.[239]

My daughter Christine was born while I was living with my second husband. I never found out I was going to have a baby until after I left my first husband. It's funny I didn't know. He must have known. He had preparations made for me to go to the hospital and everything. I never went there, although he'd paid for it.

Before Christine was born, I wasn't supposed to eat apples, because when Christine grew older she'd get sores. So I ate a lot of oranges and pickles. They didn't mind that. I wasn't allowed to eat butter. That always makes you sick anyway. Then, while I was carrying Christine, I wasn't supposed to eat the head of any animal. They didn't tell me why. I wasn't supposed to eat the insides of the deer. I never do anyway. They told me not to eat much of anything. "Afterwards you'll suffer for it," they said. They told me not to eat eggs, but they didn't say why. In that book the white man prints—the book I read at Pipestone—it says you can eat whatever you want. But I didn't tell them that. I didn't want to argue with them. They had more experience than I had. I wasn't supposed to eat turtle. They didn't say why. But I've never eaten turtle in my life anyway, so I didn't care.

I kept moving around all the time—never sat down or lay down much. That's why I had no trouble with the baby. I was only sick two or three hours. My grandmother said that we wouldn't need the pole. We didn't even put the mattress on the floor. My husband came in once while it was going on, but my grandmother pushed him out. He wasn't allowed to come in until it was all over.

Christine was a tiny baby. When she was two months old she weighed two and a half pounds. The nurse here wanted to put her in an incubator; but my mother-in-law forbade it—just chased the nurse out of the house. She pulled through just the same. The nurse gave us cotton batting. We had to keep her warm. We kept the room warm too. She lived mostly in her cradle-board—a little tiny one. We had no doctor at the birth. My husband called a doctor, although my grandmother said we wouldn't need one. The doctor arrived a half an hour after Christine was born. He put the silver nitrate in her eyes; that's all he did. My grandmother said that her eyes were all right. I don't know how she knew; but she knew.

I nursed her for eight or nine months. She slept with my mother-in-law after that, for two months. She was all right [weaned] after that. She didn't cry much. After I came back she didn't even like me any more.

Two days before my daughter was born, my father-in-law, Mashos, said to me, "Two days from now a woman is coming to stay with us. She will come with a hum-

---

[239] Mrs. Badger made the above remarks in Tom Badger's presence. On another occasion, when I talked with her alone, she spoke somewhat differently, as follows:

"My second husband is the best husband I had. Tom's all right. But he beats me when he's drunk. He's been especially bad the last two years. He claims he doesn't know what he does when he beats me or why he does it. They say he beat his first wives too. I tell him, 'My first husbands never beat me. My second husband drank all the time, but he never licked me once.' Tom doesn't get into fights with other men; he just comes after me when he's drunk. Sometimes he grabs me around the neck. I tell him that's bad to grab someone around the neck. I often tell him I'll leave him. I don't have to live with that old man.'"

ming-bird; so she's going to be a small baby." Then he gave me a blue ribbon. "Take this ribbon," he said, "and hang it up by the door. This is the kind of ribbon she's going to wear."

My grandmother's sister also asked John Whitefeather at that time how I would make out with my child-birth. He said I'd be all right. He said I'd have a small baby and that it would come with a humming-bird, just as my father-in-law had said. After my daughter was born, my father-in-law always called her Humming-Bird.

She was a tiny baby, not much bigger than my hand. That humming-bird is inside of her, between her shoulder-blades. I guess most people have an animal inside of them like that. I just know about Christine's, because that old man told me. A sucking doctor can see your animal when he swallows the bones. Then he can see right through you.

When Christine was four months old, my grandmother (father's mother) picked her up shortly after she lost her husband. Then Christine was paralyzed in the legs. It wasn't really her that was sick. It was the humming-bird inside of her that was sick. My baby couldn't move from her breast down. She was paralyzed. My grandmother said, "I had to pick her up. She was crying, and nobody else could pick her up." I'd just gone to the store and didn't even know about it. It only takes about two days for the paralysis to set in.

My grandfather said, "Now she has to go through a ceremony. Put the baby in cedar bough water [water boiled with cedar boughs]." They boiled the boughs, drained them, and put her in the water. They did that every day, every time she needed a bath, for four months. After that she started to move her legs.

My mother-in-law helped me too. She knew a lot about medicines. She showed me herbs in the woods. I used to be afraid of her before I got married. Once she asked me why I hadn't come to see her one time when she sent for me. I said, "Because I'm afraid of you." She just laughed. I didn't know how nice she was then. After I got married, I found out how nice she was.

My mother-in-law gave me some medicine for my milk for Christine. My breasts just opened up then. They didn't have to use a breast pump on me. She put a teaspoonful of a root of some kind into the stuff that I ate. It started working inside of four days. My daughter didn't eat until she was four or five days old. But then the milk came.

My baby was born on January 25. Shortly after she was born, I telephoned her father to come to see his baby. It was an awful thing to do, but I had to do it. I needed his help at this time. I wasn't very well. He came the morning after he got that call. When he got here, I told him that I wasn't feeling very good. "Can't you do anything to help me out a little bit?" He said, "Yes, I can do a lot for you, now that I see you face to face again." I told him to make some medicine for me. He was sitting alongside of me on the bed. I told him what the trouble was. He got a tea-kettle full of hot water and put some medicine in it.

[V. B.: Was it peyote?]

No, not peyote, He said, "I'll do all I can for you now that you are the mother of my baby." When that medicine had boiled, he took it outside, cooled it off, and put it into a white china cup. It was half full. He said, "This medicine is neither sweet nor bitter. If you take it as I instruct you, you will be on your feet in a week's time." He stayed with us for about a week. He didn't sleep here, though. He slept in a different place. But he came everyday for a week to see how I was. He talked to me and told me that I should take good care of myself and also of the baby. He gave me another kind of medicine the week after. This last medicine was to bring back the color to my skin.

On the morning that he left, he spoke to the man I was to live with. "You must take good care of my baby and my wife. I call her that because she was my wife before you had her. Try to furnish her with everything that she needs. That's what I did during the short time that I lived with her. I tried to do everything I could for her. She and I got along very well together. If you treat her right, you will be the same; but if you're mean to her, I'll get a letter telling me how you are treating her. Then I'll come here as fast as I can. I'll take her from this home and make a different home for her. You have the responsibility that I had. And you also have the responsibility of bringing my little girl to womanhood. This is all that I have to say to you. Take good care of yourselves, and do right by one another."

That's what he did too. That man was always good to me.

[V. B.: How did your second husband feel about having the first one come to visit you?]

He didn't mind. He was glad that he came to help me when I was sick. My first husband came up a second time in September, but my grandmother and my father's sister were so mean to him that he left in a little while. When Christine was three months old, I called him up again. She had pneumonia then. He came up to help her. Those two men were both good. They didn't hate one another.

Christine was born in January. In February I got gall-stone trouble. In February, March, and April I had trouble. I kept throwing up. I couldn't sleep or eat anything. They had to give me a morphine tablet. I've got high blood pressure too. They told me that a few weeks ago when I went to Hayward. I've got that same gall-stone trouble now. Maybe I'd better have an operation. The doctor can tell me; and then maybe they'll send for an ambulance to take me to Hayward. I haven't had that trouble for fourteen years.

At that time I lived with my second husband at his mother's house. She was married to Mashos then. He didn't live there all the time; stayed about three days and then moved on somewhere else. Mashos was a mean old man, a medicine man and *Mide* priest. He worked bad medicine against a lot of people. People had told me that when he'd got drunk at a party Mashos boasted of having killed lots of men. Then one time at a party he told me the same thing himself.

My husband had a close friend called Ed. He was a strong, husky fellow. He came to see me when Christine was five days old. He said he wanted to see the new baby. At that time I noticed that Ed didn't look so well. He had to get up from the dinner table and go outside for a while. We asked him what was wrong. He said old Mashos had asked him to join the drum. Ed said he didn't want to join because he wasn't ready for it yet. He was too crazy; he ran around too much and talked too much. So he said he didn't want to join yet.

I guess that made old Mashos sore. He was working bad medicine against Ed. Ed told us, "That old man will kill me some day." It wasn't long after that that I met my husband one day over at the Village, all dressed up in his best clothes. I said, "Why are you all dressed up like that?"

"I've been to Ed's wake."

"Ed? Why? What happened to him?"

"Haven't you heard about that? He's dead."

My husband said that when he looked at him at the wake, he was all black around the eyes—and his finger nails were black.

That old man killed him—and for nothing!

When Christine was four or five months old, my brother George got sick. He had a bad foot and a swollen knee. At that time there was a *jizikiwinini* [shaking tent shaman] here. I don't remember his name. He was up here to cure somebody else. At the tent-shaking we asked why my brother had got sick like that. He said that an old man was jealous of him for being young and active. He described the old man, and you could tell that he meant old Mashos, although he didn't mention his name. He said that if we didn't do something to help George, we would lose him. After that we called in John Whitefeather to doctor my brother with the bones. He didn't suck through the bones. He blew through them, because George was so sick. He didn't swallow the bones either. He just blew through them. He got up a lot of black matter. I don't know how he did it, but he coughed up a lot of black stuff. He came for two nights.

At the end, you're allowed to ask questions. I asked John Whitefeather whether my brother would get over his sickness; and I asked how he got it. He said that he would get well, but only if we did what he suggested. He suggested that we give a War Dance. Then he described Mashos and said that that man had caused this sickness.

My "grandfather," my father's mother's brother, was there. He had a lot of money. So I told him what John Whitefeather had said and asked him if he'd help me give a War Dance for George. He said he would. So we gave a War Dance.

I gave one of my shawls. My "grandfather" and others gave other things. After the War Dance we called in an Indian doctor. He doctored my brother too. He cut my brother's knee and then put an Indian poultice on it to collect the matter that gathered there. He was a good doctor. After that my brother got well. He's better off in Hayward than he is here. This is where he nearly died because of that old man; and he's got a good job at the mill in Hayward. He doesn't come here any more.

At the time that my brother had all that trouble with his left leg, his left moccasin was missing. My mother-in-law found this moccasin in her husband's wigwam. "Whose is this?" she said, bringing it in and showing it to us. "That's mine," said George. "I hung it up with my other moccasin, but then I found it was gone."

"It was in Mashos' wigwam," said my mother-in-law. She told everybody about it. She wasn't afraid of Mashos. She said "I've got some medicine too."

[V. B.: Did Mashos ever use any bad medicine against you?]

He tried to, but he didn't get very far. One time I felt that Mashos must be doing something against me. I wasn't feeling very good, and Mashos didn't speak to me for two mornings in a row. He usually said something to me in the morning, but two days went by, and he didn't say anything. When he stopped talking to someone, that was generally a sign that he was starting to work on them. I told my mother-in-law, and she said, "He must be starting something up." So she looked through his pockets. She found a package of something. She didn't even open it up. She just soaked it in kerosene and threw it in the stove. So Mashos didn't get very far when he tried it on me.

[V. B.: Did anyone ever try to get back at Mashos?]

Yes, he had nose-bleed sometimes. A bad nose-bleed. My mother-in-law used to doctor him then. She thought that somebody was trying to get revenge on him. When you make bad medicine like that, it generally comes back to you. The Lord takes your loved ones away from you. That's how you suffer. It doesn't help to do that sort of thing.[240]

My brother George, who had that bad knee, had a lot of bad luck. Later on he got sent for two and a half years to Leavenworth for nothing at all—for doing wrong to a girl whom he'd never even seen. She said he'd got her in trouble, and they took her word for it. But it wasn't so. It makes me mad every time I think of it. My other brother is in Waupun Penitentiary now—for raising hell. He has two and a half years too. My grandfather spent four years in jail. I don't know why.[241] That's where he learned to make black horse hair fobs. He went to school in jail too and learned how to read and write.

[V. B.: Didn't one of Tom's sons go to jail?]

Yes. He spent two and a half years in Sandstone for living with a girl and then leaving her. But he really did that. . . .

My grandfather came to see my baby when she was five days old. He brought some pink and white flannel to make my baby's clothes when I got better. He brought me a pair of shoes too, a blue coat, and gave me some money. My grandmother came to see Christine too, a half an hour later.

My grandfather started to preach at the table. He said, "Now that you have seen your first child you have a great responsibility on your shoulders. Easy life is over for you. You have something to work for and look forward to. Please, for my sake, raise this little baby, so that she can be a woman some day. It's an honor and a blessing to bring children into the world. You never know real joy until you have children of your own. That baby needs the help of both of you people. Work for one another. Work to make a home for yourselves. I worked for you. That baby is your own flesh and blood. It's your duty to take care of it; not anybody else's. Don't tell anybody 'Take care of my baby a little while,' and then go off and forget about it. This *Manido* can do a lot of things. He gave that baby the breath of life. You're young and liable to leave the baby with some old lady. Both of you are young. Young people today are foolish. They think they know it all, but they don't. If you listen to me and do just what I've told you, you'll be all right. I listened to you when you cried. I didn't turn my head and say 'I'm not going to listen to that baby when it's crying.' It's your business to go and see why it's crying. Don't send someone else to find what's wrong. This path that you are going along is full of brush. You don't know what's going to happen tomorrow or the next day. You get some stuff into you that doesn't work very well [liquor], and you think you're a second *Manido*." He pointed to a car outside. "That's what makes the young people of today crazy. You get in there without thinking about anything except yourself, and drink some of that stuff, and pretty soon something will happen to you.

---

[240] Mashos seems to have been universally feared in the community. Another informant told me that when Mashos died, no men were willing to clean his body and prepare it for the funeral. Finally some women were persuaded to do it, after the body had lain untouched for about two days.

[241] Mrs. Badger appears to be ignorant of the fact that her grandfather was sentenced to jail for killing a white man in a brawl. She may have repressed this knowledge; since she often blots out unpleasant realities. On the other hand, she may not have wanted to let me know about this skeleton in the family closet.

I'm not telling you that I didn't drink when I was young. But I also raised my children, and I raised you. If anything happens to that baby, it'll be your fault and nobody else's. They'll say 'She was out having a good time some place.' I've heard about you. I've heard that you drink a lot." I didn't really drink much. My husband was the one who drank a lot. "What is a good time?" said my grandfather. "You'll pay for it in years to come." He always used to talk to us like that. My brother and I were always in tears when he talked to us like that.

My grandfather died on April 15, 1930, that same year, at a War Dance at his brother-in-law's place. They had a War Dance at his funeral that lasted about a half an hour.

I used to think of my grandfather as my father. After my father died, we called him "pa." My grandfather was the most wonderful thing that was created on the face of the earth. My husband and I stayed in a house by the lake and watched the funeral procession go by. A lot of white people were watching.

Old man Gauthier talked to me. "Do you know that today is your greatest day?" he said. "Today is the day of your famous grandfather's burial. From here to Chicago and to other places where he traveled, people know that he died and was buried today. He was a great man among white people. They thought a lot of him. Some people here have come from Chicago and Columbus, Ohio. I hear that some of the people around the grave said that they have lost a great friend. Some of them cried. It's a nice name that you have among the white people. That name won't be forgotten. He always had a smile and a kind word for everybody. You must do the same." There were sixty or seventy people there—mostly white people, not many Indians. This was four months after Christine was born, January, February, March, April.

He died April 15th. My husband died April 28th, the same month. He died in his sleep of heart failure. When I woke up I thought he was just sleeping; but he was dead. That's why it hit me so bad. I couldn't talk. It was just like my tongue was made of lead. His mother was the same. She couldn't talk either. I just sat around. I couldn't do much.

I didn't listen to the *Mide* priest during the funeral. My thoughts were all the time with that body in the casket in that room. Everything was a lot of blabbering to me. But I stood up when they told me to stand up. They told me that I was helping him when I stood up. But I didn't know what it was for.

I could have danced if I'd wanted to. But I couldn't dance. I didn't understand anything. I didn't know what it was all about. When they asked me to stand up, they even had to pull me to my feet.[242]

---

[242] Granted that there is an element of stereotyped exaggeration of grief in this description, it is very likely that Julia's reactions did have something of this paralyzed quality. Julia's husband seems to have been a young man of about her own age. When describing him to me once, she referred to him as a much older man; but from photographs she showed me, it is apparent that he was about as old as she. His sudden death must therefore have seemed rather strange to the people at Lac du Flambeau. To the Chippewa way of thinking, "heart failure" is no explanation of such an occurrence. Sorcery would immediately be suspected; and a very likely suspect as perpetrator of the crime would be his young wife, who had been dragooned into the marriage by her relatives, apparently against her will.

Julia must have sensed a mobilization of suspicions centering upon herself. Moreover, she

Four days after my husband died, I had a vision of a long weary trail. I was walking along a trail that led to nowhere. I couldn't see. As I was going along the trail, I heard a voice saying "Do you need me? I am at your side." Amid all my sorrow and pain I told him that I needed his advice. I cried and told him what was the trouble. "Oh," he said, "That thing can be mended in no time." Then I saw an old man with white hair. He said "I am your grandfather."

[V. B.: Your real grandfather?] No.

He asked me if I would take some of the food that was set before me. He said "Take this, and I will tell you what to do. If you listen to the advice of others, your life will be just the way it was before. It will take away your sorrows and put a loving thought in its place. Do you see that rainbow in the distance? As you go along in life you will see it somewhere and you will hear it. Turn to this thing for advice. If you do, it will take you along life's highway. It will take you to loving people round about you. You are young, and you will not understand. But as years go by, you will understand what I am trying to tell you. So wipe away your tears and think of the Great One who is above—not of the one on the bottom who is the one that makes you cry. The one above furnishes you with the food of life. Don't look back. Just look forward to the pleasant things of life. That thing has happened. It will happen all the time. Pull yourself together and walk along this road that I am telling you about. And when you think of me sometimes, put out some tobacco. I will accept it gladly. Before I go any further, I will show you my home." Then he took me into a hut. In that hut I saw myself the way I was when I was about thirteen. He said "Don't look at that one. Always look forward. There are better things ahead."

That's the man who had presented himself at the door of my [seclusion] hut at the time when I was there for 32 days. He said "I am your grandfather who helps you. When you're in trouble, call upon me. I'm ready to do as you say. I am not the Holy Being, but I know the thoughts of men and women. I know what you are thinking about. I am the one that you had the vision of in your younger days [in the hut]. I am your great adviser, your grandfather." But he didn't tell me what his name was. In those days I always had visions or dreams of walking on the earth with this man. Now he presented himself to me again when I was in trouble. Sometimes when I am in trouble, to this very day, I call upon him and ask him for his advice. If I do what is right, he will take me safely along the road that he told me about. When I'd seen him in my younger days, he was a young man. He was my companion all through my younger days. He helped me in time of need and when I was in want. He still remains the best companion I ever had.

[V. B.: When did you first see him?] Back in the hut.

---

may also have felt somewhat guilty; for Mrs. Badger is impregnated with the Chippewa "omnipotence of thought." Her phantasies are as real as actual events to her, and it is very likely that she had harbored some hostile feelings toward her husband. Now that he was dead, Julia may well have been paralyzed by guilt and fear. Of course, grief may be intense at the death of a loved person; but since it is quite clear from the way she speaks of him that Mrs. Badger did not feel close to her second husband, the intensity of her reaction must be explained some other way.

What made matters worse was the fact that her in-laws were powerful people, particularly old Mashos, who had magically "killed" a friend of hers and who had also sorcerized her own brother on no provocation at all. Julia's sense of insecurity must therefore have been very great.

Sometimes he comes in the form of a bird. He sings the sweetest songs that ever were sung. He sings the song to my heart when I'm in trouble. I know that he is there, because I have seen him. Sometimes he comes in the form of a man and walks beside me, when I'm all alone. His voice is small and clear. If I listen to him, I know that I am on the right trail. Sometimes I don't listen. Sometimes I do. It makes him feel bad when I don't listen, because he has appointed himself to be my guide, through all the years to come. He sometimes gives me the advice I need; not always. Sometimes he makes me do a lot of thinking, because he's an old man. When I see his face I am glad. When I hear his voice I know that he is there. He is the one that showed me this wonderful rainbow that I saw in the midst of all my sorrows. He told me that I would see it in later years to come. When I see this rainbow sometimes I always think back of the days when I was in trouble. He told me to rely on this rainbow and keep my faith. He told me then that every bird in the universe and every living animal knew the sorrow that had come upon me. "But forget about it and always think of the rainbow. That rainbow I showed you is a wonderful thing in life. You will love its voice. It will give you advice. In later years you will realize what it was." It was the Drum that he spoke of, the Drum that God has put here on earth. In later years I realized that. Before then I'd never been to the dance. In fact, we were never allowed to go to the dance. My grandmother and grandfather didn't let us go. We always had to stay home. I never got a good view of it. I never had any intentions of joining it until my husband died. This vision that I had then was the one that put the best thoughts into my life; because from that time on I knew that I was on the right trail. I saw that thing with my own eyes—during the daytime. I suppose I was crying most of the time. A while later I told my mother-in-law about that vision.

I went to a Drum Dance a month after my husband died. There was another woman there whose husband had died a week before. They gave a dance for both of us. I was scared and cried. I just kept my head down and didn't look up when they talked to me. It made me remember what had happened a month before. Every time that speaker spoke, he spoke about that fellow I had lost. He told me that my husband was joining a Drum on the other side, just the same as I was joining one here on earth. He said that if I didn't join the dances after they made me a member, my husband would do the same thing and not go to the dances. I was supposed to belong to that drum for the rest of my life.

They put some blue paint across from one of my cheeks to the other—across my upper lip. "That blue streak," he said, pointing to it, "is the color of the drum. It represents the drum." When they washed my face, they washed the sorrow from my heart. "God has meant the Indians to do this to one another," he said. They also had ribbons and feathers in my hair. My "grandfather," Arthur Catfish, told me not to look down on the ground so much. "That's where that person is that makes you cry. Look up to where the drum is. Raise up your head and look at it. If you think you can sing, you're welcome to sing." But I didn't try it that time. He said, "if you look at the drum, it will help you to forget what has happened. God put it here on this earth for our purposes—to show our love for one another. You'll now belong to this drum and to any drum that you ever see."

Then he pointed to the head of Pat Williams, my "grandfather." He was sitting right close to me. Arthur Catfish was standing right behind me on my left side. "If you will listen and do what I tell you, your head will be just like that old man's head—as white as snow. Right now you don't know what to do, but after a while you will learn about what to do [in connection with the drum], because you'll see a lot of this as you go on in life." I did. I just listened to them when they talked.

After my husband's death I didn't have to make up a bundle for my mother-in-law. She took my bowl away from me after about two months. She said, "You don't have to get any things to give to me. You've helped me enough." I was always with her then, helping her in the kitchen.

At that time some of my first husband's folks came up and asked me to marry his younger brother, now that both of my husbands had died. But I didn't want to. Some other people told me that he was mean. He had a nice house, but he was mean. And I didn't want to marry him anyway, so I didn't do it.

I didn't want to marry anybody then; I was so blue. I made up my mind that I'd never marry again. I decided that I'd go into church work and go around telling people about Jesus. That way I could get away from people and I could do some traveling. That's what I wanted to do—travel. When I get to feeling bad, I want to get on a train.

Some time after that I got sick. When I got up, my leg felt funny. I could hardly walk; so I asked for a stick. My mother-in-law told my people that I was sick and couldn't move. I could hardly see or hear. The noise in my ears was like the noise of thunder. I sweated a cold sweat. My mother sent for the doctor. My uncle John went with him. My step-dad never did anything.

This doctor said, "There's nothing wrong with this woman. She is out of her head." Then they decided to call Dr. Huber from Minocqua. My uncle John jumped up to call him. My step-dad never called him. My aunt and uncle, my mother and step-father, my mother's mother and my mother-in-law were all there. When the doctor came, he said "Open the window." My uncle John raised the window. Then the doctor said "Raise her to a sitting position." My uncle John did that too. My step-dad just sat there watching. He never did anything. Then the doctor examined me and told my mother, "Your daughter is very sick. She's got typhoid fever." I could hardly open my mouth. The nurse came the next morning from the hospital. My mother in law took care of Christine while I was away.

They wanted to know if they could take care of some of my money, so that my mother-in-law could take care of my daughter. I said, "Don't take it all. Take thirty dollars and leave me ten." My mother didn't want to take Christine, because she was too busy with her own children, and she knew that my step-dad would abuse my daughter.

When the nurse came, my mother's mother said that she'd like to say a few words before I left. She said, "I fasted when I was young. Last night I offered tobacco to the spirits whom I saw then. I asked *Manido* to give her a longer life and let her come back to us. If my prayer is answered, she'll be back in two months. This is my prayer for my weʔe." My mother's mother said, "Everybody is broken-hearted now, but before nobody wanted her to live with them." My mother's sister was so mean to me when I stayed with her. My mother's mother raised her hand and said "*Manido* will take care of you. Think about him; not about your sickness."

The night before I left for the hospital, my mother's mother gave a feast for six people. I was laying there in bed. She told again the dream she had had which gave her the name to give me. She said "Whenever the sun comes up, I hope he looks upon us as his children, just as he did when he looked upon me. May this tobacco that I have passed around reach the four winds and also the Frenchmen behind the clouds who make the northern lights in the winter time. I'm asking them to bring back my first grand-child to whom I gave a name. Bring her back to the road she was traveling on before. We need her here more than they do. I seem to take a great liking to her, because she's my daughter's first daughter."

My mother worried about me, after I went to the hospital. She must have had a dream about me. Mothers always know when their daughters aren't feeling well. That's a feeling that's put into every woman on earth. These things here [holding her breasts] tell a whole lot. That's what my mother must have told her mother: "One of my children must be sick." Her breasts were aching. She was like that all the time I was in bed until I came back. I've been like that when Christine is sick. It's like needles pricking your breasts. White women are like that too.

When I was in the hospital the fourth day they got a call from Uncle John himself, to find out how I was getting along. He called up because my mother was sick from worrying. They told him that I was getting along fine; and that I was never left alone. Someone was always there. I was pretty weak for quite a while after that. After I got well I started working at a resort, at Rouse Allen Lake. I met Tom a year after my sickness.

The first time I met Tom was at a War Dance on New Year's Eve. Oh, I'd seen him before then, but I never paid any attention to him before that, and he never paid any attention to me. So this New Year's Dance was really the first time we met. I had a lot of liquor in me, and you know how liquor will make you act foolish. I was pretty crazy that evening.

I was working over at the resort then, and this white man used to pick me up when he drove out there. He'd bring me back in the evening. I'd asked him to buy me a crate of beer, and I had some whiskey too. While I was working I left my baby with George White and his wife. They had her in a swing. A party was going on there, when we came in; everybody was drinking and singing and playing cards. I'd already taken a big swallow of whiskey before I went in the door. When I came in, I said "Oh, look at all that beer! I'm thirsty!" George White said "Help yourself!" He had an inner-tube drum and was pounding on it. So I took some beer too. George said, "Give us a speech now! You have the floor, and I know that you are a good speaker." I said in English, "Ladies and gentlemen!" I talked as if I were addressing a big crowd. I was pretty crazy. I said "Tonight at twelve o'clock it will be the end of the old year." George White said, "That's the way! keep it up!" I said some more silly things.

After a while we decided to go to the War Dance over at Chief Niganigizik's house. I guess I walked unsteadily. I was pretty loaded up. When we came in, I saw a place between two old ladies and went to sit down. My grandmother came in and gave me a dirty look. She knew that I'd been drinking, and she didn't like it. We were all shaking hands. They had five singers at that War Dance, and Tom was one of them. I guess that when I was shaking his hand I held it a little longer than usual. I never said anything to him. Maybe I said, "Is the singing all over?"

Nobody talked English that evening. We all talked Indian except for that old white man who sat in the corner. He said, "This is a great bunch, isn't it?" I said, "Of course it's a great bunch." Then I asked him, "I thought you were going to get me a crate of beer. Where it it?" "Still out in the car," he said, "do you want it?" "How much do I owe you for it?" "Say!" he said, "you just asked me to get you the beer. You didn't say anything about paying for it. Never mind about that. All you have to do is drink it."

I guess I went home about one or two o'clock. I kept going back and forth, though. At one point I fell in the snow and I must have laid there a while. When I got back to my grandmother's house there was a party going on there too. But I paid no attention to it. I got into bed with my shoes on.

The next morning my brother said, "Well, you certainly were doing things last night. You made a fool of yourself." "Why? What did I do?" "You held onto that old man's hand. I saw you myself. And you were drunk. Your grandmother saw you walking along the road. So she went to get your baby at George White's and brought it across the lake, so that she could take care of it herself." "Well, she's welcome to take care of my baby. I have to leave it, because I need to make some money. She can take care of my baby. She has a right to look after it, if she wants to. Everybody makes a fool of himself once in a while." "I saw you holding onto that old man's hand," said my brother. "I could have slapped you too."[243]

I didn't start going around much with Tom until that spring. The old man used to say that he pitied me, because I was having the hard knocks of life. I was thin then and I didn't look strong. Tom said, "But you were fixed up good at that party. Your grandmother [alcohol] was helping you." I met Tom the second time in April. Eddy Brown introduced him to me. Eddy did all the work. He called Tom his brother and told me to go around with his brother. "My brother wants to do a lot of things for you," he said. "If you're good to him, he'll be good to you too." This was Eddy's own idea. I don't think Tom made Eddy say this.[244] I said, "What shall I do to be good to your brother?" "Talk to him nice. If he asks you a question, answer him nicely." Then Tom came up and said he'd like to tell me some things I didn't know, if I could take him for a friend.

He told me he didn't like the way the people had treated me after my husband died. "Even your own relatives don't treat you as you should be treated. I saw you when you were a little girl, when your grandfather was living. You had everything that was nice then; you were never in need of anything. Now that your grandfather's dead and gone, these people don't care about you. He was your sole protector."

[V. B.: Was that true?]

Yes, my grandfather was the only one who gave me food to eat and clothes to wear. After he left, I didn't have much of anything.

I went with Tom, April, May, June, and July—four months. Eddy always used to come along. After he'd bring him, he'd go. When Tom asked me to live with him, I said my intentions were different, and I didn't intend to get married again, because maybe I couldn't find a man like the one I lost.

He didn't say anything until about four days later. The second time he asked me, I told him, "If you can do as my second husband intended to do and be good to us,

---

[243] While Julia Badger described this New Year's Eve party, Tom, her husband, sat listening without making any comment.

[244] Tom Badger was not present at this session.

I'll do just as you tell me to do. But in the first place I want to know what you're going to do with that other one that you're going to leave behind."[245]

He said, "I'm not going to do anything. I'll just leave."

"What are you going to do about the papers you made out with her?"

He said, "I never made out any papers with her."

Eddy was standing about twenty yards away. He clapped his hands then and shouted "Hooray! Oh boy!"

Tom's second wife was mean. Everybody knew that she was nasty to Tom. He had to take care of her, her daughter, son-in-law, and grandchildren. He said "She was worse than you are. You get angry, but it don't last long. My second wife would stay mad for four days."

I remember how Tom's son used to talk about his step-mother. He said he hated her, because she was so mean to him.

My father's sister and my mother's sister wanted to break up our marriage. But my mother and my father's sister's husband told them not to butt in. My father's sister's husband told his wife, "You butted in last time and caused them a lot of trouble. Now leave them alone!" My mother said, "It's their business, not yours, if they want to get married."

After my second husband died, my aunt [father's sister] wanted me to live with my first husband's younger brother [in spite of the fact that she had wanted Julia to leave her first husband. V. B.] But I didn't want to. I didn't know anything about his background, but I knew Tom.

I went to live with Tom in the country. We camped in a tent, and Tom went hunting. I left Christine with my mother-in-law. Living in the country brought the color back to my face, and I got fat in a short time.

[Tom Badger interjected: "When I married her she was like this one," pointing to their daughter, who is not at all fat, "but she got fat right away."]

I told Tom that what worried me most was that I couldn't help him much. I was too weak. I said, "I can't help you get meals the way I did for my other husband. I can't begin all over again."

Christine used to be kind of scared of Tom at first. She used to cry, but my mother-in-law told her that Tom would take care of her. Tom didn't ask my mother if he could live with me. I guess he was afraid she'd say no. He just started living with me. That was in 1932 when I was 21. Two years later we got married. We were married twice. First we had a sort of Indian ceremony at a big fair they had at Madison; then we had a legal marriage. I wasn't the one who wanted to get married. Tom was the one who wanted it.[246] The marriage ceremony we had at Madison was to give a show to the white people. There must have been 5,000 people watching us get married. We were married on a little wooden stage they put up on the fair grounds. They had a Winnebago who could speak good English. He'd say a few words in Winnebago and then he'd speak English to the crowd to explain what he'd been saying. We were all dressed up in Indian costume. We got a special price for doing that. . . .

---

[245] The reference is to Tom's second wife, with whom he was still living at this time.

[246] Tom was sitting by, whittling. He made no comment. Later, he discussed his decision to get a marriage license. A prominent reason for this action was the fact that his own son had been jailed for living with a girl to whom he was not married and whom he abandoned.

My mother died some years later. When she was dying, I was moving around at home, getting some breakfast. I had just lifted the spoon to my mouth to eat some oatmeal, when I heard four shots in the air. I didn't even put the spoon in my mouth. I just sat there staring without moving. Then I heard some noise over at my mother's place, weeping or something. I put down that spoon and just rushed over there.

After I'd come out of that place, I stood on the door step, just looking ahead. I didn't cry or anything. John Thompson and another man came along, and John said to me, "Don't stand there like that. Come on. They're having coffee in the next room." I just looked ahead. Then he took me by the arm and made me go along to get some coffee. One time when I got stage-fright, I couldn't speak; and my lower lip was trembling. I was just like that at this time.

My mother and my grandmother—my mother's mother—died sixteen days apart. Both of them died of pneumonia. When my grandmother was dying, my mother just rushed over to her house in two thin sweaters and in her moccasins. She was so excited because her grandmother had been busy working only two days before. My mother did something then I've never seen anybody else ever do. She put her face right close to my grandmother. You're not supposed to put your face close to a person that's dying; but I guess she wanted to hear something she was saying. And then my mother was so thinly dressed too. She caught a cold. Sixteen days later she was dead.

After that I was so dumb, I couldn't talk. My ears were closed. I just went haywire. I just sat in a chair. I didn't even know what to say. I didn't even cry. I just sat there.

[I asked Mrs. Badger to tell me some dreams.]

Sometimes you dream about going to school again. Not so long ago I dreamt I was back in Pipestone again. When I got out at the station, I looked around to see if anybody had come to meet the train. There was a bunch of people there. One of them was a fellow called Calvin Cutup. He was always laughing. He started to joke with me. He said "Oho! So you've come back! They always come back for more! What did you come back for this time—to look for a man?" I said, "No, I've come back to visit Mr. and Mrs. Balmer, Mr. and Mrs. Baird, and Mr. and Mrs. Trochaud."

I went to see Mr. Balmer first. He was superintendent there. He asked me, "I suppose you want to see how the place looks. But first of all, we'll eat." We ate. I suppose I was smacking my lips while I was dreaming, because whatever we had at his house was nice. He asked me how the different people at Flambeau were getting along. The chief clerk at the office was a Sioux Indian. He came in then. He said, "You've come a long way, haven't you?"

I said, "Yes, I've come from Lake du Flambeau, my home town and birthplace." Then he said, "May I ask you a few questions? In what year were you born? Who were your father and mother? How many times were you married—only once, twice, or three times?" I told him "Three times." He threw up his hands and said "Wuwuwuwu!" That was how he used to act. The other people were laughing. "What's your husband's name?" he asked. I told him my present husband's name. "Have you any children?" he asked. I told him I had one—fourteen years old. He said "Only one—and you've been married three times!" That was just his way, that fellow—always asking me questions. He said, "That's better than me. I've been married all these years, and I haven't got any." Mr. Balmer spoke up and said "What's all this nonsense about?" The chief clerk said, "The reason I'm asking all these questions is I want to put her in the 'Pipestone Star'. She is one of our former students here. She should have been invited to that Alumni Banquet that we had." He laughed and said, "But I'm not going to put down that you're visiting three families."

[Mrs. Badger went on to describe her visits to Mr. and Mrs. Baird, Mr. and Mrs. Trochaud, and to Mrs. Abraham's.]

I didn't stay long at Mrs. Abraham's, and soon I came back to the Trochaud's. He said, "If there's a pay-day before you go, we'll have a farewell party for you." They did too. That's when I woke up, while they were having that farewell party.

Balmer gave us a real farewell party when we left school—to five girls from this reservation. Mr. Balmer was just like a father to us in those days. He helped us all he could.

Last night I dreamt that I walked to town to see my "grandmother"—John Thunderbird's aunt. I asked her if I could speak to my other grandmother—my father's mother. She said in English "No! No! No! She's drunk." I said "Can't I say just a few words to her?" She said "No! No! No! No can talk. She's drunk." I guess I was laughing, and that's what woke me up.

COMMENTARY

Julia Badger was crippled emotionally as well as physically in early childhood. While numerous ailments sapped her resources in infancy, Julia's emotional needs for dependency were harshly frustrated. In consequence, she soon retreated into a world of phantasy in which she is still immersed.

Here is Dr. Bruno Klopfer's analysis of Julia Badger's Rorschach record:

"The subject plastically manipulates material from the outer world and uses external reality only as a feeder for her richly imaginative inner life. She is a person of no ambition; no desire to succeed in the outer world. (The combination of small d's, FK, and M is consistent throughout.) The painstaking observation of small details is used almost exclusively for her preoccupation with inner happiness, although she does leave the emotional door to the outside world ajar. In our culture she would be called schizoid.

"Acculturation hasn't really advanced far; only intellectually, not emotionally.

"The eye-trouble she suffers in no way influences her responses; for her observations are remarkably minute, exact, and painstaking. There may be a psychosomatic basis for her fatness; an attempt to wall herself off from external reality by building up a buffer wall of protective fat.

"These are the main Rorschach factors underlying the subject's personality configuration:

"1) Conspicuous absence of challenging quality of outside emotional stimulation (Color), indicating a narcissistic type of personality.

"2) Use of intellectual capacities and keen observation as a feeder for her imagination. (Small details and shading, with movement and no color.)

"3) Absence of drive for achievement. (Scarcity of W.)"

I think the reader will agree that the characteristics singled out by Dr. Klopfer appear in the biographical material. We have already seen abundant evidence of Julia's passivity and of her self-abandonment to day-dreams and phantasy. These personality characteristics must have become established early in childhood in response to very frustrating experiences.

Judging from her life-history Julia appears to have always searched for a benevolent father or grandfather-figure. This seems evident from the nature of her marriages, from her dreams, and from Julia's rapturous descriptions of the white men (like the school principle) who played a paternal role toward her.

Julia does not give us a friendly picture of her grandparents, who raised her. We get the impression of a dominating old man and a sour, irritable old woman, who whipped and scolded her. Yet, Julia Badger voices the most exaggerated admiration of her grandfather, remarking at one point, "My grandfather was the most wonderful thing that was created on the face of the earth." These eulogies must be the compensatory products of a period subsequent to Julia's girlhood, for we also learn that at one time the spirits of the shaking-tent were consulted "to find out why I cried so much and why I didn't get along with my grandfather." The spirits suggested that old Sedemo became a new $we?e$ for the girl.

As we have seen, old Sedemo placed Julia under the control of his guardian spirits, the "Holy Frenchmen," white men who live behind the Northern Lights, and he told her that she would always get along well with white people. Here is a case where an aboriginal culture-pattern facilitated the acculturation process. Since Julia's guardian spirits were white men, she was assured of success in the white man's world. She could feel confident of supernatural backing in her dealings with white people. And Julia was also encouraged along these lines by her grandfather, who believed in school education.

It is not surprising that Julia welcomed school, when she was old enough to go. She was able to get away from her grandparents, with whom she was unhappy, and she found some new playmates and parental substitutes. But although the impetus toward acculturation was very strong in Julia's case, it received a set-back in her bad health. Julia had to stay home from school a great deal, because of recurrent paralysis, headaches, and dizzy spells. This not only removed her temporarily from school influences, but also exposed her to a variety of aboriginal medical and religious practices, which were initiated by her maternal grandmother and other conservative relatives. Julia Badger seems to have run the gamut of all the Chippewa curing devices—shaking tent, sucking doctors, bleeding, cedar bough medications, War Dance, Medicine Dance, etc. Every conceivable method was used to cure her ailments.

One might say that two kinds of parental figures became available to her in childhood: on the one hand, the teachers at school; on the other, the Chippewa medicine men. Julia was not forced to make an ideological choice between these different classes of parent-surrogates. Her dependency needs were so strong that she clung to both. I believe that this gives a clue to the confused acculturation picture which she presents. We have already noted a similar situation in the case of John Thunderbird.

When John fell deathly sick at the age of nine, his grandfather "brought him back to life" by fasting and summoning up his guardian spirits. John Thunderbird is immensely grateful to the old man for saving his life. It was this episode which led John to say to me, "That's why I believe in my Indian customs as well as in the white man's customs." Note that John says "*as well as* in the white man's customs"; not "*instead of* in the white man's customs." Right after his "return to life" in the hospital, John was visited by the school superintendent, who showed some interest in him and presented John with a new suit of clothing. John is therefore deeply grateful to the superintendent, as well as to the white nurse who attended him; just as he is grateful to his grandfather. Loyalties such as these always vitiate John's outbursts of anger against the white man, and they lead him to make forms of restitution and manifestations of friendship after an expression of anti-white hostility.

In Mrs. Badger's case, however, there seem to have been no conflicts, no tensions in relation to the white man, such as we find in Jim Mink and John Thunderbird. Julia's deep passivity and dependency led her to cling, more desperately than they, to any stronger figure, whether Indian or white. She always accepted the authority of native medicine men; but when Julia went away to school at Pipestone, she also adjusted very readily to the new scene and followed the instructions of her teachers as she had formerly obeyed her Chippewa elders. The conflict of white versus Indian culture-patterns raised no problem for her; she simply accepted what was given to her and did whatever she was told. Similarly, upon her return to the reservation, Julia found no difficulty in abandoning the aspects of school education which were incongenial to her elders. In describing her studies at Pipestone, Julia stressed her interest in human anatomy and physiology; yet she readily jettisoned what she had learnt in this respect. "In that book the white man prints—the book I read at Pipestone—it says you can eat whatever you want [during pregnancy]. But I didn't tell them that. I didn't want to argue with them. They had more experience than I had." No conflict of cultures occurs in the case of Julia Badger. All religions are equally acceptable to her—the Drum Dance the Christianity of the missionary, the peyotism of her first husband, the *Midewiwin* of her third.[247]

Julia finally found an acceptable grandfather-figure in Tom Badger, whom she married. It must be said, however, that Julia has managed to exploit Tom rather badly, particularly from the point of view of an old-timer; for she seldom performs the traditional chores of a Chippewa wife. Julia spends most of her time lounging about, over-eating, day-dreaming, and quarreling with her daughter. It is Tom who fixes up most of the meals, sweeps the room, scrapes the hides, and makes the fire. When Julia performs these tasks, it is generally as an act of condescension; and if Tom complains of her laziness, Julia reminds him of her youth and beauty and of the many marital opportunities which she once possessed.

Mrs. Badger also exploits her numerous ailments, which have been recurrent since her marriage. "I told Tom that what worried me most was that I couldn't help him much. I was too weak. I said, 'I can't help you get meals the way I did for my other husband. I can't begin all over again.'"

She never has begun all over again. Julia lounges and dreams; and when Tom beats her in a fit of drunken anger, she runs away. On some occasions Julia gets on a train and escapes from the reservation for a while. But most of the time she finds her escape in the form of day-dreams and phantasy. Then Julia can re-order her life along more pleasant lines and leave the depressing world far behind.

---

[247] Such eclecticism in religious matters is characteristic of many people on the reservation.

BIBLIOGRAPHY*

ADAMS, MOSES, 1901, The Sioux Outbreak in the Year 1862. *Collections of the Minnesota Historical Society*, Vol. 9, pp. 431–452.

ARMSTRONG, BENJAMIN G., 1892, *Reminiscences*. A. W. Bowron, Ashland, Wisconsin.

BARRETT, SAMUEL A., 1911, The Dream Dance of the Chippewa and Menominee Indians of Northern Wisconsin. *Public Museum of Milwaukee Bulletin*, Vol. I, Article IV, pp. 251–406.

BELCOURT, GEORGES A., 1872, Department of Hudson's Bay. *Collections of the Minnesota Historical Society*, Vol. I, pp. 207–244.

BENEDICT, RUTH, 1934, *Patterns of Culture*. Houghton Mifflin, New York.

———, 1938, Continuities and Discontinuities in Cultural Conditioning. *Psychiatry*, Vol. I, pp. 161–167.

———, 1946, *The Chrysanthemum and the Sword*. Houghton Mifflin, New York.

BLACK ELK, 1932, *Black Elk Speaks*. As told to John G. Neihardt. William Morrow, New York.

BLAIR, EMMA, HELEN, 1912, *The Indian Tribes of the Upper Mississippi Valley and Region of the Great Lakes*. Clark, Cleveland, Ohio.

CAMERON, DUNCAN, 1890, The Nipigon Country. In Masson, R. L. *Les bourgeois de la compagnie du Nord-Ouest*. Cote et Cie, Quebec.

CHITTENDEN, HIRAM M., 1902, *The American Fur Trade of the Far West*. Harper, New York.

DAVIDSON, J. N., 1895, *In Unnamed Wisconsin*. Silas Chapman, Milwaukee, Wisconsin.

DEL TORTO, J. AND P. CORNYETZ, 1945, *Psychodrama as Expressive and Projective Technique*. Psychodrama Monographs, No. 14.

DENIG, F. T., 1929, *Tribes of the Upper Missouri*. 46th Annual Report of the Bureau of American Ethnology, Washington, D. C.

DUBOIS, CORA, 1944, *The People of Alor*. University of Minnesota Press, Minneapolis, Minnesota.

ELKIN, HENRY, 1940, The Arapaho of Wyoming. In Linton, Ralph, *Acculturation in Seven American Indian Tribes*. Appleton-Century, New York, pp. 207–258.

ERIKSON, ERIK HOMBURGER, 1939, Observations on Sioux Education. *Journal of Psychology*, Vol. VII, pp. 101–156.

———, 1940, Studies in the Interpretation of Play. *Genetic Psychology Monographs*, Vol. 22, pp. 557–671.

FROMM, ERICH, 1941, *Escape from Freedom*. Farrar and Rinehart, New York.

GILFILLAN, JOSEPH A., 1901, The Ojibways in Minnesota. *Collections of the Minnesota Historical Society*, Vol. 9, pp. 55–128.

GOLDFRANK, ESTHER S., 1943, Historic Change and Social Character. *American Anthropologist*, n.s., Vol. 45, pp. 67–83.

———, 1945, *Changing Configurations in the Social Organization of a Blackfoot Tribe during the Reserve Period*. American Ethnological Society Monographs, Vol. VIII, New York.

GOTTSCHALK, LOUIS, CLYDE KLUCKHOHN, AND ROBERT ANGELL, 1945, *The Use of Personal Documents in History, Anthropology, and Sociology*. Social Science Research Council, New York.

* The following articles, which appeared after this manuscript was accepted for publication, contain relevant information: Caudill, William, "Psychological Characteristics of Acculturated Wisconsin Ojibwa Children," *American Anthropologist*, Vol. 51, No. 3, 1949, pp. 409–427; Hallowell, A. Irving, Psychosexual Adjustment, Personality, and the Good Life in a Non-Literate Culture, in *Psychosexual Development in Health and Disease*, Grune and Stratton, 1949, pp. 102–123.

See also Barnouw, Victor, "The Phantasy World of a Chippewa Woman," *Psychiatry*, Vol. 12, No. 1, 1949, pp. 67–76. This article contains some of Julia Badger's phantasies not included here, with some interpretive comments.

GRANT, PETER, 1890, *The Sauteux Indians:* About 1804. In Masson, R. L. *Les bourgeois de la compagnie du Nord-Ouest,* Cote et Cie, Quebec.

GRINNELL, GEORGE B., 1923, *The Cheyenne Indians.* Yale University Press, New Haven, Connecticut.

HALLOWELL, A. IRVING, 1938a, Fear and Anxiety as Cultural and Individual Variables in a Primitive Society. *Journal of Social Psychology,* Vol. 9, pp. 25–47.

———, 1938b, Shabwan: A Dissocial Indian Girl. *American Journal of Orthopsychiatry,* Vol. VIII, No. 2, April, pp. 329–340.

———, 1942, Acculturation Processes and Personality Changes as Indicated by the Rorschach Technique. *Rorschach Research Exchange,* Vol. 6, April, pp. 42–50.

———, 1945, The Rorschach Technique in the Study of Personality and Culture. *American Anthropologist,* Vol. 47, pp. 195–210.

———, 1947, Some Psychological Characteristics of the Northeastern Indians. In Man in Northeastern North America. *Papers of the R. S. Peabody Foundation for Archaeology,* Vol. 3, pp. 195–225.

HARMON, DANIEL WILLIAMS, 1903, *A Journal of Voyages and Travels.* A. S. Barnes, New York.

HAWLEY, FLORENCE, 1946, The Role of Pueblo Social Organization in the Dissemination of Catholicism. *American Anthropologist,* Vol. 48, pp. 407–415.

HENRY, JULES AND ZUNIA HENRY, 1944, *Doll Play of Pilaga Indian Children.* Research Monograph No. 4, American Orthopsychiatric Association, New York.

HENRY, WILLIAM E., 1947, The Thematic Apperception Test Technique in the Study of Culture-Personality Relations. *Genetic Psychology Monographs,* Vol. 35, pp. 3–138.

HUNT, GEORGE, 1940, *The Wars of the Iroquois.* The University of Wisconsin Press, Madison, Wisconsin.

HYDE, GEORGE E., 1937, *Red Cloud's Folk.* University of Oklahoma Press, Norman, Oklahoma.

JAMES, EDWIN, 1823, *Account of an Expedition from Pittsburgh to the Rocky Mountains.* Longman, Hurst, Rees, Orme, and Brown, London.

JENNESS, DIAMOND, 1935, *The Ojibwa Indians of Parry Island, Their Social and Religious Life.* Canada Department of Mines, National Museum of Canada, Bulletin #78, Ottawa.

JONES, PETER, 1861, *History of the Ojebway Indians.* A. W. Bennett, London.

JONES, WILLIAM, 1919, *Ojibwa Texts.* Publications of the American Ethnological Society, Vol. VII, Part II, New York.

KARDINER, ABRAM AND RALPH LINTON, 1939, *The Individual and his Society.* Columbia University Press, New York.

———, 1945, *The Psychological Frontiers of Society.* Columbia University Press, New York.

KEESING, FELIX M., 1939, *The Menomini Indians of Wisconsin.* Memoirs of the American Philosophical Society, Vol. X.

KELLOGG, LOUISE PHELPS, 1935, *The British Regime in Wisconsin and the Northwest.* State Historical Society of Wisconsin, Madison, Wisconsin.

KOHL, J. G., 1860, *Kitchi-Gami: Wanderings around Lake Superior.* Chapman and Hall, London.

LANDES, RUTH, 1937a, *Ojibwa Sociology.* Columbia University Contributions to Anthropology, Number 29, New York.

———, 1937b, The Ojibwa of Canada. In Mead, Margaret (editor) *Cooperation and Competition among Primitive Peoples,* McGraw-Hill, New York, pp. 87–126.

———, 1939, *The Ojibwa Woman.* Columbia University Contributions to Anthropology, Number 31, New York.

LINTON, RALPH, 1940 (editor), *Acculturation in Seven American Indian Tribes.* Appleton-Century, New York.

———, 1943, Nativistic Movements. *American Anthropologist,* Vol. 45, pp. 230–240.

LLEWELLYN, K. N. AND E. ADAMSON HOEBEL, 1941, *The Cheyenne Way*. University of Oklahoma Press, Norman, Oklahoma.

LONG, JOHN, 1904, John Long's Journal: 1768–1782. In Thwaites, R. G. (editor) *Early Western Travels*, Arthur H. Clark, Cleveland, Ohio, Vol. II, pp. 1–329.

LOWIE, ROBERT H., 1935, *The Crow Indians*. Farrar and Rinehart, New York.

MACGREGOR, GORDON, 1946, *Warriors Without Weapons*. University of Chicago Press, Chicago, Illinois.

MACLEOD, WILLIAM CHRISTIE, 1928, *The American Indian Frontier*. Kegan Paul, Trench, Trubner, London.

MALHIOT, FRANCOIS VICTOR, 1910, A Wisconsin Fur-Trader's Journal: 1804–05. *Collections of the Wisconsin Historical Society*, Madison, Wisconsin, Vol. XIX, pp. 162–233.

MALINOWSKI, BRONISLAW, 1927, *Sex and Repression in a Savage Society*. Kegan Paul, London.

MASSON, R. L., 1890, *Les bourgeois de la compagnie du Nord-Ouest*. Cote et Cie, Quebec.

McGILLYCUDDY, JULIA B., 1941, *McGillycuddy—Agent*. Stanford University Press, Palo Alto, California.

McKENNEY, THOMAS L., 1827, *Sketches and Tour of the Lakes*. Fielding Lucas, Jr., Baltimore.

MEAD, MARGARET, 1930, *Growing up in New Guinea*. W. Morrow, New York.

———, 1932, *The Changing Culture of an Indian Tribe*. Columbia University Press, New York.

———, 1937 (editor), *Cooperation and Competition among Primitive Peoples*. McGraw-Hill, New York.

MEAD, MARGARET AND GREGORY BATESON, 1942, *The Balinese Character*. New York Academy of Science, New York.

M'GILLIVRAY, DUNCAN, 1929, *The Journal of Duncan M'Gillivray of the Northwest Company at Fort George on the Saskatchewan*. 1794–1795. The Macmillan Company of Canada, Toronto.

MIRSKY, JEANNETTE, 1937, The Dakota. In Mead, Margaret (editor) *Cooperation and Competition among Primitive Peoples*, McGraw-Hill, New York, pp. 382–427.

MOONEY, JAMES, 1896, *The Ghost Dance Religion and the Sioux Outbreak of 1890*. 14th Annual Report of the Bureau of American Ethnology, Part 2, Washington, D. C.

MORSE, RICHARD E., 1857, The Chippewas of Lake Superior. *Collections of the Wisconsin Historical Society*, Madison, Wisconsin, Vol. III, pp. 338–369.

NEILL, EDWARD D., 1885, History of the Ojibways. *Collections of the Minnesota Historical Society*, Vol. V, pp. 395–510.

NUTE, GRACE LEE, 1931, *The Voyageur*. Appleton, New York.

PARKMAN, FRANCIS, 1907, *The Conspiracy of Pontiac*. Little, Brown, Boston.

PITEZEL, JOHN H., 1860, *Lights and Shades of Missionary Life*. Western Book Concern, Cincinnati, Ohio.

RANEY, WILLIAM FRANCIS, 1940, *Wisconsin, a Story of Progress*. Prentice-Hall, New York.

ROHEIM, GEZA, 1945, *The Eternal Ones of the Dream, a Psychoanalytic Interpretation of Australian Myth and Ritual*. International Universities Press, New York.

SADY, RACHEL REESE, 1947, The Menominee: Transition from Trusteeship. *Applied Anthropology*, Vol. 6, Number 2, Spring, pp. 1–14.

SCHOOLCRAFT, HENRY R., 1839, *Algic Researches*. Harper and Brothers, New York.

———, 1851a, *Information Respecting the History, Condition, and Prospects of the Indian Tribes of the United States*. Lippincott, Grambo, and Co., Philadelphia, Pennsylvania.

———, 1851b, *Personal Memoirs of a Residence of Thirty Years with the Indian Tribes on the American Frontiers*. Lippincott, Grambo, and Co., Philadelphia, Pennsylvania.

———, 1851c, *The American Indians*. Derby, Buffalo, New York.

SIMMONS, LEO, 1942, *Sun Chief: The Autobiography of a Hopi Indian*. Yale University Press, New Haven, Connecticut.

SKINNER, ALANSON B., 1912, *Notes on the Eastern Crèe and Northern Saulteaux.* Anthropological Papers of the American Museum of Natural History, Vol. IX, pp. 1–177.

TANNER, JOHN, 1830, *A Narrative of the Captivity and Adventures of John Tanner.* Prepared for the Press by Edwin James. Carvill, New York.

———, 1940, *An Indian Captivity. 1789–1822.* (Reprint of the above). W.P.A. California State Library, Sutro Branch, Reprint Series Number 20, Part I.

THOMPSON, DAVID, 1916, *David Thompson's Narrative.* J. B. Tyrell editor, Champlain Society, Toronto.

TURNER, FREDERICK JACKSON, 1891, The Character and Influence of the Indian Trade in Wisconsin. *Johns Hopkins University Studies in Historical and Political Science*, Vol. IX, pp. 1–94.

WARREN, WILLIAM WHIPPLE, 1885, History of the Ojibways. *Collections of the Minnesota Historical Society*, Vol. V, pp. 21–394.

WILLSON, BECKLES, 1899, *The Great Company.* Copp, Clark, Toronto.

WISSLER, CLARK, 1916, *Societies and Ceremonial Associations in the Oglala Division of the Teton-Dakota.* Anthropological Papers of the American Museum of Natural History, Vol. XI, Part I, pp. 3–99.

INDEX

Acculturation, 7, 10ff., 30ff., 62ff.
ADAMS, MOSES, 30n
Agent, government, 58, 60, 83, 85
ANGELL, ROBERT, 6n
Annuities, 37, 59, 63, 75
"Antler" Indians, 14
Arapaho Indians, 12, 15, 33, 56, 68
ARENSBERG, CONRAD, 9
ARMSTRONG, BENJAMIN G., 36
Assineboine Indians, 23, 41, 47, 58, 62n, 72

BADGER, JULIA, 8, 26, 50, 52, 112ff., 145ff.
BADGER, TOM, 8, 20, 23, 53, 54, 57, 112, 122, 128, 129n, 133, 138–140
BARNOUW, VICTOR, 145n
BARRETT, S. A., 69n
Basic Personality Type, 5, 6, 7, 18, 19, 27, 64–5, 76
BATESON, GREGORY, 5n
BELCOURT, GEORGES A., 41n
BENEDICT, RUTH, 8, 9, 11
BLACK ELK, 33
BLAIR, EMMA HELEN, 66
Boasting, 25

CADOTTE, JEAN BAPTISTE, 44, 46, 61
CADOTTE, MICHEL, 43, 44, 67
CAMERON, DUNCAN, 39, 44, 45, 59
CASAGRANDE, JOSEPH, 9
Catholicism, 11, 47
CAUDILL, WILLIAM, 145n
CHAMPLAIN, 32n
Chequamegon Bay, 39
Cheyenne Indians, 12, 13–4, 30, 33, 63, 68, 71
Child Training, 19, 20, 49ff., 114, 120
Children's play, 14, 20
CHITTENDEN, HIRAM M., 41
Christianity, 11, 22, 96, 102
Civil War, American, 33, 77, 81
Columbia University, 8, 9

Comanche Indians, 24, 29n, 55–6
Conjuring (shamanism), 88, 108, 115, 132
CORBINE, JEAN BAPTISTE, 39, 67
CORNYETZ, PAUL, 5n
Court Oreilles, 8, 17, 21, 27, 35, 39, 43, 61, 67, 78–9
Cree Indians, 41, 62, 72
Culture and Personality—and history, 5–8, 76
Curtis, General, 32

Dakota Indians, 7, 12, 16, 20, 23, 28–9, 30–1, 34, 43, 49, 60, 63, 65, 68, 70, 71, 75, 76
DAVIDSON, J. N., 37n
Deputy Agent, 84, 88
DEL TORTO, J., 5n
DENIG, E. T., 48, 58, 59, 64
Dependency, 53ff.
Drum Dance, or Dream Dance, 23, 28, 69, 94–5, 105–6, 135–7
DUBOIS, CORA, 5n

Economic Determinism, 6–7
ELKIN, HENRY, 15, 33n, 56
England, 30–2, 59
ERIKSON, ERIK HOMBURGER, 5n, 29, 49, 75
Eskimo, 23

"Farmer," See Deputy Agent
Fasting, for dream or vision, 20, 24–5, 53–6, 80, 92–3, 119, 135–6
"Father" relationship, 48ff.
Feast for the first kill, 97–9
Filcher-of-Meat, folktale, 49
Folklore, 25, 49, 54
Fox Indians, 12, 23, 30, 43
France, 30, 31, 43, 45
FRIEDL, ERNESTINE, 8, 9, 22, 27, 65n